CW00793410

Chronicles of the Revolution, 1397–1400

Manchester Medieval Sources series

series adviser Janet L. Nelson

This series aims to meet a growing need amongst students and teachers of medieval history for translations of key sources that are directly useable in students' own work. The series will provide texts central to medieval studies courses and will focus upon the diverse cultural, social as well as political conditions that affected the functioning of all levels of medieval society. The basic premise of the new series is that translation must be accompanied by sufficient introductory and explanatory material and each volume will therefore include a comprehensive guide to the sources' interpretation, including discussion of critical linguistic problems and an assessment of the most recent research on the topics being covered.

published titles in the series include

Janet L. Nelson *The Annals of St-Bertin: ninth-century histories, volume I*

Timothy Reuter *The Annals of Fulda: ninth-century histories, volume II*

Robert Swanson *Catholic England: religion, faith and observance before the Reformation*

forthcoming titles in the series will include

Donald Bullough *The Vikings in Paris*

John Edwards *The Jews in western Europe, 1400–1600*

Rosemary Horrox *The aftermath of the Black Death*

Simon Lloyd *The impact of the crusades: the experience of England, 1095–1274*

Richard Smith *Sources for the population history of England, 1000–1540*

J. A. Watt *The origins of anti-semitism in Europe*

CHRONICLES OF THE REVOLUTION
1397–1400
THE REIGN OF RICHARD II

translated and edited by Chris Given-Wilson

Manchester University Press
Manchester and New York

distributed exclusively in the USA and Canada by St. Martin's Press

Copyright © Chris Given-Wilson 1993

Published by Manchester University Press
Oxford Road, Manchester M13 9PL, England
and Room 400, 175 Fifth Avenue, New York, NY 10010, USA

Distributed exclusively in the USA and Canada
by St. Martin's Press, Inc., 175 Fifth Avenue, New York, NY 10010, USA

British Library Cataloguing-in-Publication Data
A catalogue record for this book is available from the British Library

Library of Congress cataloging in publication data
Chronicles of the revolution, 1397-1400 : the reign of Richard II /
    translated and annotated by Chris Given-Wilson
        p.   c.m. — (Manchester medieval sources series)
        Includes bibliographical references and index.
        ISBN 0-7190-3526-0. — ISBN 0-7190-3527-9 (pbk.)
            1. Great Britain—History—Richard II, 1377-1399—Sources
        2. Great Britain—History—Henry IV, 1399-1413—Sources. I. Given-
        Wilson, Chris. II Series.
        DA235.C54   1992
        942.03'8—dc20   92-31786

ISBN 0 7190 3526-0 *hardback*
ISBN 0 7190 3527-9 *paperback*

Typeset in Monotype Bell
by Koinonia Ltd, Manchester
Printed in Great Britain
by Bell & Bain Ltd, Glasgow

Contents

List of plates

The plates appear between text pages 136 and 137

Foreword

Richard II's reign ended in crisis and a coup d'état. His briefly exercised 'tyranny' and his deposition and death in 1399 at the hands of Henry of Lancaster caused widespread shockwaves not only in the British Isles but also in Continental Europe, from Paris to Prague and from the Rhineland to Milan. Richard, unlike Edward II, found defenders both in his own time and since. For Richard (unlike Edward) was a man of vision - and very nearly succeeded in putting his elevated ideals of kingly authority into effect. The critical years were 1397-99. They were packed with drama, violence, reversals of fortune. Yet from the student's standpoint, they have often appeared confusing and Richard's fate hard to explain. The documentation is rich, but much of it is heavily partisan. Some of it has never before been translated or even edited. With the present volume, Chris Given-Wilson make available all the key contemporary and near-contemporary narratives, including those of French alongside English chroniclers, and supplies in the notes cross-references to documentary evidence. Suppressions and distortions of information become clear. Material too readily discounted in the past as 'Lancastrian propaganda' can now be reappraised: the Evesham monk's account, though anti-Ricardian, emerges as a relatively independent one, while Adam Usk is revealed here as not only exceptionally well-informed but also a complex, perhaps guilt-ridden, participant-observer of events. Chris Given-Wilson's lucid Introduction reflects his own earlier work on the dynamics of later medieval English political history. Thus ideally qualified to present the crisis of Richard's reign in context, he enables readers to grasp for themselves why that crisis marked a turning-point and cast such a long shadow, and in what sense the events of 1397-99 constituted a revolution. This book, along with Alison McHardy's forthcoming companion-volume on the two decades before 1397, should ensure that Richard's reign and its denouement will now receive from a wider audience the close attention they deserve.

Janet L. Nelson, King's College London

In memory of Roy Barrie

Preface

Fortunately Manchester University Press imposed a 100,000-word limit on this book. Otherwise it would have been very difficult to know where to stop. As it is, it has been hard enough deciding what to omit. It would have been nice, for example, to include some of the more 'literary' pieces on Richard II's downfall, such as *Richard the Redeless* or John Gower's works, but, entertaining and instructive as these are, they do not contribute greatly to our understanding of the actual *story* of the years 1397-1400. My first task, as I saw it, was to provide such contemporary material as could be used to determine the sequence and context of the events which decided Richard's fate, and thus to try to answer some of the whys and hows of that confusing year. As it turned out, lack of space prevented me from progressing beyond this.

The introduction may be thought over-long, but there is a reason for this: the chronicles (from which nearly all the texts are drawn) are so divergent in their viewpoints that to allow them to stand without explanation would have been unhelpful. Moreover, other sources apart from chronicles (government records, for example) act as a constant check upon the narrative sources, and have been worked upon by historians with equal zeal. With a few exceptions, however – such as the Rolls of Parliament – government records are unsuitable for inclusion in a volume of this sort. The chief purpose of the introduction, therefore, is to show how the chronicles must be tempered by other sources. Many of the footnotes to the introduction contain references to records of this sort. It will soon be noticed, however, that I have not provided cross-references between the texts and the introduction: this is partly in order to keep the footnotes to a tolerable minimum, and partly to encourage readers to search through the texts for themselves. In short, I hoped that the texts could, to a great extent, be allowed to speak for themselves, but to allow them to do so unchecked might have proved in the end rather misleading.

I am very grateful to those friends who have given their time to discuss Richard II with me, or who have on occasions supplied me with references to material unknown to me. In particular, I should like to thank George Stow, Nigel Saul, Tony Goodman, Jim Gillespie, Alison McHardy, Anthony Tuck, Philip Morgan, and the late James Sherborne. That does not mean that they agree with my views on either King Richard or King Henry, but they have all, in one way or another, helped to shape them. I am grateful also to the students at St Andrews University who over the past few years have taken my special subject on 'Richard II and his Historians', out of which this book slowly emerged. They too helped to shape my views on Richard, even if they were not always aware of it. My thanks also go to Peter George of the Department of Humanity at St Andrews, who helped me with some tricky passages of Latin translation. The translations in this book are for the most part my own, although for the chronicle of Adam Usk and the *Traison et Mort* I used the printed translations by E. M.Thompson and Benjamin Williams respectively. For Creton's 'Metrical History' my translation is based upon that made by J. Webb in 1823, but substantially modernised with reference to the original French text printed by J. A. Buchon.

Alison McHardy is currently preparing a companion volume to this one, covering the years 1377-97. Her task is a great deal harder than mine (twenty years of texts rather than three), but I hope that our joint project will be seen as a worthwhile one, and will help to make Richard II, his friends and his enemies more easily accessible to future generations of students and historians than they have been hitherto. We both owe a debt of gratitude to Manchester University Press for agreeing to publish these books.

Finally, as always, a special word of thanks to Alice, for her consideration and her tolerance.

Chris Given-Wilson, St Andrews, May 1992

Chronological table

25 Nov. Anglo-Papal concordat

1399

3 Feb. Death of John of Gaunt

18 March. Richard seizes custody of the Lancastrian inheritance

April-May. Dukes of Burgundy and Berry leave Paris for the summer

1 June. Richard lands in Ireland

17 June. Alliance between Bolingbroke and the duke of Orléans

28 June. York summons troops to meet him at Ware, Hertfordshire

3 July. Sheriff of Sussex ordered to besiege Pevensey castle

?4 July. Bolingbroke lands at Ravenspur

12 July. York musters his troops at Ware

?17 July. Salisbury and Creton sent from Ireland to North Wales

?24 July. Richard lands at Milford Haven, South Wales

27 July. Meeting of York and Bolingbroke at Berkeley

29 July. Execution of Lescrope, Bussy and Green at Bristol

?31 July. Richard abandons his army near Carmarthen and sets out for
     Conway. His army disbands

?2 Aug. Northumberland appointed Warden of the West March of Scotland
     by Bolingbroke

5 Aug. Bolingbroke, at Shrewsbury, receives the surrender of Chester

8-9 Aug. Bolingbroke enters Chester

?15 Aug. Meeting of Richard and Northumberland at Conway

?16 Aug. Meeting of Richard and Bolingbroke at Flint

20 Aug. Richard and Bolingbroke leave Chester for London

2 Sept. Richard imprisoned in the Tower of London

21 Sept. Meeting of Council to discuss Crouchback legend'. Adam Usk visits
     Richard in the Tower

22 Sept. Death of Mowbray at Venice

28-29 Sept. Formal deputations visit Richard in the Tower to secure his
     abdication

30 Sept. **Deposition of Richard II. Bolingbroke becomes King Henry IV**

6 Oct. Parliament at Westminster
           13 Oct. Coronation of Henry IV
           18 Oct. Execution of John Hall
           23 Oct. Parliament agrees to Richard's imprisonment
           29 Oct. Trial of the appellants of 1397 begins
           3 Nov. Sentence passed on the appellants of 1397
           19 Nov. Parliament dissolved

?December. Richard moved to Pontefract castle

1400

4–13 Jan. The 'Epiphany Rising'
    4 Jan. Henry flees from Windsor to London after being warned of the
        plot
    6 Jan. Rebels arrive at Cirencester
    8 Jan. Execution of Kent and Salisbury at Cirencester
    ?9 Jan. Execution of Huntingdon at Pleshey
    13 Jan. Execution of Despenser at Bristol

29 Jan. Rumours in France of Richard's death

?14 Feb. Death of Richard at Pontefract castle

17 Feb. Council orders Richard's body to be brought to London

6 March. Requiem mass for Richard at St Paul's, prior to his burial at King's
Langley

1413 Death of Henry IV (20 March). Richard's body reinterred in Westminster abbey by Henry V.

Dramatis personae

The following were the chief titles used by members of the higher nobility involved in the events of 1397-1400, including the promotions and demotions of 1397 and 1399:

John of Gaunt, duke of Lancaster 1362-99

Edmund of Langley, duke of York 1385-1402

Thomas of Woodstock, duke of Gloucester 1385-97

Henry Bolingbroke, earl of Derby 1377-1413, duke of Hereford 1397-1413, duke of Lancaster and king of England 1399-1413

Edward of York, earl of Rutland 1390-1415, duke of Aumale 1397-99, duke of York 1402-15

John Holand, earl of Huntingdon 1388-1400, duke of Exeter 1397-99

Thomas Holand, earl of Kent 1397-1400, duke of Surrey 1397-99

Thomas Mowbray, earl of Nottingham 1383-99, duke of Norfolk 1397-99

John Beaufort, earl of Somerset 1397-1410, marquis of Dorset 1397-99

Richard Fitzalan, earl of Arundel and Surrey 1376-97

Thomas Beauchamp, earl of Warwick 1369-97 and 1399-1401

Roger Mortimer, earl of March 1394-98

Henry Percy, earl of Northumberland 1377-1405

Aubrey de Vere, earl of Oxford 1393-1400

John Montague, earl of Salisbury 1397-1400

Ralph Neville, earl of Westmorland 1397-1425

Thomas Percy, earl of Worcester 1397-1403

William Lescrope, earl of Wiltshire 1397-99

Thomas Despenser, earl of Gloucester 1397-99

Michael de la Pole, earl of Suffolk 1398-1415

Abbreviations

The following works are cited in short format throughout the book:

Adam Usk: *Chronicon Adae de Usk*, ed. E. M. Thompson (1904)
Annales Ricardi Secoundi: 'Annales Ricardi Secundi et Henrici Quarti', in *Johannis de Trokelowe et Anon Chronica et Annales*, ed. H. T. Riley (Rolls Series 1866)
BIHR: Bulletin of the Institute of Historical Research
BJRL: Bulletin of the John Rylands Library
CCR: Calendar of Close Rolls
CFR: Calendar of Fine Rolls
Chronique de Saint-Denys: Chronique du Religieux de Saint-Denys 1380-1422, vol. ii, ed. M. L. Bellaguet (Documents Inedits sur l'Histoire de France, 1840)
Continuatio Eulogii: Eulogium Historiarum Sive Temporis, ed. F. S. Haydon, vol. iii (Rolls Series 1863)
CPL: Calendar of Papal Letters
CPR: Calendar of Patent Rolls
Dieulacres Chronicle: 'Chronicle of Dieulacres Abbey, 1381-1403', in M. V. Clarke and V. H. Galbraith, 'The Deposition of Richard II', *BJRL* (1930), 125-81
EHR: English Historical Review
English Chronicle: English Chronicle from 1377 to 1461, ed. J. S. Davies (Camden Society Publications, 1st series, vol. lxiv, 1855)
Foedera: Foedera, Conventiones, Litterae et Cuiuscunque Generis Acta Publica, ed. T. Rymer, 20 vols (1704-35)
Froissart, *Chroniques*: Froissart, Jean, *Oeuvres*, ed. Kervyn de Lettenhove, 25 vols (1867-77)
GEC: G. E. Cokayne, *Complete Peerage*, ed. V. H. Gibbs *et al.*, 13 vols (1910-59)
Hardyng's Chronicle: *Chronicle of John Hardyng*, ed. H. Ellis (1812)
HR: Historical Research
'Metrical History': Creton, Jean, 'Metrical History of the Deposition of King Richard the Second', ed. J. Webb, *Archaeologia* (1823)
P.R.O.: Public Record Office
Reign of Richard II: The Reign of Richard II, ed. F. R. H. du Boulay and C. Barron (1971)
RP: Rotuli Parliamentorum, ed. J. Strachey *et al.*, 6 vols (1783)
Short Kirkstall Chronicle: *Kirkstall Abbey Chronicles*, ed. J. Taylor (Publications of the Thoresby Society 1952)
Traison et Mort: Chronicque de la Traison et Mort de Richart Deux Roy Dengleterre, ed. B. Williams (1846)
Vita Ricardi Secundi: Historia Vitae et Regni Ricardi Secundi, ed. G. B. Stow (1977)

At the end of November (1398), for eight successive nights, a comet could be seen in the sky, burning with extraordinary intensity, its tail turned toward the west. According to the astrologers its appearance presaged the death of kings or the imminence of revolutions. Men of wisdom and experience, when they looked back later at what happened, preferred to see it as the harbinger of revolutions. For, at a time when - as we have already seen - the Supreme Judge was humiliating France in the person of its king, almost every nation in Christendom was simultaneously racked by the horrors of war, rebellion, and open treason. For those who wish to explain the present through the past, therefore, it can truly be said that this was a prodigious year.

(Chronique de Saint-Denys for the year 1399)

Introduction

Richard II has always had his defenders; it is what distinguishes
him from, say, Edward II, or Henry VI. He was brave, he followed
recognisable policies, he was loyal to his friends. Yet his wilful,
vengeful temperament, and his unorthodox approach to the task of
kingship, had a destabilising effect on the politics of the reign and
made him too many enemies – who, in 1399, combined to depose
him. Richard's deposition was arguably the most portentous event in
the political history of late medieval England. It was also one of the
most vigorously debated, and the debate has never shown signs of
slackening.

One of his misfortunes was his inheritance, a brittle and forbidding one
even for an adult, let alone the ten-year-old that Richard was at his
accession in June 1377. The 1370s saw the war with France, in which
Edward III had enjoyed such conspicuous success for much of his reign,
turn decisively against the English, and failure abroad brought in its
wake a renewal of political discord and government insolvency at home.
These problems were to haunt Richard during his minority. Disagreements over foreign policy, chronic financial instability, and the intensifi-
cation of parliamentary criticism and magnate faction culminated in the
brief civil war of December 1387 and the personal humiliation of the
king during the 'Merciless' Parliament in the spring of 1388. Richard's
chief opponents among the higher nobility – his uncle Thomas of
Woodstock the duke of Gloucester, his cousin Henry Bolingbroke (the
future Henry IV), and the earls of Arundel, Warwick and Nottingham
– seized power and used it to destroy the influence of the clique of
'favourites' who had gathered about the king since the early 1380s.
Eight of the king's supporters, including his former tutor Sir Simon
Burley, were executed; a further three (Robert de Vere duke of Ireland,
Michael de la Pole earl of Suffolk, and Alexander Nevill archbishop of
York) only escaped death by fleeing abroad, never to return. Upwards
of forty more of the king's followers were ejected from the court.

In May 1389 Richard, now aged twenty-two, was allowed to resume
personal control of government, and the next four or five years were
the most cordial of the reign. The ending of hostilities with France

in June 1389 allowed a fair measure of financial recovery, and the king showed a greater willingness to be guided by the advice of those whom he might not necessarily count as friends. Gradually, however, from about 1394, old tensions began to resurface. Despite the cessation of the war, foreign policy remained a contentious issue. From about 1392-93 the king's domestic expenditure also began to burgeon, leading by 1396-97 to renewed financial difficulties. Nevertheless, there is little *contemporary* evidence that Richard was encountering widespread opposition to his rule in the mid-1390s. On the contrary, it was his opponents, most notably Gloucester and Arundel, who, having failed to capitalise on their successes in 1387-88, now appear to have become isolated in their antagonism to the king and his new following among the magnates – chief among whom were his half-brother John Holand earl of Huntingdon, his cousin Edward earl of Rutland, and the under-chamberlain of the royal household, William le Scrope. Richard's relationship with his senior surviving uncle, John of Gaunt duke of Lancaster, was also – at least on the surface – much better now than it had been during the 1380s, while Thomas Mowbray earl of Nottingham, after a brief spell of opposition in 1387-88, had returned to favour at court. Ever since his resumption of power in 1389, the king had also been building up his support amongst the gentry, partly through a policy of recruitment in the shires, and partly by increasing the size of his household. All in all, the king's position by 1397 was immeasurably stronger than it had been ten years earlier.

The ratification of a thirty-year truce with France in November 1396 may have provided Gloucester and Arundel with new cause for disquiet, but it also freed the king from concern that foreign emergencies might undermine his domestic position. The time had come to strike back – and if Richard had been prepared, during the past few years, to bury the hatchet, he had not forgotten where he had buried it. In July 1397 he arrested Gloucester, Arundel and Warwick. At the so-called 'Revenge' Parliament in September, Arundel was executed for treason, Warwick exiled for life to the Isle of Man, and an announcement made that Gloucester had 'died' in captivity at Calais. But if Richard thought that by such actions he could quiet the realm and bend it to his will, he was soon proved wrong. During the winter of 1397-98, the misgivings that his coup had bred among the nobility erupted in a confrontation between his two remaining opponents from 1387-88, Henry Bolingbroke and Thomas Mowbray. Richard ordered them to fight a duel, but at the last minute he changed his mind and exiled them both from England. A few months later, in February 1399, John of Gaunt died. Instead of allowing Bolingbroke to enjoy his father's inheritance – as he had promised – he decided instead to seize custody of the Lancastrian lands for himself. Having done so, he took ship for Ireland at the end of May. Scarcely had Richard left the country when Bolingbroke crossed from France and, trading on the sympathy which Richard's treatment of him had aroused, embarked on the campaign which was to win him the crown. Richard, returning too late from Ireland, was cornered at Conway Castle in North Wales in mid-August, and brought to the Tower of London. At a parliamentary meeting at Westminster on 30 September, he was formally deposed, and Bolingbroke was chosen to be King Henry IV. By mid-February 1400, Richard was almost certainly dead.

The high drama of Richard's last years stimulated an outpouring of literature recounting the king's fate, the quantity of which is matched by the perplexing variety of viewpoints from which the story is told. At one end of the spectrum is the so-called 'Record and Process', the official account of Richard's deposition drawn up with the express purpose of justifying Henry's action and condemning Richard's rule; at the other end is the *Chronique de la Traison et Mort de Richart Deux Roy Dengleterre*, a similarly propagandist tract written in France lamenting Richard's fate and seeking to stir the French nobility into action against the usurper. While it may be easy to reject parts (though by no means all) of what each of these says, it is much more difficult to decide what ought to be accepted or rejected from the middle ground. There is, of course, no ultimate 'truth' on such matters. There are, however, truths of a sort to be uncovered, and a correct sequence of events to be determined. A number of questions, answered in different fashion according to the author's viewpoint, run insistently through the literature relating Richard's fall. Why, for example, did Richard decide to strike against his old enemies in the summer of 1397? Were they once more plotting against him, or had he simply decided that the time had come for revenge? What was the extent of his 'tyranny' in 1398-99? Why was he unable to muster more support for his cause in July and August 1399: was it the price he paid for his evil government, or was it because Bolingbroke successfully concealed his true aims until it was too late to stem the tide? How was Richard taken in North Wales: did he, realising the game was up, hand himself over and voluntarily resign the crown, or was he tricked out of Conway with false assurances and treacherously seized? How unanimous was the decision to depose him, and to choose Bolingbroke as his successor? And how did he die: did he, as the Lancastrians claimed, starve himself to death of pure melancholy, or was he murdered on Henry's orders?

Of the three most substantial contemporary chronicles which cover the earlier part of Richard's reign, two cease before 1397: namely the *Westminster Chronicle*, which ends in 1394, and the *Chronicon Henrici Knighton*, which peters out in 1395.[1] Fortunately, the third – the *Chronica Maiora* of Thomas Walsingham – continues through the revolution of 1399 and well beyond, right up to 1420. Walsingham was a monk of St Albans. He wrote a number of chronicles, the texts of which later became transposed and have only quite recently been disentangled. The section of Walsingham's *Chronica Maiora* which contains his most complete and contemporary account of the events of 1397-1400 was printed in the nineteenth century under the title of *Annales Ricardi Secundi et Henrici Quarti*: it is from this edition that the extracts below are taken.[2]

St Albans, just twenty miles from London on the main road north, was one of the great monastic houses of medieval England and received a constant stream of often high-ranking visitors. Walsingham was therefore in a good position to acquire news, and the chief value of his chronicle is the sheer *amount* of information which he provides. He wrote clearly and with detail, and always enjoyed a good story. He also had a waspish tongue, and herein lies one of the main drawbacks of his work. Walsingham began writing his *Chronica Maiora* around 1380, at which time he had been well-disposed to the young king, looking to him for salvation from the malaise which had befallen England during Edward III's decline. As the reign progressed, however, he became increasingly disillusioned with Richard, and by the time he came to write his account of the years 1397-99 his view of the king had come full cycle. He was now prepared to believe almost anything that redounded to the king's discredit. His account of these years is

1 *The Westminster Chronicle 1381-1394*, ed. L. C. Hector and B. F. Harvey (1982); *Chronicon Henrici Knighton*, ed. J. R. Lumby, 2 vols (Rolls Series 1895).

2 For discussion of Walsingham's chronicles see V. H. Galbraith, 'Thomas Walsingham and the St Albans Chronicle 1272-1422', *EHR* (1932), 12-30; and G. B. Stow, 'Richard II in Thomas Walsingham's Chronicles', *Speculum* (1984), 68-102. Walsingham's later *Historia Anglicana* has nothing of significance to add to his account of these years in the *Annales*.

peppered with asides designed to show Richard in a bad light, and with what on occasions appear to be little better than rumours masquerading as fact. Moreover, like almost all the other chroniclers of these years, he did not start writing his account of them until after the deposition: thus not only was he writing in the knowledge of Richard's failure, but also under the yoke of the propaganda put about by Bolingbroke and his supporters to justify the usurpation. He seems to have been quite willing to allow his chronicle to become a vehicle for such propaganda. For example, parts of his account of Richard's 'tyranny' (Walsingham himself said that from 1397 onwards the king 'began to tyrannise and burden his people') were simply lifted wholesale, though without acknowledgement, from the 'Record and Process'. Yet even if much of what Walsingham tells us about Richard is so extreme as to be unconvincing, he cannot be ignored.

Walsingham was the chief exponent of what is commonly called the 'Lancastrian' view of the revolution, but he was not the only one. The second part of the *Vita Ricardi Secundi*, which covers the years 1390-1402 and was written by a monk of Evesham Abbey during the first decade of the fifteenth century, also takes a line thoroughly hostile to Richard.[3] Like Walsingham, the monk of Evesham has frequently been accused of allowing his chronicle to become a vehicle for Lancastrian propaganda, but this is not really true. In fact Walsingham's is the only contemporary chronicle to make direct use of the 'Record and Process'. The author of the *Vita* was undoubtedly prepared to believe much that was discreditable to the king, and parts of his chronicle are certainly based on official documents, but whether these documents were compiled in the interests of Lancastrian propaganda is a quite different matter.[4] The *Vita* is, in fact, a largely independent source, and as such has great value, especially for Bolingbroke's movements around the Severn Valley and the Welsh border in July-August 1399 – which, of course, the monk was particularly well-placed to observe. The third principal 'Lancastrian' chronicle of these years is the

3 The *Vita* was probably not written until after 1404: see below, Doc. 11, n. 1.

4 C. Given-Wilson, 'Adam Usk, the monk of Evesham, and the parliament of 1397-8', *HR* (forthcoming). The 'Lancastrian narrative' – as Sayles called it – upon which the monk based his account of Richard's 'abdication' is really no more than a copy of his instrument of resignation and a list of witnesses, together with a copy of his so-called 'protestatio'; but it was certainly not in the interests of the Lancastrians to circulate the latter. (See G. O. Sayles, 'The deposition of Richard II: three Lancastrian narratives', *BIHR* (1981), 257-70.)

Continuatio Eulogii, the central section of which covers the years 1390-
1400 and was probably written during the first few years of the
fifteenth century. This was almost certainly the work of a Franciscan
friar, very probably based at the Greyfriars at Canterbury.[5] As might
be expected, the friar seems to have acquired some of his original
information from Archbishop Thomas Arundel of Canterbury, the
younger brother of the earl of Arundel executed in 1397. Since the
archbishop played a leading part in the events of 1397-1400, this is
often of considerable interest. It also helps to explain the tone of the
chronicle, which is thoroughly inimical to the king.

To describe as 'Lancastrian' the chronicle of Adam Usk is – although
it has been done frequently enough – somewhat misleading. Adam was
a secular clerk from Usk in Monmouthshire; his patrons were
Archbishop Arundel and the earl of March, neither of whom were well
treated by Richard during the later years of his reign. However,
although Adam clearly disliked Richard, that did not mean that he
supported Bolingbroke's bid for the throne: it is important to be aware
not only of what he tells us, but also of what he omits to tell us. He was
in a remarkably good position to recount at least one side of the story
of what happened in the summer of 1399: having joined Bolingbroke's
forces, probably at Bristol, at the end of July, he accompanied the duke
on his march to Cheshire, and then, having returned to London, was
appointed to the committee set up by Bolingbroke to determine 'the
matter of setting aside King Richard, and of choosing Henry, duke of
Lancaster, in his stead.' That Adam gave his opinion in favour of the
usurpation there can be no doubt; what he really thought about it is
another matter. It was, after all, not Henry Bolingbroke, but Edmund
Mortimer, the seven-year-old heir to the earldom of March, who,
following Richard's deposition, was the primogenitary heir to the
throne. It may well be that Adam's chronicle should in some measure
be read as an act of expiation for the guilt he felt in acquiescing with
Bolingbroke's usurpation. He certainly presents us with a fairly
equivocal account of Henry's campaign – pointing out, for example,
that having promised to 'spare the people and the country' of Cheshire,
he then proceeded to pillage it without mercy, and emphasising that
Richard did not surrender to Henry but had to be taken by force.
Adam's chronicle reads like the work of a man for whom the clash of
loyalties had become too acute.

5 A. Gransden, *Historical Writing in England II* (1982), 158, n.5.

There was clearly no problem of allegiance, however, for the authors of the two major French chronicles which cover these events, namely the *Histoire du Roy d'Angleterre Richard* (written in verse, and commonly known as the 'Metrical History'), and the *Chronique de la Traison et Mort de Richart Deux Roy Dengleterre*. Both were firmly in the king's camp, and, being interrelated, they are best taken together.[6] The author of the Metrical History was very probably Jean Creton, a *valet-de-chambre* at the French court. Like Adam Usk, Creton was in a strong position to tell one side of the story. Having come across from France in the spring of 1399, he accompanied the royal expedition to Ireland (of which he provides a much-quoted description), and then, when news of Bolingbroke's landing reached the king, he was dispatched back to the mainland in the company of the earl of Salisbury to try to rally support for Richard in the North Wales/Cheshire area. He and Salisbury remained in North Wales until joined there by Richard, and he was still with the king at Conway when a deputation from Bolingbroke, led by the earl of Northumberland, arrived there to talk terms. His account of what happened at Conway is strikingly different from that given in the Lancastrian chronicles. Far from resigning willingly and acknowledging Henry as his successor, Richard was, according to Creton, lured out of the castle by false promises, then promptly ambushed and led away a prisoner to meet Henry. At the time when Creton wrote his chronicle, in the winter of 1401-2,[7] he still believed it likely that Richard was alive: indeed, part of the reason why he wrote it was in an attempt to galvanise the French nobility into taking action against the usurper. It was for a French, not an English, audience that he wrote.

The same is true of the *Traison et Mort*. Despite much speculation, there is no certainty as to who wrote the *Traison*, but it was undoubtedly a Frenchman, probably a servant of the duke of Burgundy who had been sent to England in the household of Richard's new queen, the seven-year-old French princess Isabelle, in early 1397. He seems to have remained in England for about four years, returning to France with Isabelle in July 1401. For part of this time he may have

---

6 Much the best discussion of these chronicles is by J. J. N. Palmer, 'The authorship, date and historical value of the French chronicles on the Lancastrian revolution', *BJRL* (1978-79), 145-81, 398-421.

7 R. Vaughan, *Philip the Bold* (1962), 200, notes that the duke of Burgundy purchased from a 'Jehan Creton' in 1402 a book 'faisant mencion de la prinse de feu le roy Richart.'

been seconded to the household of Richard's half-brother John Holand.[8] The chronicle covers the years 1397-1400, and was originally written at about the same time as the 'Metrical History', that is, in 1401-2. In its first version, it was a quite separate composition from Creton's work. Within a few years, however, it had been revised to include a number of passages from the 'Metrical History', and in time it was to go through two more editions, each of which included additional passages from Creton's work. There is much in the later editions of the *Traison*, therefore, that is simply copied verbatim from the 'Metrical History', and is thus of no value as independent source material. As John Palmer has shown, the author of the *Traison* was also less than scrupulous in his regard for the truth – as witness, for example, his extraordinary account of Richard's death. Nevertheless, there remain passages from the original version of the *Traison* which do have historical value, such as the details which he provides on the course of the Bolingbroke-Mowbray dispute, or his description of the early events of the 'Epiphany Rising'.

There is nothing to suggest that either the *Traison* or the 'Metrical History' was known in England before about 1470, which helps to explain why the 'Lancastrian' version of the revolution was able, by constant repetition through the generations, to acquire and for long maintain a measure of moral authority over its rivals. Indeed it is only in the twentieth century that these rivals have been given the attention they merit. This is especially true of the 'Metrical History', which is now recognised as a source of the first importance for events at Conway – the pivot of the revolution. That is not to say that Creton's evidence is unimpeachable: his chronology, for example, was clearly wrong at times, and his partisanship on Richard's behalf very probably led him to overstate his case. What has persuaded historians that his story must be taken seriously, however, is the publication this century of a number of hitherto largely unknown chronicles, which corroborate, albeit briefly, the essential points of Creton's story.

The chronicles in question are the *Dieulacres Chronicle*, the *Whalley Chronicle*, and the *Short Kirkstall Chronicle*. All three are, in differing degrees, composite chronicles, and all three were compiled at Cistercian abbeys in the north of England. Since some of the crucial

---

8 The author certainly took an unusual interest in the Holand family. Palmer, 'Authorship, date and historical value', 66-8, thought that he disliked John Holand, but only one of the references to Holand in the chronicle could be construed as unfavourable (*Traison et Mort*, 195), and many others are distinctly favourable.

events of the revolution – such as Bolingbroke's landing and the confrontation at Conway – took place in the north, they were in a good position to gain first-hand knowledge of these episodes. Whether their accumulative evidence should be seen as presenting a peculiarly 'Cistercian' view of the revolution is debatable. There was evidently a certain amount of manuscript-exchange between these northern Cistercian houses,[9] but there are significant points at which their stories contradict each other, and even within these houses there was no unanimity of view on the merits or otherwise of the fallen king, or of his supplanter.

The *Short Kirkstall Chronicle* seems to have been written in two parts. The first covers the period up to June 1398, and was probably written in the winter of 1398-99. It thus contains the only surviving description of the parliament of September 1397 to have been written *before* the revolution, and the relatively favourable picture of the king which it presents must, consequently, command additional authority. The second part resumes the story from 1397-98 and takes it through (in somewhat disordered fashion) to the early months of 1400; it was written shortly after the revolution, and is less favourable to Richard. Kirkstall abbey was under the patronage of the dukes of Lancaster, and it may be that the chronicler's change of tone after 1398 was occasioned by Richard's treatment of Bolingbroke in the winter of 1398-99; alternatively, the author may simply have been trimming his sails to the political wind.[10]

The *Dieulacres Chronicle*, compiled at Dieulacres abbey in Staffordshire, was also written in two parts, and on this occasion by two different authors. They cover the years 1381-1400 and 1400-3 respectively. Once again there is a difference in tone between the two sections, the first author being strongly sympathetic to Richard, the second to Henry. On this occasion the change of tone is sharper, the second author even remarking, at the point where he took up his pen, that 'there are numerous places in which this writer (*his predecessor*) has condemned actions which ought to be commended, and commended actions which ought to be condemned ... I know this for certain, because I was present on many of these occasions and saw for myself'.[11]

---

9 J. Taylor, *The Kirkstall Abbey Chronicles* (1952), 32-5.

10 Taylor (*Ibid.*, 24) thought it unlikely that the two sections were written by different authors. Support for his view is suggested by the fact that the chronicle takes a consistently favourable view of the Percy family (e.g. 114, 116-17, 122).

11 Dieulacres Chronicle, 174-5.

There could be no clearer indication of the passions which the king's downfall aroused. It may be, as John Taylor has suggested, that the first section was originally written at Chester – which would explain its Ricardian sympathies – and then copied out and continued by a second author who was a monk at Dieulacres.[12] It is certainly the most fearlessly partisan of the English chronicles supporting the king. Along with Creton, it states that Richard was enticed from Conway castle by a promise that he would remain king, only to find once he reached Flint that this undertaking was disregarded. Although the third Cistercian chronicle, that of Whalley abbey in Lancashire, is a late source, probably compiled soon after 1430 (when it ends), it seems to have been put together from various scraps of information some of which may originate from earlier dates, and its evidence for the meeting at Conway should not be discounted. It too confirms the 'Metrical History''s version of events at Conway.[13] Taken as a group, then, these Cistercian chronicles seem to confirm at least the central points of Creton's story, and by implication undermine much else that is at the heart of the 'Lancastrian' chroniclers' version of these years.

The Lancastrian, French and Cistercian chronicles are the principal narrative accounts of the years 1397-1400, though they are not the only ones. Brief extracts have also been included from the chronicles of John Hardyng and John Catesby, which provide information on Bolingbroke's movements and intentions in the summer of 1399, and from the French *Chronique du Religieux de Saint-Denys*, which tells of the preparations which he made in France immediately prior to his embarkation for England. Also germane to this is the treaty of alliance which Bolingbroke made with the duke of Orleans in Paris just before his departure, which was later to cause a political furore in France. The alliance is a reminder that documentary sources also make a significant contribution to our knowledge of these events. The most extensive 'official' source are the *Rotuli Parliamentorum*, the formal minutes of parliament (on which, for example, the 'Record and Process' was enrolled). Although the *Rotuli Parliamentorum* rarely deviate too far from the official line, they do not suppress every hint of opposition to the crown, and frequently provide background information on the decisions taken by the king. During the last year of Richard's reign the acts of the parliamentary committee appointed in January 1398 were

---

12 J. Taylor, *English Historical Literature in the Fourteenth Century* (1987), 190-1.

13 The Whalley chronicle has never been printed; the manuscript is British Library Harleian MS. 3600.

also recorded on the *Rotuli Parliamentorum*, giving us an insight into, for example, the thinking behind Richard's handling of the Bolingbroke-Mowbray dispute. Of a semi-official nature, too, is the memorandum entitled *The Manner of King Richard's Renunciation*, which describes the negotiations between Richard and Bolingbroke leading up to the deposition, and which provides an important corrective to some of the assertions of the 'Record and Process'. Finally, a small number of private letters written at the time of the 'Epiphany Rising' – an event which appears to have given rise to a great deal of private correspondence – are also included. They contain small but significant scraps of information not included in the chronicles.

The great attraction of the sources which describe Richard II's triumph and downfall is that they approach events from such starkly opposed points of view. Frequently they cover the same ground, and often enough the outlines, at least, of the stories which they tell are recognisably the same, but behind the superficial similarities lie nuances of phrase, the workings of patronage and prejudice, decisions concerning the insertion or omission of material, the advantages or disadavantages of location and access to information, and, on both sides, the steady drip of propaganda insinuating its way, consciously or unconsciously, into the minds of both chronicler and reader. In using medieval sources – especially chronicles – it is just as important to be aware of who the author was, and why (or for whom) he wrote, as of what he says, for the former must act as a constant check upon the latter. Just as with, for example, modern-day newspapers, it is the only way to arrive at a meaningful distinction between the true and the false, the dispassionate and the frankly sectarian. Read in this way, the texts in this volume serve not merely as an introduction to one of the most dramatic episodes in late medieval English history, but also as a case study in the detection of partisanship, credulity and deliberate misinformation in medieval historical writing. Before moving on to the texts themselves, however, some account is necessary of the principal events which they cover: the aim of which is, in part, to test their evidence against that of other surviving sources (chiefly government records), and in part to give some indication of how their testimony has been used by historians in the past.

The event that sparked off the crisis of 1397-1400 was Richard's decision in July 1397 to arrest his uncle the duke of Gloucester and the earls of Arundel and Warwick. The chronicles ascribed this decision to a variety of motives. The simplest, if least credible, was the claim in the *Traison et Mort* that these three and other lords had conceived a plot to arrest the king and a number of his supporters, including Gaunt, and thus that Richard's strike at his opponents was pre-emptive. The purpose of this story was clearly to provide an immediate and convincing justification for the king's coup. However, the details as given in the *Traison* are frankly unbelievable, and although Walsingham commented that Richard, fearing a violent reaction to the lords' arrest, issued a proclamation that they had been seized 'not for any crimes which they had committed in the past, but for recent offences which they had committed against the king' (which, as he went on to say, was 'totally false'), it is difficult not to believe that had there been any truth in his allegation Richard would have used it in the charges which he subsequently brought against the three lords.

Broadly speaking, the English chroniclers explain the arrest of the three lords either in terms of Richard's desire for revenge against those who had humbled him in 1386-88, or as a means of asserting the fullness of his royal power. The Kirkstall chronicler and the monk of Evesham both preface their descriptions of the arrests with the comment that Richard 'recalled to mind' his earlier humiliations, and the trials of September 1397 certainly add substance to the view that the events of 1386-88 were never far from the king's thoughts, for the charges against Gloucester, Arundel and Warwick related almost exclusively to their actions at that time. In particular, the execution of Simon Burley still rankled with the king: 'You shall have such mercy as you showed to Simon Burley,' he is said (in the *Continuatio Eulogii*) to have retorted to Gloucester's plea for his life, while Arundel was condemned to be beheaded 'on Tower Hill, where Simon Burley was beheaded.' Coupled to this yearning to avenge the friends who had been condemned to death or exile in 1388 was a belief on the king's part that his sovereignty had been trampled upon in these years, and that those responsible should be punished.[14]

Richard had been working towards this for a number of years. Since 1389 he had embarked on a policy of retaining the more prominent members of the county gentry, and had developed a foreign policy to suit his own inclinations. By late 1396 he seemed to have won much

14 See for example the exultant letters which Richard wrote in the winter of 1397-98 to Albert of Bavaria, count of Holland, and to the Emperor Manuel of Constantinople; printed respectively in Froissart, *Chroniques*, xviii, 584, and *The Official Correspondence of Thomas Bekynton*, ed. G. Williams (Rolls Series 1872), i, 285.

of what he had worked for. Early in 1397, however, a number of events convinced him that more drastic action was needed to enable him to establish genuine freedom of action. In the January 1397 parliament there was much murmuring against the king's proposal to proceed with a joint Anglo-French campaign against Milan, to which Richard replied that he was obliged to keep his promise to the French king, and that he ought to have the freedom to induce his subjects to fulfil his promises. Criticism of the extravagance of the royal household also resurfaced in this parliament, after an absence of nearly a decade.[15] In the following month the king held a council at Westminster which Gloucester and Arundel refused to attend, pleading illness; Richard, according to the monk of Evesham, was furious, and it may well have been at about this time that he made up his mind to act.[16] According to Walsingham, the king was also eager at this time to improve his standing on the continent with a demonstration of kingly authority, for he believed that he was a candidate for the German imperial throne.

There is little contemporary evidence (despite the assertions of chroniclers writing after 1399) to suggest that Richard's arrest of his three leading opponents aroused great opposition. By 1397, Gloucester and Arundel — Warwick had largely faded from view since 1389 — had lost much of the standing which they had enjoyed in the late 1380s. Arundel's continuous and ill-mannered carping at the king and Gaunt, and Gloucester's obstructive attitude towards the negotiations with France, had left them dangerously isolated from a court which was increasingly dominated by men sympathetic to Richard and his policies. Most apposite, perhaps, is the comment of the Kirkstall chronicler, who wrote that in 1397 it was as if the king 'was then ruling for the first time ...' Thus when chancellor Edmund Stafford, bishop of Exeter, rose at the opening of parliament on 17 September to deliver a speech on the theme 'Rex unus erit omnibus', there were probably many who agreed that it was only by silencing public nuisances such as Gloucester and Arundel had become that progress could be made and further dissension averted. Yet even by this time Richard had already committed the deed which, more perhaps than any other, was to endanger that support which he had so carefully

15 *RP*, iii, 338-40.

16 It is worth noting that the charters of creation of John Beaufort as earl of Somerset and Thomas Mowbray as earl marshal, both dated 10 February at Westminster, were witnessed by most of the higher nobility but not by Gloucester, Arundel or Warwick (*RP*, iii, 343).

built up over the previous few years and which had provided the
foundations for his summer coup: namely, the murder of his uncle
Gloucester.

The arrests of the three lords probably took place on 10 or 11 July.
Richard arrested his uncle in person, and he was careful to ensure that
Gloucester had no foreknowledge of his intentions. Summoning a
troop of retainers – who apparently had no idea of the task which they
were about to perform – to meet him in or near London, he rode
through the night and arrived at his uncle's castle of Pleshey in Essex
at daybreak. The astonished duke came down into the courtyard of the
castle accompanied by his wife and various members of his household,
and greeted the king cordially, only to be told – despite the pleas and
lamentations of the duchess and others – that he was being placed
under arrest. He was immediately handed over to the earl marshal,
Thomas Mowbray. Within a few days he had arrived at Calais, where
he was to meet his end.

On 5 August, in the great hall of Nottingham castle, eight of the king's
foremost supporters among the higher nobility formally appealed
Gloucester, Arundel and Warwick of treason. It was probably soon
after this that the decision was taken to murder Gloucester. The
reason behind the decision was no doubt the fact that he was so closely
related to Richard. Whatever his former crimes, and however discred-
ited he might be, the public trial and sentencing to death of a reigning
king's uncle – and a former king's son – was something at which too
many of the nobles (especially perhaps his own brothers, Gaunt and
York) would have baulked. There is at any rate fairly general
agreement among the chroniclers, even those favourable to the king,
that Gloucester was murdered, only the Dieulacres chronicler attempting to deny the king's ultimate responsibility for his death. It
was also widely believed, and probably rightly, that the king's agent in
this affair was Thomas Mowbray[17] (Mowbray was captain of Calais at
this time). On 24 September, in parliament, he was formally requested
to produce Gloucester to stand trial for treason. He replied that he
could not, because 'I held this duke in my custody in the lord king's
prison in the town of Calais; and there, in that same prison, he died.'
The official line, then, was that Gloucester had died a natural death
while awaiting trial, and the fact that rumours (perhaps even a royal

---

17 Rumours of Mowbray's involvement in Gloucester's death were already circulating
in October 1397: A. Goodman, *The Loyal Conspiracy* (1971), 164.

proclamation) of his death were circulating in England and Calais even before it occurred may indicate the government's anxiety to make this story credible. It is worth remembering that both Walsingham and the monk of Evesham state that the duke was ill at the time of his arrest, but even so it is stretching credulity too far to believe that he died of natural causes at so convenient a moment, especially in view of the evidence later produced. Nevertheless the full truth only emerged gradually. Gloucester probably died on the night of 8 September 1397. The grisly details of his suffocation with a 'featherbed' at the hands of half a dozen or so esquires and valets in the back room of a Calais hostel were only divulged publicly in the parliament of October 1399. The revulsion felt at the deed is reflected in its wide circulation among the chroniclers, and at the punishments meted out to those who perpetrated it. To arrest his uncle was one thing; to have him secretly suffocated was quite another.

If Mowbray was generally thought to have taken immediate charge of Gloucester's murder, more debatable is the question of where ultimate responsiblity lay. The unfortunate John Hall, whose confession in the parliament of 1399 is our chief source of information for the murder, stated that not just the king but Rutland too had ordered his death, and that those who carried it out were servants of either Mowbray or Rutland. William Bagot, when brought to trial in October 1399, also accused Rutland of advising the king to have Gloucester murdered, and many of the lords apparently agreed with him. Naturally Rutland hotly denied it – his life depended upon it. In fact it is difficult to believe that the ultimate order for such a deed can have come from anyone but the king, but it is equally likely that Richard made sure that those closest to him shared his guilt, if only to ensure that at no future time could they turn his action to account against him. According to Walsingham – no friend of Mowbray's – Mowbray was very reluctant to arrange Gloucester's murder, and only agreed to do so when the king threatened him with death himself if he refused. As will be seen, there is evidence to suggest that Mowbray rapidly became disillusioned with the king's behaviour in the latter part of 1397, and it is by no means impossible that Richard's insistence on implicating him in his uncle's death – if this is indeed what happened – was the reason for his alienation from the king. It was a decision which the king would soon have reason to regret.

For the moment, however, everything went according to plan for Richard. Parliament met at Westminster on 17 September 1397, and

sat for two weeks. Its principal business was the conviction of
Gloucester, Arundel and Warwick for treason. Arundel was brought
to trial on Friday 21 September; despite defending himself bravely, he
was sentenced to death and beheaded on Tower Hill that same day. On
the following Monday came Mowbray's announcement that the duke
of Gloucester had died at Calais. In order to secure his conviction,
however, a confession which he was said to have written before he died
was read out in parliament, and it was on the basis of this that he was
posthumously sentenced to forfeiture of all his lands and goods. Sir
William Rickhill, a justice of the common bench who had been sent to
Calais to obtain this confession, and who presented it to the parliament
on 25 September, later claimed that only those parts of Gloucester's
confession which supported the king's case were read out in parliament.[18] Three days later, on 28 September, came Warwick's turn: faced
with near-certain death, he broke down and confessed his treason,
'sobbing and whining and begging the king's mercy.' Many of the
lords supported his plea, and the initial sentence of death against him
was commuted by the king to life imprisonment on the Isle of Man.
Archbishop Arundel was also convicted of treason and exiled for life
from England, apparently without being given an opportunity to
speak in his defence. Bolingbroke and Mowbray, however, who had
also opposed the king in 1387-88, were pardoned, on the grounds that
they had at that time endeavoured to place a check upon the more
violent inclinations of their fellow rebels.

It remained to apportion the spoils. The lands of all those who had
been convicted of treason, earmarked for distribution to the king's
supporters, were declared forfeit to the king, and on Saturday 29
September, the last full day of the parliament, these supporters were
duly rewarded by Richard in a ceremonial bestowal of titles such as
had not been seen in England for sixty years: Rutland, Huntingdon,
Kent, Nottingham and Derby were given dukedoms; the countess of
Norfolk became a duchess, and John Beaufort, earl of Somerset, a
marquis; William le Scrope became earl of Wiltshire, Thomas Percy
became earl of Worcester, Ralph Nevill became earl of Westmorland,
and Thomas Despenser became earl of Gloucester. On the following
day, Sunday 30 September, the lords, prelates and commons were all
asked to swear solemnly on the shrine of St Edward in Westminster

18 Still essential reading on Gloucester's death is an article by J. Tait, 'Did Richard II
   murder the Duke of Gloucester?', in *Historical Essays by Members of the Owens College
   Manchester* (1902), 193-216.

Abbey that they would maintain and support the judgements and other ordinances of the parliament, on pain of treason; which having been done, parliament was adjourned.

This was Richard's hour of triumph, and he had managed it well. While routing his enemies, he had also shown himself capable of mercy, and had avoided the sort of bloodbath which had sullied the reputations of those who had opposed him in 1387-88. Above all, he had convincingly reasserted kingly authority. Already, however, the seeds of his final destruction had begun to be sown. The event which precipitated Richard's fall was the quarrel which erupted during the winter of 1397-98 between Thomas Mowbray and Henry Bolingbroke, leading ultimately to the exile of both men and to Henry's triumphant return in the summer of 1399. Yet the background to their quarrel is notoriously difficult to disentangle, and explanations of the behaviour of the two lords vary considerably. In fact, it is likely that the quarrel arose out of much wider disagreements among the king's chief supporters about the direction of royal policy, and that it was Richard's inability to keep these rivalries in check that doomed him.

Some time between October 1397 and January 1398 various nobles and courtiers became involved in a plot which seems to have been directed principally against the house of Lancaster. The most likely explanation for the behaviour of those who wished to see Gaunt put to death is probably to be found in their fears – or hopes – for the succession. Richard's first marriage to Anne of Bohemia, who died in 1394, had been childless, and his new queen was only seven years old in 1397, whereas Richard was thirty. In such circumstances, it is hardly surprising that the minds of those most closely involved should have turned to the question of the succession, and there is evidence that they did. According to Walsingham, when Sir William Bagot was brought to trial in the parliament of October 1399, he gave an account of a conversation in which, he said, the king had toyed with the idea of resigning his throne and handing over power to his cousin Rutland, as being 'the noblest and wisest man in the whole kingdom.' Mowbray, also present, retorted that it would be more correct if he were to be replaced by Bolingbroke, not only because he was more closely related to Richard, but 'for many other reasons.' This, Richard declared, he would never do, because if Henry became king he would wish to destroy the church.

That Richard seriously considered his own voluntary resignation is difficult to credit, but whatever the truth of Bagot's assertions, they clearly reflect apprehension about the consequences of Richard's failure to produce an heir. They also help to account for the hostility which was felt in some quarters towards the power of the house of Lancaster. By tradition, if not by law, the throne of England generally descended by primogenitary inheritance, and if tradition was to be followed, and Richard remained childless, that meant strictly that his heir would be the earl of March, even though his claim came through a female line. On the other hand, the fourteenth century had seen an increasing number of great estates in England being deliberately restricted by their holders to inheritance in 'tail male' (i.e. to male heirs only), and Gaunt, whose family stood to benefit should inheritance to the crown be similarly restricted, was surely entitled at least to argue that the current fashion for tail male might be applied to the crown as well. There is, moreover, evidence that he did so: both John Hardyng and the author of the *Continuatio Eulogii* say that in one of the parliaments of the 1390s Gaunt petitioned that his son Henry be recognised as Richard's heir, to which the earl of March replied that he was the rightful heir. Richard apparently ordered them both to be silent; not surprisingly, it was a subject upon which he had no desire to encourage discussion.[19]

But there were other reasons apart from their fears over the succession why some of those closest to Richard should have been jealous of the house of Lancaster. Gaunt's landed estate was, after all, the greatest in England, worth about £12,000 a year, and there must have been many who coveted a share in it. It is on this point that the records of the Bolingbroke-Mowbray dispute are particularly instructive. The dispute began in December 1397, when – according to Bolingbroke's version of the story, which is the only one we have for the outbreak of the quarrel – he was riding between London and Brentford when Mowbray approached him and warned him that the two of them were about to be 'undone' by the king for their part in the events of 1387-88. Although Bolingbroke affected incredulity, Mowbray went on: 'if it had not been for certain people,' he declared, 'your father the lord of Lancaster and you would have been either seized or killed when you came to Windsor after the parliament (of September 1397).' These 'certain people', it transpired, were the earls of Rutland, Huntingdon, Worcester and himself, who had jointly sworn an oath that in future

19 *Continuatio Eulogii*, 369-70, and see the extract from Hardyng's chronicle below; see also Adam Usk, 168-9, and Froissart, *Chroniques*, xvi, 10, for speculation on the earl of March's claim to the throne.

'they would never assent to the ruin of any lord without just and reasonable cause.' According to Mowbray, four lords, whom he identified as the earls of Kent, Wiltshire, Salisbury and Gloucester, had sworn to destroy six other lords, namely Gaunt, the earls of Rutland and Huntingdon, John Beaufort marquis of Dorset, and both Henry and Mowbray themselves. Mowbray also said they planned to reverse 'the judgment concerning Earl Thomas of Lancaster,' which, he added, 'will result in the disinheritance of us and of several others.' 'God forbid!' replied Bolingbroke, and with good reason, for this can only refer to the judgements given in the parliaments of 1327 and 1330, whereby the sentence of forfeiture passed on Thomas of Lancaster at the time of his execution in 1322 was overturned, and his brother Henry (Bolingbroke's maternal great-grandfather) restored to his inheritance. Finally, Mowbray claimed that Richard – whom he thus identified as being a party to the machinations of Kent, Wiltshire, Salisbury and Gloucester – was planning, along with those four, to lure the earl of March to their side.

Although much of this is customarily dismissed as deliberate falsi-fication by either Mowbray or Bolingbroke, it is not all quite as improbable as it might seem. Wiltshire, Salisbury, Kent and Despenser had much in common. All four of them had only become earls during the past few months, and they seem to have had the typical character-istic of the 'new man': hunger for advancement through royal favour. They were, moreover, those who adhered most faithfully to Richard in 1399. Wiltshire was executed by Bolingbroke at Bristol in July, while the other three accompanied the king to Conway, and later lost their lives leading a rebellion, the Epiphany Rising, aimed at restoring Richard to the throne. There can be no doubt, therefore, about their sympathies: they were thoroughgoing Ricardians. As to the six lords whose ruin they planned, their most obvious unifying characteristic was that they included the chief representatives of the house of Lancaster: Gaunt, Bolingbroke, Beaufort (Gaunt's illegitimate son), and Exeter (Gaunt's son-in-law). The same may not be true of Rutland or Mowbray himself, or indeed of Worcester; what Mowbray might have done in 1399 we shall never know, but there is no doubting what Rutland and Worcester did: they deserted the king. It was in 1399 that the English nobles showed their true colours, and it is perfectly clear that the colours displayed by Rutland and Worcester were not the same as those displayed by Wiltshire, Salisbury, Gloucester or Kent.

Richard and his new band of royal acolytes were certainly planning some sort of redistribution of landed resources in the autumn of 1397, for during the parliament of 1397-98 he gave the earl of Salisbury permission to reopen his suit against the earl of March for the honour of Denbigh, a dispute which had by now been simmering for over sixty years, and he also reversed the sentences of treason passed in 1326 against the elder and younger Despensers, the ancestors of the earl of Gloucester, and gave Gloucester permission to sue for the recovery of their lands.[20] Whether he seriously contemplated a move against the house of Lancaster at this time is less clear, but there is no doubt that Gaunt and Bolingbroke took the threat seriously, for on 20 February 1398 they secured from the king, 'with the full assent of the council after mature deliberation,' an undertaking that he would not attempt to use the judgement against Thomas of Lancaster in 1322 as a way of claiming any Lancastrian lands.[21] There is also evidence – apart from that provided by Mowbray – of a plot at court against Gaunt and his family at this time, for on 1 March 1398 the ubiquitous William Bagot was obliged to enter into two recognisances stating, firstly, that should he ever make an attempt in future to kill Gaunt or his family he would immediately be put to death, and secondly, that should he ever attempt to disinherit Gaunt or his children, he would be fined £1,000. The only explanation for such bizarre undertakings must be that he had plotted to do precisely this, as indeed he later admitted during his trial in parliament in October 1399.[22]

That there was a conspiracy of some kind against the house of Lancaster, and that the king was planning a further redistribution of resources in favour of his closest supporters, both seem highly probable. In the atmosphere of suspicion which had arisen during the second half of 1397 it is, indeed, entirely believable that factional divisions of the sort decribed by Mowbray had developed within the higher nobility. Whether the groupings at court were quite as described by Mowbray is difficult to know, but what evidence there is suggests that he was not far wrong. It was against this background that the Mowbray-Bolingbroke dispute erupted. What has often

---

20 *RP*, iii, 353, 360-8; Despenser's permission to sue for his ancestors' lands was, however, circumscribed by his promise not to attempt to regain lands currently held by the king or by specified members of the higher nobility.

21 *CPR, 1396-9*, 285.

22 *CCR, 1396-9*, 291-2. On the same day, Bagot received a pardon for all crimes committed by him before 6 January 1398, indicating that his plots against Gaunt must have predated that time: *CPR, 1396-9*, 317.

seemed puzzling, however, is why Mowbray should have felt threatened: for a man who had so emphatically returned to royal favour, who had just been given the dukedom of Norfolk and various forfeited lands from the former earldoms of Arundel and Warwick, his behaviour smacks almost of political suicide. Yet this view depends on a reading of Mowbray's relationship with Richard which the evidence does not support. In fact, Mowbray was by no means established in the king's favour at this time. Later, following the abortive duel at Coventry, the king was to claim that even before the end of the 1397 parliament, Mowbray had already revealed his misgivings about the direction that events were taking by arguing 'both privately and publicly' against the repeal of the judgements passed in the parliament of 1388, and – despite the fact that he was himself one of the appellants in 1397 – by failing to turn up at Westminster 'on the day that the said appeal was to be decided.' That he was thereby likely to cause trouble for himself seems to have been well enough understood: two years later, Archbishop Arundel reported a conversation which he alleged had taken place between himself and the king shortly before he went into exile (i.e. in October 1397), at which Mowbray was apparently present. Arundel 'observed sadly that he was not the first to suffer exile, nor would he be the last, for he thought it likely that the duke of Norfolk and other lords would soon be following in his footsteps.' Mowbray's reaction to this is not recorded, but he must have been well aware that he was playing a dangerous game. Richard later declared that he had been prepared to overlook these indiscretions at the time 'because the said duke of Norfolk is of the blood and arms of the king,' and although both he and Henry took the precaution of securing public pardons from the king, he knew well – as he later made clear – the value of Richard's pardons.

By late 1397, then, Mowbray was a man who was living in fear: fear that his behaviour in 1387-88 had been only temporarily forgiven, that his backsliding in September 1397 had irritated the king and those closest to him, that his involvement in Gloucester's murder might be used against him at any time, and that plots were being contrived at court which included him among their targets. It is hardly surprising that it was to Bolingbroke – the man most obviously in a similar position to himself – that he chose to divulge his fears. What he does not seem to have anticipated, however, was that Bolingbroke would break his confidence and tell his father about Mowbray's allegations. Once he discovered what had happened, he seems to have panicked.

He knew that parliament was due to meet at Shrewsbury on 27 January, and that – if he had not done so already – Gaunt would almost certainly tell the king about Mowbray's allegations. Mowbray, therefore, tried to stop Gaunt. Adam Usk tells us that he 'laid snares of death' for Gaunt as he travelled to the Shrewsbury parliament, but that the duke was forewarned and avoided the trap; this is supported by the author of the *Traison*, according to whom Mowbray later admitted having 'laid an ambush to kill my lord of Lancaster'.[23]

In fear of his life, Mowbray failed to attend the parliament at Shrewsbury, leaving Bolingbroke a free hand to present his side of the story. Mowbray was promptly stripped of his offices of earl marshal and admiral of England, and an order was sent to all the sheriffs in England telling them to issue a proclamation that he was to appear before the king in person within fifteen days.[24] Richard's reaction suggests a strong presumption of guilt on Mowbray's part and also, perhaps, a fear that he might be about to flee the country. In the event, however, Mowbray duly appeared before the king, on 23 February at Oswestry, where he denied everything that Henry had alleged against him. This put Richard in a quandary: clearly the issues raised by Henry's accusations could not be ignored, yet there was not a shred of evidence to go on apart from the words of the two men. Thus he decided that only a trial by battle could decide the issue between them.

Mowbray's denial of all the charges also put Bolingbroke in a quandary: how was he expected to prove his case, and was he prepared to chance it to personal combat? He evidently preferred not to, for by the time the two parties appeared before the king again at Windsor on 29 April, he had drawn up a new list of charges against Mowbray which, he no doubt hoped, would be more susceptible of proof. According to the *Traison*, our best source for this meeting, these were, firstly, that during his tenure of office as governor of Calais Mowbray had appropriated funds intended for the defence of the town and thereby imperilled its safety; secondly, that he had been 'at the bottom of all the treasons committed in your kingdom these last eighteen years'; thirdly, that he had been responsible for the murder of Gloucester. According to the official record, Mowbray on this occasion admitted 'certain civil points' which he had previously denied. The *Traison* confirms that he now confessed to having plotted to kill Gaunt

23 Adam Usk, 169; *Traison et Mort*, 148.
24 *RP*, iii, 368; *CCR, 1396-9*, 281.

– which might have been the real point of the second of these charges – but that he denied any impropriety in relation to his governorship of Calais. It does not record his response to the charge of killing Gloucester, although the *Continuatio Eulogii* confirms that Boling- broke had 'appealed' Mowbray of his murder.[25] It may well be, of course, that the king interpreted such an accusation as a covert attack upon himself, for it was his claim that Gloucester had died of natural causes.

However, no more was heard of the charge concerning Gloucester. It is possible that by now Richard had come to see the quarrel as an opportunity to achieve what Mowbray's urgent action in December had so far denied him, namely, the neutralisation for the foreseeable future of the power of the house of Lancaster; and when the earl of March died in battle against the Irish at Kells on 20 July 1398, leaving a six-year-old son as his heir, the need for some such action probably seemed even more pressing to the king and his supporters. Moreover, as far as the murder of Gloucester was concerned, Richard was probably as afraid of Mowbray as Mowbray was of him, for if Mowbray were to be openly accused of it, there was a good chance that he would try to save himself by accusing Richard directly of ordering his uncle's murder. Bolingbroke's accusation had already come close enough to the mark. It was in the nature of their complicity that Richard and Mowbray each had a hold over the other.

Thus Bolingbroke's attempt to bring the dispute to a judicial resolu- tion failed, and the issue was referred to personal combat. The sequel is well known, and is given extended treatment in many of the chronicles. Despite the fact that both men appeared at Coventry on 16 September ready to do battle, Richard at the last moment ordered them not to fight and instead took the dispute into his own hands. Then he passed sentences of exile on both men: Henry was to quit the country for ten years, Mowbray for life. No justification was offered for Henry's exile, indeed the official record specifically states that it was 'not given on account of any misdemeanour committed by the said duke of Hereford in matters concerning his appeal.' Even the author of the *Traison* commented on the general astonishment which greeted the announcement of such a sentence upon a man against whom nothing had been proven, for the implication was that he had forfeited

25 *Continuatio Eulogii*, 379.

his honour.[26] Mowbray's sentence was much harsher. This was partly because the circumstantial evidence pointing to his guilt was greater, and partly because the charges against him relating to Calais were evidently regarded as proven. It may also have been an attempt by Richard to make Henry's sentence seem less severe.

Both men left England in mid-October. By February, Mowbray had reached Venice, where he hired a galley to take him on a pilgrimage to the Holy Land.[27] Within a few months he was back in Venice, where he died of the plague on 22 September 1399. It was extraordinarily convenient for Bolingbroke that he died when he did, for it made him the ideal scapegoat. In truth, however, he was anything but a royal stooge at this time, and the fact that he was prepared to speak his mind to the king indicates a greater degree of political courage than is found among most of his contemporaries. It is worth remembering Walsingham's remark that had Mowbray not become involved in Gloucester's murder he would have enjoyed great fame, and his death 'would have been justly lamented by the whole English kingdom'.[28] Mowbray's early death also meant that, unlike Bolingbroke, he never got a second chance to present his side of the argument – a great pity not only for him but also for those attempting to understand the two men's quarrel. Richard's mistake, it is usually asserted, lay in his handling of the dispute once it had broken out. Given the consequences of his behaviour, there is obviously some truth in this, but perhaps more to the point is that it was the king's fears and ambitions, and the greed and suspicion of the little group of men who now surrounded him, that had caused the outbreak of the quarrel in the first place. By October 1398 Richard may well have believed that he was well along the road to achieving what had, perhaps for many years now, really lain at the back of his mind. Gaunt's death in February 1399 gave him the opportunity to bring that policy to fruition, but it was to be the briefest of triumphs.

Bolingbroke's arrival in Paris in October 1398 coincided with a period not only of rapid deterioration in Anglo-French relations, but also of intense polarisation of noble factions at the French court. It is these

---

26 There is no evidence apart from that of Froissart (*Chroniques*, xvi, 108-9), which is unlikely to be reliable on this point, that Richard later reduced Henry's sentence to six years.

27 *Calendar of State Papers: Venice*, i, 1202-1509 (1864), 38.

28 *Annales Ricardi Secundi*, 321.

two factors which go much of the way towards explaining the treatment accorded him there. The French chroniclers regarded his eight-month sojourn in the French capital as a personal triumph: he was granted the Hotel de Clisson as his residence and apparently enjoyed easy access to the French court as well as freedom to correspond with other European rulers. His hand in marriage was sought at the highest levels of European society. Given that he had been exiled from England under suspicion of treason, and that the English and French kings had recently sealed the thirty-year truce between their two countries with a royal marriage, this seems, on the face of it, rather surprising. It was also from Boulogne on the French coast that Bolingbroke was to set sail in the summer of 1399, en route for his meeting with Richard at Flint. This raises obvious questions. Why did no one in France try to stop him? Did he in fact receive French support in 1399, and if so why?

The real driving forces behind the thirty-year truce of 1396 were, on the English side, Richard II and Gaunt, and on the French side, Charles VI and his uncle Philip duke of Burgundy. Yet despite the conciliatory attitude taken by both kings, and by many of their nobles, there were clearly also dissenting voices on both sides. Gloucester in particular was widely thought in France to be opposed to the ending of the war, and not a few eyebrows were raised in both countries at the disparity in age between the English king and his new queen. In France, the chief opponent of the truce was the king's brother, Louis duke of Orleans, whose views received at least intermittent support from another of the king's uncles, John duke of Berry. Here too there was some amazement both at the marriage, some apparently arguing that it should only have taken place after the conclusion of peace (as opposed to a truce), and at the apparent desperation of the English king to secure a French alliance after so many years of warfare.[29]

Orleans' suspicion of the truce was heightened by various agreements entered into by the two kings for common action on European issues:

---

29 Froissart, *Chroniques*, xv, 183-8, 237-8, 299-300; *Chronique de Saint-Denys*, 415; *Continuatio Eulogii*, 369; *Traison et Mort*, 117. For discussion of Anglo-French relations in this period see F. Lehoux, *Jean de France, Duc de Berri*, ii (1966); M. Nordberg, *Les Ducs et La Royauté: Etudes sur la Rivalité des Ducs d'Orléans et de Bourgogne 1392-1407* (1964); E. Perroy, *L'Angleterre et le Grand Schisme D'Occident* (1933); R. Vaughan, *Philip the Bold* (1962); and J. J. N. Palmer, *England, France and Christendom 1377-99* (1972). Palmer takes a different view from that proposed here, believing that Anglo-French relations remained good until the end of Richard's reign.

most notably, for a joint Anglo-French expedition against
Giangaleazzo Visconti, the duke of Milan (whose daughter, Valentina,
was Orleans' wife), and for a joint embassy to both popes to try to
bring an end to the schism which had divided Europe for twenty years.
There were, therefore, a number of issues at stake in the murderous
power struggle which was developing at the French court – the
prelude to the Armagnac-Burgundian civil war of the early fifteenth
century. The essential precondition for this power struggle was, of
course, the periodic insanity of Charles VI, whose mental state had
continued to deteriorate since his first attack of frenzy in the summer
of 1392. Some idea of the atmosphere in Paris can be gleaned from the
fact that in April 1396, apparently at the instigation of Burgundy,
Valentina was forced to leave the French court because she was
suspected of using sorcery to gain a hold over the king's mind, thereby
undermining his sanity.[30]

In the event, neither of the schemes agreed between the English and
French governments in 1396 was to prove a success, largely because
of opposition to them on both sides of the channel. When Richard put
the Milanese proposal to parliament in January 1397, the attitude of
the commons was that they wanted no part in it. Several of the lords
probably felt the same way – including, perhaps, Henry Bolingbroke,
who was a personal friend of the Milanese ducal family and who was
soon to enter into negotiations for his marriage to Lucia Visconti,
Giangaleazzo's cousin. As a result, Richard had, by early 1398 at the
latest, abandoned the idea of a Milanese expedition, and wrote
accordingly to Charles VI, informing him that he had forbidden his
subjects to take part in any attack on Giangaleazzo. So irritated was
Burgundy at Richard's volte-face that he apparently tried to stop the
letter being delivered to Charles.[31] Equally irritating to the French
government was Richard's volte-face (as they saw it) over the joint
Anglo-French proposal to end the schism.[32] The preferred option in

30 D. M. Bueno de Mesquita, *Giangaleazzo Visconti, Duke of Milan 1351-1402* (1941),
    202-3; R. C. Famiglietti, *Royal Intrigue: Crisis at the Court of Charles VI 1392-1420*
    (1986), 209. For a discussion of Charles' mental illness see Famiglietti, Chapter 1.

31 *Reign of Richard II*, 172; Froissart, *Chroniques*, xvi, 95-6; *Calendar of State Papers:
    Milan*, i, 1385-1618, ed. A. B. Hinds (1912), 1-2; and D. M. Bueno de Mesquita, 'The
    foreign policy of Richard II in 1397: some Italian letters', *EHR* (1941), 628-37, who
    argues that Richard's decision to patch up relations with Milan in 1397 may also
    have been connected with his hopes of the imperial title.

32 For what follows see especially M. Harvey, *Solutions to the Schism: A Study of Some
    English Attitudes 1378 to 1409* (1983), 97-113; also Perroy, *L'Angleterre et le Grand
    Schisme*, Chapters 8 and 9.

England was for a general council of the church at which both popes might be persuaded to resign. The French government, however – or at least Charles VI and Burgundy – had by 1396 come to believe that the only effective way to reunite Christendom was through the 'way of cession', that is, the resignation of both popes simultaneously, preferably voluntarily, but if necessary forced, through the withdrawal of obedience on the part of national governments. At some point during the 1396 peace negotiations, probably when he met with Burgundy in August of that year, Richard agreed, despite the wishes of the English church, to go along with the French proposal. Exactly what he agreed to is, however – and was – a matter of debate. He certainly subscribed to the idea of simultaneous resignation, but whether, as the French later claimed, he gave an undertaking to withdraw the obedience of the English church from Boniface IX (the Roman pope) in the event of his refusal to resign, is more doubtful. At any rate, the two kings certainly agreed on the dispatch of a joint embassy to both popes in the summer of 1397 in an attempt to secure their resignation. The embassy duly visited Rome and Avignon, but was a complete failure: neither pope was prepared to resign. One of the reasons why they could afford not to was because they knew that in both countries there was powerful opposition to the joint royal initiative. In England this opposition seems to have come mainly from the church, but in France it was led by Orleans, who was particularly opposed to the idea of withdrawal of obedience.

By early 1398, therefore, the common policy initiatives agreed between the English and French governments in November 1396 had ground to a stop, and under the pressure of failure, relations began to cool. At some point during the spring or summer of 1398 Charles VI wrote a letter to Richard complaining that the terms of the 1396 truce had still not been published in Gascony and that the English garrisons there were continuing to levy tribute, contrary to its terms: there was once again, he warned, a threat of war in the duchy.[33] There were recriminations too on the question of the schism. Following the two popes' refusal to resign, the dukes of Burgundy and Berry decided to force the issue, and on 27 July 1398 the French government unilaterally withdrew its obedience from Benedict XIII (the Avignon pope). This was done against the advice not only of Orleans, but also of a number of influential French churchmen, who argued that such a move would be pointless since the English would not follow suit. It was

33 Froissart, *Chroniques*, xvi, 302-5.

therefore of the utmost importance to Burgundy and the French
government that the English should be persuaded to do so, and in
August an embassy was sent to Richard reminding him of his (alleged)
promise to withdraw the obedience of the English church from
Boniface once the French had done the same. Was this French bluff, or
had Richard secretly promised more in 1396 than he had dared to
reveal at the time? Whatever the truth, the French ambassadors
claimed that the failure of the 1397 embassy was largely the fault of
the English – who, they claimed, had treated Boniface with too much
leniency – and that now was the time for them to make amends by
doing as they had said they would and withdrawing from the Roman
allegiance. Richard, however, refused to do so, saying instead that he
wished to consult the Universities of Oxford and Cambridge.[34] French
annoyance with Richard can only have increased when news reached
them that on 25 November 1398 the English king had established a
concordat with Boniface detailing their respective rights over appointments to the English church: the apparent conclusion to be drawn
being that Richard had only feigned adherence to the 'way of cession'
in order to bolster his bargaining power with Boniface. In return for
his abandonment of the 'way of cession', Richard also obtained papal
support for his actions in the parliament of 1397-98. The concordat
marks the effective demise of the policy of Anglo-French co-operation
agreed in 1396.[35]

Thus matters stood when, in the middle of October, Bolingbroke
arrived in Paris. His presence there soon generated further Anglo-
French tension, for it was widely thought in France that Richard had
acted foolishly in his treatment of Bolingbroke.[36] Not surprisingly, it
was to the duke of Orleans in particular that Henry turned, for the two
men had much in common: both were political allies of the duke of
Milan (Henry's proposed marriage to Lucia Visconti, in return for
which he would marry one of his daughters to one of Giangaleazzo's
sons, was still being discussed as late as May 1399), and both had an
interest in disrupting Anglo-French relations: Orleans because he had
never favoured what he thought of as the duke of Burgundy's truce and
was eager to reopen hostilities, and Bolingbroke because Anglo-
French tension was likely to weaken Richard's position and might thus

34 Harvey, *Solutions to the Schism*, 93-101; Lehoux, *Jean de France*, 382-7.
35 Perroy, *L'Angleterre et le Grand Schisme*, 384-90.
36 Froissart, *Chroniques*, xvi, 116, 139-41; *Chronique de Saint-Denys*, 675-7.

create an opportunity for him to return to England.[37]

It was the events of March and April 1399, however, which both persuaded Orleans to throw his support more unequivocally behind Henry and presented him with the opportunity to do so. Richard's famous decision on 18 March to seize custody of the Lancastrian inheritance following Gaunt's death was condemned by English and French chroniclers alike, and won Henry much sympathy among the French nobility. At the same time, word had reached Richard that plans were afoot for a marriage between Henry and Mary, countess of Eu, the widowed daughter of the duke of Berry, whereupon he promptly dispatched the earl of Salisbury to the French court to put an end to the proposal. According to Froissart, Salisbury reminded the French king that Henry was a traitor, to which Charles protested angrily at Richard's treatment of Henry and said that he ought to be recalled. Nevertheless, although Charles hurriedly reassured Bolingbroke that the French did not consider him a traitor, he and the duke of Berry agreed, though reluctantly, that the negotiations should be broken off. That Orleans had been in favour of the marriage there can be little doubt: he even arranged a meeting between Henry and Mary at his castle of Asnières in April 1399.[38]

Events at the French court now combined in Bolingbroke's favour. Following a violent quarrel with Orleans on the question of the schism, Berry retired on about 20 May to his castle of Bicetre for the summer. Burgundy had already, in late April, left Paris for Artois, where he too remained for the summer. The way was thus clear for Orleans, who during these months gained such an ascendancy at court that it was said that he could bend his brother the king's will to almost any project that he favoured.[39] By early June news must have reached Paris that Richard was on his way to Ireland, and on 17 June Orleans drew up his celebrated treaty of alliance with Bolingbroke. Their

---

37 *Calendar of State Papers: Milan*, 2; Nordberg, *Les Ducs et la Royauté*, 131, 233. On 1 December 1398 Orléans gave a great dinner in Henry's honour (E. Jarry, *La Vie Politique de Louis de France, Duc d'Orleans* (1889), 227). There was even a rumour circulating in France at this time that Orléans and Derby were about to undertake a joint mission to Avignon to assist Benedict XIII, though it came to nothing (P. Pietresson de Saint-Aubin, 'Documents inédits sur l'installation de Pierre d'Ailly à l'evêché de Cambrai en 1397', *Bibliothèque de l'Ecole des Chartes* (1955), 138-9).

38 E. Collas, *Valentine de Milan, Duchesse d'Orléans* (1911), 253. Our best source for this episode is Froissart, *Chroniques*, xvi, 141-51. See also Lehoux, *Jean de France*, 406-7, and, for a different interpretation, Palmer, *England, France and Christendom*, 224.

39 Lehoux, *Jean de France*, 414-16.

alliance was later to become the subject of fierce debate between the two men, and it is by no means clear either how much Orleans knew of Henry's intentions or what he hoped to gain from it. Perhaps he intended merely to help Henry, whom he clearly regarded as unworthily disgraced, to regain his Lancastrian inheritance; perhaps he genuinely expected that Henry would supplant Richard, whereby England would, he hoped, have a king more amenable to his own views; or he may simply have seen Henry's expedition as a convenient way to strike a blow at the English king, for whom he had little sympathy. His foreign policy was, after all, opposed to Richard's in almost every respect, as it was to that of his enemy Burgundy, Richard's ally.[40]

But if Orleans knew of Henry's plans, while Burgundy clearly did not, how much did the duke of Berry and King Charles himself know? The Saint-Denys chronicler relates the story at this time of the dismissal of most of the French personnel of Richard's child-queen Isabelle, at which, he says, 'the king and queen of France, and all the princes of the blood, were incensed.' The author of the *Traison*, who was probably with the queen's household, tells the same story in more detail, and the fact that Froissart mentions it too suggests that it caused quite a stir in France. According to the *Traison*, it was Richard himself who dismissed Isabelle's governess, Lady Courcy, shortly before his departure for Ireland.[41] Such insensitive treatment of his young wife may have been the last straw as far as the French were concerned. His broken promises over the schism and the Milanese expedition, his seizure of the Lancastrian inheritance, his treatment of Bolingbroke in relation to the Mary de Berry marriage, and the continuing disagreements over the enforcement of the truce in Gascony had all served to debase the English king's reputation at the French court. The passive

---

40 Vaughan, *Philip the Bold*, 56; Nordberg, *Les Ducs et la Royauté*, 130-1; Bueno de Mesquita, 'The foreign policy of Richard II in 1397'.

41 *Traison et Mort*, 163-70; Froissart, *Chroniques*, xvi, 189-90. The Courcy family, who seem to have been Isabelle's principal advisers in England, received many favours from Richard in the years 1397-99. Sir William, baron de Courcy, and his wife Margaret were granted £100 a year at the English exchequer for their good service to the young queen, and Sir William was granted permission to import corn to England without paying the custom. Master Richard Courcy, described as the queen's secretary, was granted 40 marks a year (*CPR, 1396-9*, 46, 103, 519). According to the *Traison*, the king dismissed Lady Courcy from her post as governess because of her extravagance and lack of discretion. Williams, in his edition of the *Traison* (p. 165, n. 1) identified this lady wrongly; for the correct identification see the note by Kervyn de Lettenhove in Froissart, *Chroniques*, xvi, 347.

support of others at court, including perhaps the duke of Berry,[42] and possibly even the king himself – although just what they thought they were supporting must remain a matter for speculation – was probably as crucial to Henry's plans as the active support of Orleans. Not surprisingly, his real destination was kept secret: according to the chronicler of Saint-Denys, where Henry called on his way to the coast, he had put it about that he was planning to travel to Spain. Yet he was able to embark at Boulogne without a finger being raised to stop him.

There were probably many people at the French court, therefore, who would not have disagreed with the assertion made in the 'Record and Process' that Richard was 'so inconstant in his behaviour, especially in his dealings with the pope, and with kings ..., that virtually no living person who came to know him could or wished to trust him'.[43] The chief task of those who drafted the deposition charges, however, was of course to justify that deposition to the people of England, not to the king of France. Just how unpopular, then, was Richard in England by the summer of 1399? The accusations made against him in the 'Record and Process' were not on the whole simply fabricated – indeed, several of those charges which are capable of proof have been proven correct[44] – but many of them were hardly the sort of 'crimes' which would have greatly concerned the majority of his subjects. Leaving aside the 'Record and Process', however, two accusations stand out as really earning Richard the opprobrium of his people: that he extorted 'blank charters' from the seventeen counties closest to London, and that he maintained as his bodyguard an unruly and violent retinue of Cheshiremen.[45] That chroniclers hostile to the king should have criticised him on these grounds occasions no surprise, but what needs emphasising is that some of those favourable to Richard did so as well. Even the Dieulacres chronicler, that most Ricardian of English commentators, declared that as a result of the king's demands for

---

42 It is of some significance to note that, according to the *Traison et Mort*, 226, the followers of the dukes of Berry and Orléans were the only foreigners allowed to attend Henry IV's court on the day of his coronation.

43 Article twenty-five of the deposition charges.

44 C. Barron, 'The tyranny of Richard II', *BIHR* (1968), 1-18; J. G. Edwards, 'The parliamentary committee of 1398', *EHR* (1925), 321-33.

45 For blank charters see Barron, 'Tyranny of Richard II', 10-14: 'blank charters were not blank but were couched in terms which gave the king *carte blanche* over the lives and possessions of his subjects.' The existence of the Cheshire bodyguard is confirmed by P.R.O. document E101/402/10, which lists over 760 Cheshiremen retained by the king.

blank charters, 'evil rumours began to spread through the whole community because of the harsh bondage to which they were subjecting themselves,' and that because of the rumours of extortions practised by his Cheshire bodyguard he was 'held in fatal odium by his ordinary subjects.'

There were other ways too in which Richard contributed to his own unpopularity: for instance, his increasingly arbitrary interference after 1397 in local politics – appointments to county offices, parliamentary elections, and so forth – which crucially undermined the rapport which he had gradually built up with the gentry since 1389.[46] Even so, the collapse of support for the king in 1399 is difficult to explain on these grounds alone, for Richard's policies had bound men to him as well as against him. Bolingbroke's success must have depended on other factors too: the speed with which he acted, for example, and the advantage of surprise it gave him; uncertainty as to his real intentions; the absence of the king and many of his best soldiers in Ireland; the lack of political will of the regent, Edmund of York; and fears among landholders about the king's increasingly cavalier attitude to property rights. On this last count, Richard had touched an exposed nerve in the body politic. The denial to him of the Lancastrian inheritance was what made Henry's cause a just one. It was as the champion of property rights that he presented himself to the people of England between July and September 1399.

Richard crossed to Waterford in Ireland on 1 June 1399. Henry must have begun his final preparations as soon as he heard for sure that Richard had arrived there. As late as 20 June York apparently still had no inkling of Henry's intentions, but by 28 June he was aware that all was not well, for on that day he wrote from Westminster to various sheriffs telling them that an armed force was gathering in Picardy planning to attack Calais and to invade England, and ordering them to raise forces and join him with all possible haste at Ware in Hertfordshire.[47] In addition to this element of surprise, Henry also succeeded (intentionally or otherwise) in creating confusion about his real intentions. Walsingham says that he did not try to land at once, instead 'taking his ships back and forth along the coastline, approaching different parts of the kingdom in turn, trying to discover whether

---

46 C. Given-Wilson, *The Royal Household and the King's Affinity: Service, Politics and Finance in England 1360-1413* (1986), 245-51.

47 P.R.O. E101/42/12; *CPR 1396-9*, 518; on 20 June two of Henry's esquires had been given over £1,500 at the exchequer for his use (P.R.O. E403/562, 20 June).

the coastal defences had been put in a state of readiness to resist him.'
He also seems to have made prior contact with his supporters in
England, who may have been expecting him to land on the south coast:
by 3 July York was ordering the sheriff of Sussex to besiege Pevensey
castle, which, so he had heard, had been seized by the king's enemies:
it was in fact John Pelham, a Sussex knight and a retainer of Henry's,
who had taken Pevensey, where he was still being besieged three
weeks later.[48]

Whether the capture of Pevensey was a deliberate diversionary tactic
or an exploratory preliminary towards a full-scale south coast landing,
there is no doubt that Henry eventually landed in Yorkshire, probably
at Ravenspur (modern Spurn Head, at the mouth of the Humber).[49]
The most likely date for his landing is that given by Walsingham and
the well-placed Kirkstall chronicler, namely 4 July. York, however,
apparently still had little idea where the chief danger was likely to
come from. Orders were sent out by him between 4 and 12 July for the
garrisoning of castles in Kent, Surrey, Sussex, Berkshire, Nottingham-
shire, Herefordshire, Gloucestershire, Staffordshire, Cheshire and
Yorkshire. The author of the *Traison* states that initially he and John
Beaufort set out for 'the west coast of the country' intending to
prevent Henry's landing there, but after three days, when they realised
their mistake, they returned to London and summoned troops to meet
them at St Albans.[50] This confusion allowed Henry time to gather
strength and plan his moves. He seems at first to have been in no
hurry, and to have kept his options open. He first moved north to
Pickering castle, then west to Knaresborough and south to Pontefract,
spending two or three days at each, installing his own garrisons and

48 CPR, 1396-9, 596; for the siege of Pevensey see S. K. Walker, 'Letters to the Dukes
    of Lancaster in 1381 and 1399', EHR (1991), 68-79. John Davy, presumably a
    Lancastrian servant, was later given 10s. by Henry for travelling from London to
    Dover 'on hearing of the lord's arrival at the end of the said month (June)' (P.R.O.
    DL.28/4/1, f. 15).

49 Matthew Danthorpe, a hermit, was later given permission to complete the chapel
    which he had started building at Ravenspur 'where the king landed at his last
    coming into England.' Another government record states that Henry 'put into the
    parts of Holdernesse' (CPR, 1399-1401, 27, 209). The Kirkstall chronicler, however,
    inserted in his margin a note that Henry landed 'near Bridlington in Holderness',
    and the Vita said that he landed 'between Hull and Bridlington'. It is possible that
    Henry initially put in to Spurn Head but then went on by boat to a point near to
    Bridlington.

50 Traison et Mort, 183-4; P.R.O. E403/562, 4-12 July; CPR, 1396-9, 591; CCR, 1396-
    9, 506-7, 518; P. Morgan, War and Society in Medieval Cheshire 1277-1403 (1987),
    203.

gathering his supporters. He probably reached Pontefract on 13 or 14 July, moving on to Doncaster a day or two later. From here he continued southwards, though still quite slowly, to Leicester, which he probably reached on about 20 July. At Leicester he was faced with a choice: he could move south-east to London, to take the capital, south-west to Bristol, to cut off Richard's return, or north-west to Cheshire, to neutralise the king's 'inner citadel'.

His decision to march towards Bristol was probably taken only after he had received information about the movements of York and the other royalist supporters. York's movements can be traced with a fair degree of accuracy from the place-dates attached to his writs and from the accounts later submitted by those who brought their retinues to join him.[51] Having summoned troops to meet him at Ware, he remained at Westminster until about 7 July, then moved north to St Albans where he remained for five days. Walsingham tells us that during this time he was busily sending out summonses, and that 'as a result of this many worthy lords joined him with their retinues.' On 12 July he moved to Ware, presumably to collect his troops, and on the following day he probably moved north to Bedford. Possibly he was planning to challenge Henry in the midlands, before he could reach London or Bristol; but if that was the case he soon changed his mind, for by 14 July he had turned south-west to Aylesbury, and on the 16th he reached Oxford. Here he remained for about four days, during which time a decision was taken to split the army. Lescrope, Bussy, Green and Russell made straight for Bristol, hoping apparently to link up with Richard when he returned from Ireland, while York himself moved via Stow-on-the-Wold and Gloucester to Berkeley. According to the *Vita* he reached Berkeley before Henry did, probably on about 24 July. Henry meanwhile remained at Leicester until he knew which way York had gone. According to John Catesby's account he only reached Coventry on 23 July. By this time he must have heard that York had moved west, and decided to follow him. Passing through Warwick and Evesham, Henry reached Gloucester on 25 or 26 July, and on the 27th he caught up with York at Berkeley.

The author of the *Vita* tells us that on Sunday 27 July Henry and York 'spoke together in a church outside Berkeley castle and came to an agreement.' He does not tell us what that agreement was, but there is no doubt that their meeting was one of the turning-points of Henry's

51 See Appendix A.

campaign. In effect, York agreed to abandon his attempt to resist Henry's advance. What Henry promised in return – if anything – will never be known: Walsingham states that York had already declared his unwillingness to confront his nephew, for 'he had no intention of attacking someone who came in a just cause and to ask for the restoration of his rightful inheritance', but the accounts submitted by his commanders (as well as the remarks of some of the chroniclers) also suggest that he was having trouble in holding his army together, and that he was probably not in a position to stop Henry had he wished to. Although at least 3,300 men received wages for responding to York's summonses, many of these seem to have left him – some, apparently, to join Henry – before 27 July, and it was left to a handful of diehards, of whom the most notable was Henry Despenser, bishop of Norwich, to offer any form of armed resistance to the Lancastrian army. Despenser and his companions were arrested (on 27 July) and imprisoned until after the king's capture. York, and presumably many of his followers as well, now joined with Henry and moved on to Bristol, which was reached on 28 July. Lescrope, Bussy and Green were forced out of the castle and beheaded on the following day. York's presence at these executions can only have been seen as publicly committing him to Henry's cause – whatever he judged that to be.

The size of Henry's army by this time is even more difficult to determine than that of York. Those who landed with him at Ravenspur numbered only a few hundred at most – mainly the servants of Henry himself and his chief supporters, presumably – although they included a number of battle-hardened Lancastrians such as John Norbury, Thomas Erpingham, Thomas Rempston and Francis de Courte. Henry's own second son, Thomas, was also with him, as were Archbishop Arundel and the son and heir of the executed earl of Arundel, also called Thomas. By the time he left Doncaster, however, his army had grown enormously. Among the most prominent to join him during these early days were the earls of Northumberland and Westmorland, Northumberland's son 'Hotspur', and Lords Willoughby, Roos and Greystoke, all of them bringing retainers with them. Once he had become king, Henry paid a total of nearly £4,900 in wages to those who had accompanied him on his march and remained with him during the October parliament: the list of recipients includes two earls, three barons, and forty-four knights, esquires and valets, and although it is far from complete, it is nevertheless useful in indicating the sizes of the retinues raised by Henry's supporters. It is striking for example that more than half of this sum was paid to just three men – Northumberland who received £1,333, Hotspur who received £666, and Willoughby who received £623 – suggesting that these three retinues were by far the most powerful to accompany Henry. Westmorland, surprisingly, received only £140.[52] Nevertheless, his and Northumberland's support was crucial, even if the price they exacted was a heavy one: for Northumberland, it was the office of constable of England and the wardenship of the Scottish marches; for Westmorland, the office of marshal of England and the much-coveted honour of Richmond.

York's army was drawn almost exclusively from the southern half of the country. By contrast, most of those paid by Henry were northerners, testimony to the wisdom of his policy of initially making for the areas of traditional Lancastrian influence. Several of the chroniclers, even those hostile to Henry, describe his army growing daily as it advanced, joined by a motley band of opportunists, adventurers and deserters from the royalist cause, and although the figures given by some of them are hardly credible (Creton, Usk, and the author of the Kirkstall chronicle all mention a hundred thousand men, while the Dieulacres chronicler goes to two hundred thousand), it is not difficult to imagine that by the time he reached Berkeley Henry's army was several thousand strong. It is worth remembering, though, that Henry did not have it all his own way. The Kirkstall chronicler tells us that in his own Yorkshire heartland he encountered problems in taking Knaresborough castle, and Usk reports that even after Bristol had fallen there were still some who were planning to resist him. By this time, however, there was in reality only one way in which Henry could be stopped: that is, if Richard were able to return from Ireland bringing his army with him and hold it together for long enough to mount an effective challenge.

Richard must have heard of Henry's landing by about 10 July at the latest, but it was at least a further week before he left Ireland. The date of his arrival at Milford Haven in Pembrokeshire is generally agreed to have been some time between 18 and 27 July, probably about the 24th.[53] Different chroniclers give different reasons for this delay, some

---

52 See Appendix B. S. Walker, *The Lancastrian Affinity 1361-1399* (1990), 95, notes that 192 gilt collars were issued by Henry's receiver-general in the summer of 1399.

53 P.R.O. E101/403/21 records that Richard left Dublin on 17 July for England, but he may have gone via Waterford. For a thorough review of the evidence see D. Johnston, 'Richard II's departure from Ireland, July 1399', *EHR* (1983), 785-805.

ascribing it to indecision on the king's part, others to the foolish, conflicting or treacherous advice offered to him by his followers. According to Creton, the king had already – probably on about 17 July – sent the earl of Salisbury to Conway in the hope that he could raise an army of Welshmen and Cheshiremen; since Creton claims to have accompanied Salisbury to Conway, it is difficult not to believe him. Richard's plan, then, was evidently to raise Cheshire before Henry could get there: Salisbury, he probably hoped, would bring a force of Cheshiremen southwards, while Richard himself would link up with the army which York, Lescrope and the other royal councillors had assembled at Bristol. But the king's indecision, which was in part occasioned by the fact that his returning army landed at a number of different ports, proved crucial. By 29 July – the day Lescrope, Bussy and Green were executed – he had only reached Whitland Abbey, seven miles west of Carmarthen, where he managed to establish contact with some of York's officials.[54] Two days later he was at Carmarthen, but by then he must have heard of York's defection, and possibly of the fall of Bristol too. Guessing, presumably, that Henry would now make for Cheshire, Richard tried to get there before him. One point upon which almost all the chroniclers are agreed is that it was the king's own decision to leave his army and make his way northwards. According to the Whalley chronicler he was warned that he was about to be captured; other chroniclers state that his troops, fearful of Henry's growing power, began to desert, or that the king simply lost heart. At any rate, Richard abandoned his army. He slipped away secretly with just a dozen or so intimate supporters, probably during the night of 31 July, and made his way to north Wales. Awakening the following morning to find the king gone, Thomas Percy earl of Worcester, the steward of the household, formally broke his rod of office, and he and Rutland announced to the king's followers that they were free to disperse. Rutland and Worcester, along with many others, then promptly rode to join Henry.

From this point onwards we are largely dependent upon Creton for our knowledge of the king's movements, but since Creton's chronology is frequently vague, and on occasions demonstrably wrong, it is difficult to date events with precision.[55] According to Creton, Richard

54 £500 of the exchequer's money was passed to Richard Maudeleyn and others of the king's household at Whitland abbey on 29 July (P.R.O. E361/5, m.26d.)

55 For the dating of these events see particularly Johnston, 'Richard II's departure from Ireland', and J. W. Sherborne, 'Perjury and the Lancastrian revolution of 1399', *Welsh History Review* (1988), 217-41.

'rode hard' for Conway, expecting to find Salisbury there with an army of Welshmen and Cheshiremen. Those troops that Salisbury had managed to raise had, however, already deserted when they discovered that the king was not at Conway in person. Thus Richard found himself at Conway with no more than a score or so of his followers, the most prominent of whom were the earls of Kent, Huntingdon and Salisbury, and the bishop of Carlisle. It would still have been possible, as Creton points out, to flee by ship, but before making any decisions Richard decided to make contact with Henry and find out just what it was that he wanted. Kent and Huntingdon were accordingly dispatched to parley with Henry and report back to the king. It is not clear whether Richard was aware of Henry's whereabouts at this time. In fact Henry had left Bristol on 31 July and made his way northwards, with no great speed, along the Welsh border, arriving at Chester (which had already been surrendered to him) on 8 or 9 August. According to Creton, Richard then spent 'four or six nights' restlessly travelling to Beaumaris and Caernarvon – hoping perhaps to recruit the garrisons there, or to find ships, or simply in search of a safer refuge – before returning to Conway to await the return of his half-brothers. At any rate, Richard must have been back at Conway no later than 15 August, for that is the latest possible date for his meeting there with Henry's envoys.

Kent and Huntingdon never returned to Conway; Henry detained them at Chester, and instead sent a deputation of his own supporters, led by the earl of Northumberland and, perhaps, Archbishop Arundel, to parley with Richard.[56] At Conway, some agreement was struck between Richard and Henry's envoys. The 'Record and Process' says that Richard willingly agreed to resign his crown, but this is scarcely credible. It is possible, however, that he made some promise to the effect that he would continue to reign while Henry would in practice be allowed to rule. The comments of Usk, that Richard agreed to surrender to Henry 'on condition of saving his dignity', and of the Dieulacres chronicler, that Arundel and Northumberland swore to him that he would be allowed to retain 'his royal power and dominion', might refer to some agreement along these lines. Creton, however, who claims to have been an eyewitness to the negotiations between Northumberland and the king, was adamant that Richard

---

56 Sherborne, 'Perjury and the Lancastrian revolution', 229-30, and Palmer, 'Authorship, date and historical value', 417-19, both cast doubt on the assertion in the 'Record and Process' that Arundel was at Conway.

only agreed to restore Henry to his inheritance (including the stewardship of England), and to summon a parliament at which five of his councillors would be put on trial; in return for this, Northumberland swore on the newly-consecrated host that he would remain king. Yet according to Creton, Northumberland was lying, for he had already, on his way to Conway, laid an ambush for Richard a few miles down the coast, and was simply making promises in order to lure the king out of the castle. In this he was successful: Richard, believing the earl's promises, agreed to follow him to a meeting with Henry, and was duly ambushed and led away to Flint not as a free man but as a prisoner.

The meeting at Flint was apparently a brief affair. As little seems to have been said as was decently possible, although it was clear by now that Richard was Henry's prisoner. The date was probably Saturday 16 August. Creton's date of Tuesday 22 August is certainly wrong, for 22 August fell on a Friday in 1399. The evidence of the place-dates attached to royal writs – which began to be issued again on 16 August after a hiatus of eight days – suggests that Richard and Henry returned to Chester on that day, and that they left for London on Wednesday 20 August; this fits well with Creton's statement that after returning to Chester with the king, Henry held a council there for three days before setting out for London. The author of the *Vita* also says that they left Chester on 20 August, but was apparently ignorant of the fact that they had spent three days there before departing, which led him to date the meeting at Flint to 19 August.

During the council at Chester it was agreed to summon a parliament, the writs for which were sent out (in Richard's name) on 19 August. Both Creton and Walsingham say that Henry decided too at this point to send home many of those who had gathered to his standard, apparently because of misgivings about the devastation that such a large army marching from Chester to London might wreak. Either at Chester or at some point along the road to London Henry also apparently received a deputation from the city of London offering him the city's support. Some of the chroniclers state that the Londoners were firmly behind Henry almost from the moment he landed, but it has recently been suggested, perhaps more realistically, that they waited until they knew the outcome of his campaign before committing themselves to his cause. By 20 August, however, the news of Richard's capture must have reached London, for on that day Henry's esquire John Leventhorpe was given £1,333 by the chamberlains of the exchequer for his master's use, and at his order.[57] Surely the king's own administrators would not have passed cash to his adversary without good information that his cause was lost.

It was on the same day, 20 August, that Henry and the captive king set out from Chester on the road south. Apart from one attempt to rescue Richard, which probably occurred on the first night out from Chester, at Cholmondeston near Nantwich, the journey seems to have been uneventful, and Westminster was reached on Monday 1 September.[58] On the following day the king was transferred to the Tower, where he remained for the next two months. By this time the decision had probably been taken that Richard would be deposed. Quite when Henry and his supporters reached that decision is impossible to know, although naturally it has been the subject of much speculation. Later, at the time of their rebellion in 1403, the Percies claimed that when they joined Henry at Doncaster in July 1399 he had sworn an oath 'upon the holy gospels' that he had come only for his inheritance, and that Richard would remain king. The story of the oath, and of the way in which Henry tricked the Percies and seized the throne, is told in detail by John Hardyng, but Hardyng was a Percy supporter, and he was writing some fifty years later, by which time his memory may have become (intentionally or otherwise) clouded. There are nevertheless at least three independent sources which state that at some point during July or August Henry swore an oath that he would not seize the throne (which was not quite the same as swearing that he would not depose the king – the Percies might have been more concerned about who would replace Richard), which makes it hard to believe that there is not some truth in the story. On the other hand, as early as 2 August, a full two weeks before Richard's capture, Northumberland accepted appointment from Henry, under his Duchy of Lancaster seal, as Warden of the West March of Scotland, which was an office in the gift of the king; this makes it equally hard to believe that Northumberland acted in good faith when he promised Richard at Conway that he

---

57 P.R.O. E403/564, 6 April. For a discussion of the Londoners' role in these events see Barron, 'Deposition of Richard II', 140–44. It is worth noting, though, that as early as 11 August a group of Londoners had come to Westminster abbey searching for the king (Sherborne, 'Perjury and the Lancastrian revolution', 239).

58 For the attempt to rescue Richard see Morgan, *War and Society in Medieval Cheshire*, 204; Creton, however, says that it (or another attempt) occurred at Lichfield. Henry and Richard's itinerary was: (nights of) 20 August Nantwich; 21st Newcastle-under-Lyme; 22nd Stafford; 23–24th Lichfield; 25–26th Coventry; 27th Daventry; 28th Northampton; 29th Dunstable; 30–31st St Albans.

would remain king. The crucial point, surely, is that those who knew Richard and had witnessed his coup of 1397 must have known that if they let him remain on the throne it would only be a matter of time before he reasserted his authority and avenged himself on them. Whatever oaths were sworn by Henry in the summer of 1399, at Doncaster, Flint, Knaresborough, Chester, or elsewhere, were intended for public consumption, not to deceive the thoroughly hard-headed earl of Northumberland.[59] Henry and Northumberland – and Archbishop Arundel, no doubt – perjured themselves in equal measure. It is quite possible that Henry's ultimate decisions to depose Richard and to claim the throne for himself were only arrived at gradually, but they must have played a part in his thinking from the moment he left Paris, and those who committed themselves to his cause must have known this.

Once Richard was in the Tower, however, Henry could act more openly. From 10 September he ceased dating his Duchy of Lancaster letters by Richard's regnal year and dated them instead by the Christian era.[60] The proceedings of the following two weeks are not well documented, but clearly a number of meetings were held, devoted principally to devising the means whereby an act of undoubted illegality might be veiled in legality. Adam Usk, who was a member of the committee appointed to draft Henry's claim to the throne, preserves an account of one of these meetings, as does John Hardyng, although his account is later and less reliable. According to Hardyng it took place on 21 September, and was chiefly concerned with the so-called 'Crouchback legend'. This was the story – and it was completely untrue – that Edmund 'Crouchback', the first earl of Lancaster, had really been the elder rather than the younger brother of King Edward I, but had been passed over for the throne by his father because he was deformed. If accepted, this would have meant that all the kings of England since Edward I had in reality been intruders, and that successive earls and dukes of Lancaster had been the rightful kings: thus in taking the throne Henry was claiming no more than his birthright. Both Usk and Hardyng make it clear that Henry's attempt to use this story was firmly rejected. Walsingham also says that Henry encountered opposition (from Justice Thirning) to his suggestion that he might claim the throne by conquest.

---

59 Sherborne, 'Perjury and the Lancastrian revolution', discusses these oaths in detail.
60 *Ibid*, 240.

Thus Henry did not by any means have it all his own way during these
weeks, and nor did he find it easy to extract a deed of resignation from
Richard. The memorandum describing the negotiations with the king
entitled 'The Manner of King Richard's Renunciation', which was
probably written by someone who witnessed these negotiations, states
that when he was first asked to resign, the king 'replied shortly that
he would not do it under any circumstances; and he was greatly
incensed, and declared that he would like to have it explained to him
how it was that he could resign the crown, and to whom'.[61] Eventually
it was impressed upon him that he had no option but to do so, but even
Walsingham states that right to the end Richard was still insisting
that there were certain 'special dignities of a spiritual nature' which
had been bestowed upon him at his anointment, of which no form of
words could deprive him.[62] Naturally the 'Record and Process' makes
no mention of this. Indeed the story it tells – of Richard's ungrudging
resignation at Conway, of his unsolicited aspiration that Henry should
succeed him – the whole tone of the document, moreover, presenting
as it does such enormous events with the bland assurance of a deed of
conveyance, frankly strains belief to breaking point and beyond.[63]

Following the meetings in the Tower on 28 and 29 September, the
record of the king's resignation was presented to the assembled estates
in Westminster great hall on 30 September, after which the deposition
charges (or at least some of them) were read out, and it was agreed
that they were sufficient to merit deposition. Despite the assertion in
the *Traison* that at this point the bishop of Carlisle spoke up in
Richard's favour, it is in fact entirely credible that there was no *public*
opposition to Henry's plans in this assembly.[64] Discussion was clearly
not the order of the day. Henry had done the sensible thing: he had, in
effect, presented the estates with a *fait accompli*. Even so, the 'Manner
of King Richard's Renunciation' raises an element of doubt by saying
that Henry asked the lords whether they assented to his kingship 'with

61 C. Given-Wilson, 'The manner of King Richard's renunciation: a "Lancastrian
   narrative"?', *EHR* (1993).

62 Walsingham added this passage to his version of the 'Record and Process'. He must
   have seen the document used by the author of the *Vita*, and printed by Sayles, 'Three
   Lancastrian narratives', 264–6.

63 For a thoroughly sceptical discussion of all these documents see Sayles, 'Three
   Lancastrian narratives'.

64 The author of the *Traison et Mort* may have heard of what Walsingham calls the
   'excellent speech' made by the bishop in his own defence in the parliament of
   October 1399, and assumed that it was made in defence of Richard.

your hearts as well as your mouths', for if they did not, he went on, 'that would be no great surprise to me.' The reaction to this was apparently another round of applause. Hardyng claims that the Percies had also objected to Henry's seizure of the throne – although not in public, evidently – but that Henry outwitted them. If this was true, Northumberland hid his feelings well, for he clearly took a leading part in the proceedings.

Finally, there is the question of the title by which Henry claimed the throne. According to the 'Record and Process' he based his claim on his descent 'by right line of the blood coming from the good lord King Henry the third' (possibly a reference to the 'Crouchback legend', but more probably a deliberately equivocal allusion to his royal ancestry), on the fact that he had been able, with God's grace, to 'recover' the kingdom, and on the necessity of rescuing the realm from Richard's evil rule. This vague concoction no doubt represents a compromise: it has all the hallmarks of a claim devised by a committee. Whether these really were the words which Henry used is, however, open to doubt. The 'Manner of King Richard's Renunciation' states that he claimed the throne as the 'nearest male heir and worthiest blood-descendant of the good King Henry the third.' This may simply have been a misunderstanding of Henry's words on the part of the document's author, but given the problems that Henry had encountered in trying to arrive at an acceptable title, it might well have made more sense to have based his claim upon indisputable fact – for he was indeed the strictly *male* heir to the throne. The words reproduced in the 'Record and Process' might have been inserted later, as representing a compromise more acceptable to the nobility. The 'Record and Process' was probably not drawn up in its final form until several months after the proceedings which it describes, and there have long been suspicions that various other 'facts' were later included in it – such as, possibly, the presence of Archbishop Arundel at Conway, the presence of Justices Thirning and Markham at Richard's act of resignation in the Tower, and additional charges against the king.[65]

Be that as it may, Henry's claim was duly accepted, he was installed upon the throne, and it was announced that he would be crowned on 13 October. 'Thus ended the day, and the lords then rose, at which

65 Sayles, 'Three Lancastrian narratives', 260-3, questions in particular the presence of Thirning and Markham in the Tower, though it is difficult to believe that the 'Record and Process' completely invented the prominent role which it allots to Thirning.

time it was between three and four o'clock in the afternoon.' On the following day, 1 October, the proctors appointed in parliament went to the Tower to inform the king of the decision and formally to renounce their homage and fealty to him. According to the 'Record and Process', Richard 'answered by saying that he looked not thereafter; but that he hoped, after all this, that his cousin would be a good lord to him.' Since most of the chroniclers based their accounts upon one or other of the documents describing the proceedings, they have virtually nothing of note to add to this story. Of the major chroniclers, only Adam Usk wrote an independent account of these events, and what he says for the most part simply confirms the outline of the story as given in the documents. Of greater interest is Usk's account of the king's mental state. He visited Richard in the Tower on 21 September, where, he says, he found the king brooding gloomily on 'his ancient and wonted glory, and on the fickle fortune of the world.' 'Perceiving then the trouble of his mind,' Adam continues, 'I departed thence much moved at heart.' If the Dieulacres chronicler is to be believed, the time of hope for Richard had passed: the king, he says, 'asked not to be brought into parliament in so humble a condition, but instead, simply placing his royal crown upon the ground, he resigned his rights to God.'

Meanwhile the assembly of 30 September had been dissolved and a parliament summoned for 6 October. Its elected membership was the same as for that of 30 September.[66] It met just long enough to hear Archbishop Arundel's opening address and to be prorogued until the day after the coronation. On that day, Tuesday 14 October, the real business of parliament began. Its main task was twofold: to reverse the acts of the previous two years, and to decide who had been responsible for them. The first of these was largely accomplished on 15 October, when the judgments of 1397-98 were reversed, the heirs of the condemned were restored to their inheritances, and the remaining acts of the 'Revenge' parliament were annulled. All this was easy enough; the business of deciding who was responsible was more taxing.

Henry had no desire to preside over a witch-hunt. He had already executed a number of Richard's more notorious supporters, and, with

---

66 The writs for the new parliament included one to 'Henry duke of Lancaster'. It is interesting that the chancery clerks had no compunction in referring to the assembly of 30 September as a parliament (CCR, 1399-1402, 89, 107), although, as is pointed out in the 'Manner of King Richard's renunciation', the initial summons to parliament was invalidated once Richard, in whose name it had been called, resigned.

one or two exceptions perhaps, his preference seems to have been to let matters rest and hope that conciliation would restore a semblance of political unity. It was also the case, of course, that he himself had given tacit, indeed more than tacit, support to the judgements of 1397-98, and to inquire too closely into them might have proved embarrassing for him. The commons, however, and a substantial group among the lords, were bent on revenge. In the end, therefore, it was decided that the six surviving lords who had presented the Appeal of 1397 should be put on trial, namely Rutland, Kent, Huntingdon, Somerset, Salisbury and Despenser (Mowbray and Lescrope were dead). The official account indicates that there were three main charges: firstly, that they had presented the Appeal against Gloucester, Arundel and Warwick; secondly, that they had consented to Gloucester's murder; thirdly, that they had agreed to Henry's exile in September 1398, and to the revocation of his letters patent in March 1399. No mention was made of the similar action taken against Mowbray. Salisbury, whose defence was significantly different from that of the others, was also asked to answer the charge that he had plotted against the life of John of Gaunt – a reference to the accusations allegedly made by Mowbray in the winter of 1397-98 which had sparked off the quarrel between him and Henry. The replies made by the other five were predictable. They denied insistently their complicity in Gloucester's death: on that, we may be sure, their lives depended. They admitted – as they could scarcely deny – that they had been parties to the Appeal of 1397, but declared that they had only done so in fear of their lives. Some of them implied that William Lescrope, now safely dead, had masterminded the Appeal. They also insisted that, although they had given their support to Henry's banishmnent and the revocation of his letters patent, they had not in their hearts agreed to it, and had only done so because they dared not gainsay Richard's wishes. The essence of their defence, in other words, was coercion.

The dry tone of the official account is brought to life by the narratives of Walsingham and the *Great Chronicle of London*. If they are to be believed, the trials were conducted in an atmosphere of near-frenzy, with lords hurling gages across the floor at each other almost as often as they rose to speak, and the embattled king barely able to save Rutland from being lynched on the spot. The proceedings apparently began with William Bagot, who had fled from Bristol to Ireland in July and been brought back in chains by Prince Henry, being asked to explain a certain 'bill' which he had written and sent to King Henry.

He replied that he stood by what he had said, and immediately went on to accuse Rutland of being 'one of the principal accomplices to many of the king's evil designs' and of advocating the deaths of Gloucester, Arundel and Warwick. Rutland apparently 'rose from his seat and threw his hood into the middle of the hall, challenging him to a duel to prove his innocence,' but Henry, trying to calm things down, ordered him to retrieve it. Such histrionics serve as a reminder of the deep and personal antagonisms between those who had surrounded Richard during his last few years on the throne, as well as of the enduring horror at the murder of Gloucester, the full details of which now emerged. This was a question which neither lords nor commons were prepared to let rest. Lord FitzWalter rose to accuse Rutland of complicity in Gloucester's death, and Lord Morley laid the same charge against Salisbury. Mowbray's former valet John Hall, who by his own confession had been present, though unwillingly, at Gloucester's suffocation, was condemned by the lords to the most hideous of fates, because 'it seemed to them that he merited the harshest death to which he could possibly be sentenced, since the duke of Gloucester was so great a personage.'

Remarkably, Bagot escaped with his life. So did the six lords, though they did not escape unpunished. Five of them – Rutland, Kent, Huntingdon, Somerset and Despenser – were stripped of the titles and lands which they had been granted since 1397, and anyone who wished to bring more specific complaints against them was invited to do so. On the sixth, Salisbury, judgement was reserved: since he had been challenged by Lord Morley, their quarrel was referred to the Court of Chivalry, which decreed that it should be decided by duel in the king's presence at Newcastle in February 1400. FitzWalter's challenge to Rutland would have been similarly referred, but Henry decided first to consult Mowbray, whose testimony was crucial to the allegations; evidently news of Mowbray's death had not yet reached England. Once it did, Henry probably persuaded FitzWalter to drop his challenge, for no more was heard of it. Henry had no desire to hound Rutland. Against Salisbury, however, the new king had evidently developed an intense personal dislike, and may well have hoped that this would be the death of him.

The chroniclers are agreed that the decision to spare the lives of Richard's principal followers was Henry's own, and that the sentence passed against them was widely regarded as too lenient. Yet Henry had some reason to think that they had been punished sufficiently. Not only had they been degraded and deprived, they had also been humiliated, forced to cite their own cowardice as the only plea that would save them from the gallows. The threat of future action, moreover, continued to hang over them: for some of them at least – such as Salisbury, Kent and Despenser, whose personal dependence upon Richard had been intense – the outlook can have held little hope. To have executed them would only have opened new wounds, created new groups of disinherited: far better to let them prove themselves, one way or the other.

Meanwhile there was another pressing matter: the question of what was to be done with the deposed king. On Tuesday 21 October the commons requested that he be brought before them to answer for his crimes – and, no doubt, to shed some light on Gloucester's murder. Henry stalled, saying that 'he did not wish to reply to this until all the prelates were present.' He can hardly have wished to bring Richard into parliament, not least because of the constitutional issues which a public trial would have raised. Two days later Archbishop Arundel and the earl of Northumberland asked the lords what they thought should be done with him, 'for the king does not in any way wish to deprive him of his life.' They replied that he should be imprisoned in a secret and secure location, where he would be guarded by trustworthy persons and waited upon by strangers. He seems to have been moved from the Tower about a week after this, but was probably kept in the vicinity of London for some weeks.[67] Some time before Christmas, however, he was moved north, to the security of the king's Lancastrian heartland. The Kirkstall chronicler says that he was escorted by Sir Peter Bukton, one of Henry's most trusted knights, first to Knaresborough and then on to Pontefract.[68] He seems to have reached Pontefract, where he was to remain until his death, by the beginning of January at the latest.

Even before Richard reached Pontefract, however, a plan had been laid to restore him to freedom. Accounts of the 'Epiphany Rising', especially its early stages, are thoroughly confused, but according to the record of one of the trials held in its aftermath the plotting had

---

67 In late November 'Ricardem nuper Regem Anglie chivaler' was a party to a final concord made in the king's court at Westminster (P.R.O. CP25(1)/186/10), but it is not clear whether he would have had to be present in person to seal the deed.

68 On 17 December Bukton was given £20 'for certain expenses incurred by him by order of the late king' (P.R.O. E403/564, 17 December), which might have been connected with his journey north with Richard.

C

been going on, mainly in London, since early December.[69] The chief conspirators were the earls of Kent, Salisbury and Huntingdon, Thomas Despenser, Ralph Lord Lumley, and Thomas Merks, the former bishop of Carlisle. Merks had been deprived of his temporalities in September, and by early December had also been demoted from his bishopric, probably because of the public outcry resulting from suspicions that he had been an accomplice to Gloucester's death.[70] The plan was to seize and kill the king and his sons on 5 January at Windsor, where they had been spending Christmas and New Year, and to restore Richard to the throne. Just in time, however, Henry discovered the plot. Some of the chroniclers state that Rutland was also a party to the conspiracy but betrayed his fellows.[71] The author of the *Continuatio Eulogii*, however, who probably got his information from Archbishop Arundel, said that the plot was discovered by chance when a member of the king's household slept with a London prostitute who had spent the previous night with one of the conspirators, and who, in the morning, informed him of the fate that awaited him. He therefore raced to Windsor to tell the king, who in turn sent a messenger to warn Arundel, who was on his way from Canterbury to join Henry at Windsor for the Epiphany.

By the evening of 4 January the king was back in London issuing orders for the arrest of those whom he suspected of complicity,[72] while Arundel had retired to the security of Reigate castle. Baulked of their quarry, Kent, Salisbury and Lumley moved westwards, sending out letters to their supporters to join them with all haste and proclaiming along the way that Richard had escaped from prison. They were probably making for Shrewsbury, where they apparently planned to regroup on 14 January.[73] On 6 January, the Epiphany, they reached Cirencester. The events at Cirencester are described in detail by both

---

69 *London Letter-Book I*, 1-4; *CPR, 1399-1401*, 385. For general accounts of the rising see A. Rogers, 'Henry IV and the revolt of the earls', *History Today* (1968), 277-83; and D. Crook, 'Central England and the revolt of the earls, January 1400', *HR* (1991), 403-10.

70 *CCR 1396-9*, 508; *CPL*, v, 317.

71 The extraordinary account in the *Traison* of the discovery of the conspiracy through Rutland's carelessness is impossible to believe, but the Dieulacres chronicle and the later *English Chronicle*, 20, also say that he revealed the plot to the king. He was certainly involved in the mopping-up operations after the débâcle at Cirencester, along with John Norbury (P.R.O. E403/564, 20 March).

72 *CPR, 1399-1401*, 214; *CCR, 1399-1402*, 32, 34, 37, 106.

73 Crook, 'Central England and the revolt of the earls', 405.

Walsingham and the author of the *Vita*, although other sources are an important supplement to their accounts. The townspeople of Cirencester soon became suspicious of the rebel earls' intentions. A letter from John Norbury, the royal treasurer, states that this was because Sir Walter Hungerford, whom they had seized and forced to ride with them, managed to alert the town authorities to the situation. The townspeople therefore blockaded them in their lodgings, and after a protracted skirmish managed to arrest them and lead them to the abbey, where they were placed in custody until the arrival of Thomas Lord Berkeley on the following day. Some time later, however, probably on the morning of 8 January, the rebel lords somehow managed to start a fire in the town, hoping that in the ensuing confusion they might be able to escape, but the townspeople, realising that this was simply a diversionary tactic, hurried to the abbey and, furious at their behaviour, promptly dragged Kent, Salisbury and Lumley out into the market-place and beheaded them. They were later generously rewarded by the king for their efforts.[74]

Whatever serious threat there had been from the rising was now over, and the remaining conspirators were soon rounded up. Huntingdon, who had apparently remained in London, failed to escape by boat to France and was captured in Essex and beheaded – 'by clowns and workmen', according to Adam Usk – on 9 or 10 January at Pleshey castle.[75] Thomas Despenser was beheaded in the market-place at Bristol, again at the instigation of the townsfolk, on 13 January: the author of the *Vita* provides a vivid account of his attempt to flee by sea from his castle of Cardiff and his betrayal by the ship's captain, who handed him over to the mayor of Bristol. The behaviour of Huntingdon and Despenser suggests that the rebels' plan involved a number of simultaneous risings in different parts of the country, and there were in fact risings in their support in Devon and Cornwall, in the midlands, and in Cheshire, though none of these amounted to much.[76] Henry, meanwhile, had raised a force in London and set off in pursuit of the rebels, but by the time he reached Oxford it only remained for him to preside over the trials of the surviving conspirators. Ninety or so men were accused of participating in the plot, but

74 P.R.O. E403/564, 20 March; *CPR, 1399-1401*, 86, 182-3, 225, 318. The leader of the townspeople at Cirencester was evidently the king's esquire John Cosyn.

75 Adam Usk, 198.

76 P. McNiven, 'The Cheshire rising of 1400', *BJRL* (1969-70), 375-96; Crook, 'Central England and the revolt of the earls'.

most of them, being regarded as camp-followers rather than ringlead-
ers, were pardoned. In the end about twenty-seven were executed.
Although all twenty-seven were sentenced to the full horrors of a
traitor's death, they were, on the orders of the king, beheaded only,
'because the sight would be very horrid and the hearing greatly odious
in the mortal execution of so many persons, and lest they should curse
God their Creator in their pains at the departing of their souls'.[77]

There was also a substantial degree of clerical involvement in the
conspiracy: Richard Maudeleyn and William Ferriby, both favoured
clerks of the former king's household, were tried and executed at
London at the end of January. Also suspected of involvement were
Thomas Merks the demoted bishop of Carlisle, Roger Walden the
former archbishop of Canterbury, William Colchester abbot of Westminster, and Henry Despenser bishop of Norwich. They were all
pardoned by the king, though only, in the case of the first three, after
spending several months in prison.[78] There may also have been an
element of foreign involvement in the conspiracy. The Scottish esquire
Gilbert Purveys was among those accused of complicity, and the
formal charges against the rebels at Oxford included the accusation
that they had 'adhered to the adversary and enemy of the lord king, the
king of France, to bring the same adversary into the land of England
deceitfully.' Froissart also declared that the rebels had tried to enlist
French support, though he is not always reliable on such matters. It
was, of course, good propaganda from the king's point of view to
present the rebels as in league with a hostile foreign power.[79]

For Richard, the failure of the rising must have represented the closing
of the last window of hope that Henry's usurpation could be undone
almost as quickly as it had been effected – which, up until that time,
might well have seemed a real possibility. Instead, it turned out to be
the catalyst for his death. The manner and date of the former king's
death were matters of disagreement at the time and are unlikely ever

77 *CPR, 1399-1401*, 228-9; Rogers, 'Henry IV and the revolt of the earls', 282. Henry
     was at Oxford by 11 January at the latest, for on that day he sent out letters
     ordering the sheriffs not to bother to send him the troops he had requested a few
     days earlier: *Black Book of Winchester*, ed. W. H. B. Bird (1925), 6-7.

78 *CCR, 1399-1402*, 41, 157, 167-8; *CPR, 1399-1401*, 224. Maudeleyn and Ferriby
     were arrested on their way to Yorkshire, presumably to try to release the king
     (*London Letter-Book I*, v). In a letter written to his nephew, Bishop Despenser hotly
     denied any involvement in the plot (Legge, *Anglo-Norman Petitions*, 64).

79 *London Letter-Book I*, 4; Rogers, 'Henry IV and the revolt of the earls', 282;
     Froissart, *Chroniques*, xvi, 223.

to be known for certain. Leaving aside the obviously spurious story by the author of the *Traison* that Richard was hacked to death at Gravesend castle, on Henry's order, by eight henchmen led by Sir Peter Exton,[80] there are essentially two versions of the story. Firstly – as told by John Hardyng and the author of the Whalley chronicle, both of whom were opposed to Henry's usurpation – that Richard was starved to death; secondly, that he was so despondent at hearing of the deaths of his supporters that he starved himself to death. Walsingham and the author of the *Continuatio Eulogii* both present the latter view, but so, interestingly, does the Dieulacres chronicler, no friend to Henry. The author of the *Vita*, however, believed that Richard had really been starved to death. It was certainly not a matter upon which the chroniclers divided along partisan lines. Perhaps the best solution was that adopted by Adam Usk, who, in one of his more Delphic utterances, incorporated both versions in one sentence. When Richard heard of the failure of the rising, says Usk, 'he grieved more sorely and mourned even to death, which came to him most miserably on the last day of February, as he lay in chains in the castle of Pontefract, tormented by Sir (Thomas) Swynford with starving fare.' Quite what he expected his readers to make of this is difficult to know. The last day of February is at any rate at least two weeks too late. On 9 February the royal council was still unsure of the former king's fate, but by 17 February at the latest Richard was known to be dead, for on that day or shortly before it William Pampilion esquire was despatched by the government to Pontefract 'to transport the body of Richard former king of England from the town of Pontefract to London'.[81] If, as is possible, Pampilion was sent north as soon as the news was received, then the date for Richard's death given by Walsingham and the author of the *Vita*, namely 14 February, is probably about right.

Given the secrecy and confusion surrounding the former king's fate, it was important that the fact of his death should be accepted as widely as possible: that is why Henry ordered Richard's body to be borne slowly and publicly along the road from Pontefract to London, with,

---

80 When Richard's body was exhumed in the nineteenth century, no marks of violence were found on it: A. R. Stanley, 'On an examination of the tombs of Richard II and Henry VI in Westminster Abbey', *Archaeologia* (1880), 309-27.

81 *Proceedings and Ordinances of the Privy Council of England*, ed. N. H. Nicolas, i (1834), 107; P.R.O. E403/564, 17 February, 6 April. But according to Froissart, *Chroniques*, xviii, 587, rumours were already circulating in France in late January that Richard was dead.

as Walsingham puts it, 'that part of his body by which he could be recognised (being) exhibited, namely, from the base of his forehead down to his throat.' Despite such precautions, it was inevitable that not everyone would be convinced. Jean Creton declared in 1402 that he still believed the former king to be alive, and although Creton himself later came to accept that he was wrong, rumours continued to circulate for many years that Richard was alive and well in Scotland, where he was awaiting the day when fortune would restore him to his inheritance.[82] It is hard not to believe, however, that it was only the overcredulous and the desperate who truly believed such stories, and that it was indeed Richard's body over which the new king had a requiem mass said in St Paul's cathedral on 6 March 1400, prior to its burial at King's Langley. Henry attended the exequies himself. His almoner distributed twenty-five marks to 'various religious priests' to say a thousand masses for Richard's soul, while his confessor doled out one pound to 'paupers and cripples'.[83] His namesake, Henry IV of France, was to remark some two hundred years later that Paris was worth a mass. The circumstances were somewhat different, but Henry IV of England must also have thought it a small price to pay for a throne.

---

82 See for example *London Letter-Book I*, v-vii, 165-6; also Walter Bower, *Scotichronicon*, ed. D. E. R. Watt, viii (1987), 29, 67, 115.

83 P.R.O. E403/564, 20 March.

Part one: July 1397 to May 1399

1. Richard II's coup of 1397 according to the Monk of Evesham

Source: *Vita Ricardi Secundi*, 137-51

Language: Latin

The well-known account of the parliament of 1397 which follows, including its dramatic descriptions of the trials of the earls of Arundel and Warwick, is not in fact the chronicler's own narrative but is based on a tract probably written by a clerk of the royal chancery present at the proceedings. Adam Usk used the same tract in his chronicle, although both he and the monk of Evesham felt free to insert into it a number of comments designed to portray the king in a less favourable light – in keeping with the general tone of both chronicles. The chronological accuracy of the monk's description of the parliament is, with one or two minor exceptions, confirmed by the Rolls of Parliament.

In February of that year (*1397*), a council was held at Westminster to which the duke of Gloucester and the earl of Arundel were summoned by the king. They refused to come, however, claiming that they were ill, which annoyed the king greatly and made him extremely angry with them.

That same year, about the feast of St John the Baptist (*24 June*), the king, who in his youthful folly was egged on particularly by John Bussy, ordered the arrests of Richard earl of Arundel and Thomas earl of Warwick, and had them imprisoned. Then soon after this he took John Bussy and some other men-at-arms and went to Pleshey, where, in the quiet of the night, he personally arrested Thomas duke of Gloucester, who was laid low by illness and resting in his bed, disregarding the grief, tears and prayers with which the duchess his wife and the whole of the duke's household entreated him. Straight away that night he sent him to Tillingbourne, and from there to Dover, and then finally on to the duke of Norfolk at Calais – where he was captain at the time – to be killed – as will be explained in more detail below ...

In the same year the king, recalling to mind and reflecting upon the way in which he had formerly been constrained and coerced by certain people into granting them a commission to rule and govern himself, his kingdom, and his estate, and thinking that now that he was of full age he also possessed wisdom and judgement, was filled with an ardent desire to exact revenge for the bitter rebuke which he had endured in all these matters. Following the advice of incompetents, therefore, and deciding that he would not be able to bring his plans to fruition properly without a parliament, in July he sent out through the whole kingdom the customary messengers with writs and letters, ordering all those who ought by right to be there without exception to come to his parliament.[1]

Thus both these and others gathered at this parliament in such numbers as had not been seen for many years. This parliament began on (*17 September*) a Monday, the feast of St Lambert the martyr, and, including its continuation, it lasted until the week after the feast of St Hilary, as will be seen below.

Prior to the parliament the king ordered the construction of a hall in the centre of the palace (*yard*), between the tower and the entrance to the great hall, from which he could deliver his judgements; and there he sat, presiding in greater splendour and solemnity than any king of this realm ever had before.[2] Once the parliament was over, however, he had this hall taken down and completely removed from the site ...

(*The bishop of Exeter delivered the opening address to parliament.*)[3] As soon as this speech was over, the king ordered the commons that before their departure they should agree as to who should be their spokesmen in parliament, so that they could present them to him on the following day. He also ordered proclamation of his pardon to be made to all those who might be implicated in the aforesaid deeds,[4] excepting only fifty persons who were to be impeached in this parliament, as long as they sued out their letters of pardon in due order before the feast of St

---

1 Messengers carrying the summonses to parliament were paid in the exchequer on 23 July (P.R.O. E403/555, 23 July).

2 This 'hall', or marquee as it is described elsewhere, was necessitated by the fact that Westminster great hall was in process of being rebuilt by the king.

3 From this point up to '... return to their homes' (below, p. 62), the narrative is based upon a tract probably written by a chancery clerk. See C. Given-Wilson, 'Adam Usk, the monk of Evesham, and the parliament of 1397-8', *HR* (1993).

4 That is, the 'conspiracy' of Gloucester, Arundel and Warwick.

Hilary (*13 January*). He also ordered it to be proclaimed that in future no person should carry either offensive or defensive weapons in parliament, save only the king's retinue.

On the Tuesday following (*18 September*), Lord John Bussy, a knight from Lincolnshire and a man of undoubted discretion and enormous eloquence, was presented in person to the king by the commons as speaker in parliament; the king readily accepted him. He immediately rose to his feet therefore, and after making the accustomed protestations, spoke as follows: 'My lord king, since we are bound by your own command to tell your royal highness who are the people who undermined your power and transgressed against your regality, we tell you that Thomas duke of Gloucester and Richard earl of Arundel, in the tenth year of your reign, with the assistance of Thomas Arundel, then chancellor of England and now archbishop of Canterbury, compelled you to concede a commission touching the government and state of your kingdom which was to the prejudice of your regality and majesty, whereby they did you great injury.' Then, on the same day, this said commission was, with the assent of the king and the whole parliament, revoked, repealed, and perpetually annulled, together with each and every act dependent or consequent upon it.[5]

On the same day a general pardon and a special pardon which had been granted before this parliament to Richard earl of Arundel, at the request of the said archbishop his brother, were also revoked and perpetually annulled. The commons also requested, again through John Bussy, that this special pardon should be declared to have been traitorously obtained, and that the said Thomas Arundel, archbishop of Canterbury, who had requested it, who was at the time chancellor of England and who should therefore, by virtue of his office, rather have opposed it, should be adjudged a traitor.[6] Whereupon the said archbishop immediately rose to his feet intending to answer this charge, but the king stopped him from speaking, saying, 'You may reply tomorrow.' But after this he did not appear there again. As to the petition, the king said that he wished to take advice.

On the same day it was ordained that anyone who should in future be convicted of violating, usurping or undermining the king's regality, should be adjudged a false traitor, and should be sentenced to suffer

---

5 The 'Commission of Government' of November 1386.

6 Arundel was chancellor from October 1386 to May 1389, and again from September 1391 to November 1396. His brother's pardon was dated 30 April 1394 (*CPR, 1391-6*, 406).

the appropriate penalty for treason. Also on the same day it was ordained, with the consent of the prelates, that in future criminal charges should be decided in parliament, for which their consent was required.[7] Whereupon the prelates, after receiving permission to do so, sorrowfully withdrew.

This withdrawal of the prelates caused considerable bustle among the commons, as a result of which the Cheshire archers, numbering about 2,000 – whom, among others, the king had summoned, and in whom, above all others, he had confidence, even entrusting the security of his person to them, whereby most of the kingdom was treated with disdain – these iniquitous archers, who surrounded the parliament building, thought that some quarrel or dissension had broken out there, and, bending their bows, drew their arrows back to their ears and, to the terror of everyone present, began to shoot.[8] But the king immediately went across and quietened them down.

On the Wednesday following, the aforesaid statute of the prelates was utterly revoked, and they were ordered, on pain of loss of their temporalities, that they must, that same day, agree to the appointment of a spokesman who would consent on their behalf to everything that was to be done in that parliament.[9] Then the king spoke as follows to the speaker of parliament: 'Lord John Bussy, although several people in this parliament have asked me to disclose the names of those fifty persons who are excepted from the general pardon, I tell you straight out that I will not do so; and I wish, moreover, that anyone who asks me to do so should be worthy of death. Firstly, because on hearing this, they would most likely take to flight; secondly, because I have also excepted those who are to be impeached in this parliament; and thirdly, because if their names were to be revealed, others associated with them would probably take fright, when in fact they have nothing to fear.'

---

7 The chronicler seems to have miscopied his source here. Adam Usk (p. 11) has 'irrequisito concensu' in place of our author's 'requisito consensu', which makes better sense. If the prelates' consent was not required, that explains why they promptly withdrew.

8 Adam Usk says there were 4,000 archers, but says only that they drew back their bows, not that they actually began to shoot. The *Vita Ricardi Secundi* (ed. Stow) gives 200 archers, but this is a misprint. The figure given in both the manuscripts upon which the edition was based is 2000 (British Library MSS. Cotton Claudius B.ix, f. 296, and Cotton Tiberius C.ix, f. 27v).

9 The clergy agreed to the appointment of Sir Thomas Percy, steward of the royal household, as their proctor.

On Thursday the archbishop of Canterbury came to the palace
intending to take his place in parliament; but the king ordered him,
through the bishop of Carlisle, to return to his lodgings. Thus he went
away, and did not appear there again ...

(*Sir John Bussy accused Archbishop Arundel of treason.*) On Friday (*21
September*), the feast of St Matthew the apostle, the duke of Rutland,
the earls of Kent, Huntingdon, Nottingham, Somerset and Salisbury,
Lord Despenser and William le Scrope came into parliament dressed
in a livery of red silk robes banded with white silk and powdered with
letters of gold, and presented to the king the appeal which they had
already drawn up at Nottingham, in which, having given pledges to
pursue the appeal to its conclusion, they accused Thomas duke of
Gloucester, Richard earl of Arundel, Thomas earl of Warwick, and
Thomas de Mortimer, knight, of the aforesaid treasons, and of having
traitorously risen in armed insurrection against the king at Harringay
Park.[10]

The court being seated, Richard earl of Arundel was immediately put
on trial, clad in a robe with a scarlet hood. Then John, duke of
Lancaster and steward of England, who had been appointed to
undertake this task, formally told Lord Nevill, 'Remove his belt and his
hood,' which was done.

When the articles of the appeal had been read out to the earl, he hotly
denied that he was a traitor, and claimed the benefit of his pardon,
protesting that he had no desire ever to withdraw himself from the
king's grace. But the duke of Lancaster, who was also steward, said to
him, 'That pardon is revoked, traitor.' 'Truly you lie,' replied the earl,
'never was I a traitor.' 'Why then did you seek a pardon?' the duke
asked him. 'To silence the tongues of my enemies, of whom you are
one,' retorted the earl, 'and to be sure, when it comes to treason, you
are in greater need of a pardon than I am.'

Then the king said to him, 'Answer the appeal.' To which the earl
replied, 'I see it clearly now: all those who accuse me of treason, you
are all liars. Never was I a traitor. I still claim the benefit of my pardon,
which you, within the last six years, when you were of full age and free
to act as you wished, granted to me of your own volition.' 'I granted

10 Mortimer was the half-uncle of the earl of March: for his part in the events of 1387,
see J. L. Gillespie, 'Thomas Mortimer and Thomas Molineux: Radcot Bridge and
the appeal of 1397', *Albion* (1975), 161-73. He was in Ireland at this time, but fled
to Scotland, where he died before May 1399 (Adam Usk, 159, 165; *CPR, 1396-9,*
574).

it provided that it were not to my prejudice,' the king said to him. Whereupon the duke of Lancaster said, 'Therefore the grant is worthless.' But the earl replied, 'In truth, I was as ignorant about that pardon as you were – and you were abroad at the time – until it was willingly granted to me by the king.'

Then Lord John Bussy, speaker of parliament, said to him, 'That pardon has already been revoked by the king, the lords, and us, the faithful commons.' To which the earl replied, 'Where are those faithful commons? I know all about you and your crew, and how you have got here – not to act faithfully, but to shed my blood. The faithful commons of the kingdom are not here; if they were, they would without doubt be on my side, trying to help me from falling into your clutches. They, I know, are grieving greatly for me; while you, I know, have always been false.' Then this Bussy and his supporters exclaimed hotly, 'Look, lord king, at how this traitor is trying to stir up dissension between us and the commons who have stayed at home.' To which the earl replied, 'You are all liars. I am no traitor.'

Then Henry earl of Derby rose to his feet and said to him, 'Did you not say to me at Huntingdon, where we first gathered in revolt, that before doing anything else it would be better to seize the king?' The earl replied, 'You, Henry earl of Derby, you lie in your teeth. I never said anything to you or to anyone else about my lord king, except what was to his welfare and honour.' Then the king said to him, 'Did you not say to me at the time of your parliament, in the bath behind the White Hall, that Simon Burley was for various reasons worthy of death? And I replied that I neither knew nor could discover any reason for his death. And even though my wife, the queen, and I interceded tirelessly on his behalf, yet you and your accomplices, ignoring our pleas, traitorously put him to death'.[11] Then the king turned to the steward: 'Pass sentence on him.' And so the duke of Lancaster gave him his judgement, in the following manner:

'Richard – I, John, steward of England, adjudge you a traitor, and sentence you to be drawn, hanged, beheaded and quartered, and the lands descending from your person, both entailed and unentailed, to be forfeited for ever by you and your heirs.' Then the king, out of recognition for his birth, ordered him to be beheaded only; whereupon

11 The reference is to Richard's first queen, Anne of Bohemia, who died in June 1394. *The Westminster Chronicle*, ed. L. C. Hector and B. F. Harvey (Oxford 1982), 329, confirms that the king and queen 'and other great personages' pleaded for Burley's life, but he was executed on 5 May 1388.

he was led away through Cheap and other parts of London to Tower Hill, followed all the way by a great crowd of citizens who mourned him as much as they dared, and there he was beheaded. He was buried with the Austin friars of London.[12]

On the same day the king ordered Lord Cobham, who had been accused by the commons, to be put on trial.[13] On the Saturday notice was given to Lord Thomas de Mortimer, under pain of treason and perpetual exile, to appear within six months to stand trial. However, he did not appear. Whereupon the king declared, 'Perhaps the earl of March is unable to capture him, as he has undertaken to do. I shall wait for him therefore, for as long as it takes me to be informed of his arrival from Ireland.' On the same day it was announced that all benefices and other grants bestowed or alienated since the tenth year of the reign by those who had been or were to be condemned in this parliament should be entirely annulled and revoked.

Next Monday (*24 September*) the declaration of the earl of (Nottingham), captain of Calais at the time, to whose safekeeping the duke of Gloucester had been entrusted, was read out, in which it was announced that the duke would not be able to stand trial since he had died in the earl's custody at Calais. Nevertheless at the request of the aforesaid appellants the same sentence was pronounced against him as had been delivered against the earl of Arundel. On the same day Thomas Arundel, archbishop of Canterbury, after first having his temporalities confiscated, was banished from the realm. On the Tuesday the earldom of Chester was raised to a duchy and was augmented by the annexation to it of the lands which had been forfeited by the earl of Arundel.[14]

On the same day the earl of Salisbury petitioned for a writ to be issued to him against the earl of March concerning the lordship of Denbigh in Wales; to which the king replied that he would take advice.[15] On the Wednesday it was decreed that the lands of the earldom of Arundel

---

12 That is, the church of the Augustinian friars in Bread Street.

13 John Lord Cobham (d. 1408) had been a member of the 1386 Commission. He was convicted of treason during the second session of this parliament, at Shrewsbury, and exiled to Jersey.

14 The earldom of Chester was in fact erected into a Principality, on 25 September: *RP*, iii, 353-4.

15 The Welsh Marcher lordship of Denbigh had been disputed between the Mortimer and Montague families since the 1330s: see G. A. Holmes, *The Estates of the Higher Nobility in Fourteenth-Century England* (Cambridge 1957), 14-19.

which had been annexed to the aforesaid duchy of Chester should enjoy all their liberties, provided that the Welsh who inhabited those lands should continue to exercise their ancient laws and customs. It was also decreed on the same day that anyone who offered help, counsel or support to the children of those who had been or were to be condemned in this parliament should suffer punishment as a traitor.

On Thursday,[16] the king announced that any persons who were descended from those who had been or were to be condemned, namely their male heirs and those descending from them in the male line, should be debarred for ever not only from their inheritances but also from the councils and parliaments of the king. It was also decreed on the same day that all the lords spiritual and temporal should swear to observe unswervingly all the deeds, ordinances, pronouncements and sentences of this parliament, together with the censures which at any future time might be decreed by the prelates against those who opposed this, saving always the lord king's regality in all things.

On the Friday Thomas earl of Warwick was put on trial. Once his hood had been removed and the appeal read, he foolishly, wretchedly, and pusillanimously confessed to everything in the appeal, weeping and wailing and whining that he had indeed acted traitorously in all these matters, submitting himself to the king's mercy in all things and bemoaning the fact that he had ever associated with the appellants. The king asked him by whom he had been persuaded to associate himself with them, to which he replied in pathetic and inane fashion that it had been by Thomas duke of Gloucester, the abbot of St Albans as then was, and a monk who was at that time a recluse at Westminster;[17] and all the time he kept on sobbing and whining and begging the king's mercy. So at length, since almost everybody there felt moved by his tears and was begging and pleading with the king to show mercy to him, the king granted him his life to pine away in perpetual prison outside the kingdom, once he had forfeited his movable and immovable goods in the same way as the earl of Arundel had done.

Then the king ordered him to be taken to the Tower of London, and

---

16 Thursday was 27 September. According to Adam Usk (p. 16), the parliament did not meet that day, but was adjourned on the Wednesday until the Friday: *RP*, iii, 352, seems to confirm Usk's chronology.

17 The abbot of St Albans referred to was Thomas de la Mare, abbot 1349-96; for a distorted version of this story, placing it in 1396 rather than 1387, see the *Traison et Mort*, below, Doc.6.

from there to the Isle of Man, where he was to be imprisoned for life
in the castle, in the custody of Lord William le Scrope, who was keeper
of the island. He was given one month by the king to get himself to the
castle. The king also gave him and his wife an annuity of five hundred
marks for the term of their lives.[18]

On Saturday the earl of Salisbury was granted a writ against the earl
of March concerning the aforesaid lordship of Denbigh in Wales, with
a respite of fifty days to respond ... Also on the same day Henry of
Lancaster earl of Derby was made duke of Hereford, Edward of
Langley earl of Rutland was made duke of Aumale, Thomas Holand
earl of Kent was made duke of Surrey, John Holand earl of Huntingdon
was made duke of Exeter, Thomas Mowbray earl of Nottingham was
made duke of Norfolk, John Beaufort earl of Somerset was made
marquis of Dorset, Lord Thomas Despenser was made earl of
Gloucester, Lord Ralph Nevill was made earl of Westmorland, Lord
Thomas Percy was made earl of Worcester, and Lord William le
Scrope was made earl of Wiltshire.

Then also on this Saturday, the parliament was adjourned to be
continued at Shrewsbury within the following quinzaine of St Hilary,
there to be completed and brought to a conclusion – all ranks and
orders there, both spiritual and temporal, to be exactly as they had
been here at Westminster. Whereupon the king gave permission to all
present to return to their homes ...

This same year (*1398*), about the feast of St Peter ad Vincula (*1
August*), the king ordered another much greater and more important
tournament to be held at Coventry to settle the duel between the
dukes of Hereford and Norfolk. The reason for this duel was as
follows. One day when these two dukes were out riding along the road
they began to talk about the king and the way that events had turned
out, whereupon the duke of Norfolk said to his companion, 'Do you not
see, Lord Henry, how changeable are the king's utterances, and how he
has already ordered some of the great men of the realm to be banished,
and others to be put to death? We should be careful about putting too
much faith in what he says, for it is surely the case that at some time
in the future, now that he has dealt with the others, he will seek to
destroy us.' The other replied, 'I shall continue to place my trust in the

18 Adam Usk (p. 17) adds that the annuity was never paid. Warwick's wife was
however granted 250 marks a year by the king in May 1398, with effect from 27
September 1397 (*CPR, 1396-9, 339*).

king's words, for I know of nothing that I have done to offend him in any way. As long as he wishes it, therefore, I have no intention of withdrawing my support or my fealty from him.' This entire conversation was reported to the king, who asked them both if it was true. One of them said it was, the other hotly denied it.

Pledges having been given, therefore, a duel was arranged and a day of battle given to them, namely the feast of St Lambert, bishop and martyr, in September, and on the appointed day great throngs of people converged on the place from all parts of England. When the two dukes in dispute had appeared in the lists, however, and were ready to do battle, the king, who had remained, girded with his sword, in his royally-furbished pavilion, ordered them to hold fast and under no circumstances to join battle, and he took the dispute into his own hands.

Then he ordered his will to be proclaimed, namely that Henry duke of Hereford, on account of his former disobedience towards the king, should be banished from the realm for ten years, and that Thomas duke of Norfolk should be banished from England for ever, and should receive 1,000 marks a year from his estates until such time as the town of Calais was repaired.[19] For this duke had been captain of Calais for a number of years, during which time he had inflicted great damage on the town, for which he owed it enormous sums; nor had he repaired it properly, or paid the wages of the garrison, as he should have, but instead he had wasted the money which the king had given him for these purposes; in recompense for all of which the rest of his lands were now to be reserved for the king's use ...

19 Mowbray had been captain of Calais since 1391. He was in fact granted an annuity of £1,000, not 1000 marks, by Richard (P.R.O. E403/562, 23 June).

2. The king's duplicity according to a Canterbury chronicler

Source: *Continuatio Eulogii*, 371-9.

Language: Latin

The anonymous author of the Continuation of the Eulogium Historiarum *was almost certainly based at Canterbury; hence his interest in and knowledge of the affairs of Archbishop Arundel. His story of the arrest of the archbishop's brother finds an echo in Walsingham's narrative (below, Doc. 3), while his account of a final conversation between the king and the archbishop before the latter went into exile is corroborated by the thirty-third and last of the charges brought against Richard in the 'Record and Process'. The king's treatment of the Arundels helps to explain the chronicler's tone of bitter hostility towards Richard, as typified by his remark that after dinner the king liked to sit in splendour in his chamber, 'talking to no-one but watching everyone,' and obliging all those upon whom his eye happened to alight to kneel to him.*

After his return to England (*following his marriage to Isabelle of France*), the king summoned the archbishop of Canterbury and told him to bring his brother, the earl of Arundel, to him. 'But you plan to do him harm if he comes,' the archbishop replied. The king denied this, even swearing to him upon the Body of Christ, straight after the archbishop had said mass, that it was untrue. The archbishop therefore eventually persuaded his brother, who was very apprehensive, to come with him to visit the king at Westminster. When he saw him, the king said to the earl of Nottingham, 'I commit the earl of Arundel to your care,' and promptly retired to his chamber. The earl of Nottingham led the earl of Arundel into a different chamber and closed the door. The archbishop waited until vespers, but then returned, downcast, to his residence at Lambeth. On the following day the king handed the earl over to one of his enemies with orders that he was to be imprisoned in (*Carisbrooke*) castle on the Isle of Wight, and immediately confiscated all his goods.[1] He also arrested the earl of Warwick at his own house

---

1 The custody of the Isle of Wight, including Carisbrooke castle, had been granted on 4 June to the earl of Rutland (*CPR, 1396-9*, 150).

and sent him to the Tower. Then, immediately afterwards, he gathered a large following and rode to Pleshey castle, the duke of Gloucester's residence in Essex, and, seizing the duke, said to him, 'You would not come to me, despite all the messages I sent you, so I have had to come to you; and now I arrest you.' To which the duke replied, 'I hope you will show me enough mercy as to spare my life.' 'You shall have such mercy as you showed to Simon Burley,' retorted the king, 'when the queen went down on her knees before you on his behalf. Read this!' and so saying he handed him the schedule of charges against him. 'We can reply to this,' said the duke when he had read it. But the king handed him over to the earl of Nottingham, who was captain of Calais, to be held in the prison there. Then the king travelled over to the west of England and collected an army, and summoned the French to come to his aid; and they came right into the heart of his kingdom, with their lances raised high.[2] He also sent out individual messages to every bishop, abbot, gentleman and merchant, from whom, under pretence of borrowing their money – which he never intended to repay – he extorted such sums from them that even an ordinary gentleman had to hand over forty pounds.

Then the earls of Rutland, Kent, Huntingdon, Salisbury and Nottingham, and the marquis of (*Dorset*) and the other appellants proceeded to accuse the duke of Gloucester and the earls of Arundel and Warwick of crimes of lese-majesty committed by them in the tenth and eleventh years of the king's reign.

The king also sent one of his justices[3] to ask the duke of Gloucester how he intended to answer these appeals, and the duke wrote his reply in English in his own hand, sealed the letter, and sent it to the king. When the justice handed the letter over to the king, he wisely kept a copy of it for himself, authenticated with the king's seal. The duke's reply displeased the king, however, so he ordered the earl of Nottingham, under threat of death, to have the duke murdered. The earl therefore crossed to Calais, where some of his followers secretly and wickedly suffocated the duke by smothering him with a featherbed, letting it be known that he had died of natural causes.

Later, after the feast of the Exaltation of the Holy Cross (*14 September*),

2 This is the only chronicle to state that Richard summoned the French to his aid in 1397, and there appears to be little truth in his statement. Possibly he intended to write 'Wallicos' (the Welsh) rather than 'Gallos' (the French).

3 This was William Rickhill, Justice of the Common Bench: see below, Docs 4 and 20(b).

the king came to parliament riding menacingly through the middle of London surrounded by five thousand armed men, most of whom were malefactors. He and his accomplices held the parliament in a great marquee which had been set up in the courtyard at Westminster. In order to keep the bishops, abbots, and other clerics away from parliament, he persuaded them and the clergy as a whole to delegate their authority to Sir Thomas Percy, knight, the steward of his household. The proceedings in this parliament were conducted not according to the law of England, but according to civil law;[4] and those who were learned in the law of England were excluded from it ...

(*On 21 September*) the earl of Arundel was brought in, and the duke of Lancaster, acting as judge there, read out to him the appeal of the lords and the charges brought by parliament, and ordered him to make answer. But he said that there was no point in replying, 'For I know that you have ordered me to be put to death, in order to seize my possessions.' Then they warned him of the penalties of remaining silent, and the duke said to him, 'Since it is parliament that has accused you, then, according to your own law, you deserve to be condemned without right of reply'.[5] To which the earl said, 'What I did before was done because of the circumstances of the time; and if errors were made then, I have a pardon from the king for them.' 'That pardon has been revoked by parliament,' retorted the duke, 'because it was granted under duress at a time when you were ruling the country.' 'But I still have the pardon which the king offered me of his free will, and which he sent to me, unsolicited, five years ago,' said the earl. 'That too has been revoked by statute of parliament,' replied the duke. 'To be able to grant a pardon for any offence is the greatest prerogative of the king,' said the earl, 'and if you are now declaring that he either cannot or should not grant pardons, then you are undermining his prerogative more than me. And in truth, John, if you were to be interrogated closely, it would be found that your actions have been far more prejudicial to the king's interests than mine.' Then the duke and the others advised him to throw himself upon the king's mercy, but the earl replied, 'I submit myself to the mercy of the Supreme King. To uphold the laws, and for the welfare of the kingdom, I am quite

4 The chronicler may be referring here to Richard's use of the procedure of appeal, the same procedure as used by the Lords Appellant in 1387-88; appeal was in fact a procedure known at both civil and common law.

5 A reference to the proceedings of the 'Merciless' Parliament of 1388, where counsel was denied to the accused, who were only allowed to reply 'Guilty' or 'Not Guilty': see *Westminster Chronicle*, 281-5.

prepared to die.' Whereupon the duke passed sentence: 'The king pardons you the drawing and hanging, but you shall be beheaded on Tower Hill, where Simon Burley was beheaded, and your children shall be disinherited, and their children shall be excluded from parliament and from the king's council for ever.' Thus was the earl sentenced to death, on the feast of St Matthew the apostle and evangelist; and on the same day, on the aforesaid hill, was he beheaded.

On the following day,[6] the earl of Warwick was brought into parliament and sentenced to the same fate. In accordance with the advice given to him, he confessed to having done everything he did because he trusted in the wisdom of the duke (*of Gloucester*) and the earl (*of Arundel*), and in the spiritual integrity of the abbot of St Albans and a recluse at Westminster who had told him that such action was quite permissible. 'Nevertheless, if you truly adjudge that I have done wrong,' he declared, 'then I throw myself upon the king's mercy.' At the prayer and request of the lords, however, and because he was an old man, his sentence was commuted to life imprisonment on the Isle of Man. The duke of Gloucester was also sentenced to posthumous disinheritance, since, or so they said, his deeds were so notorious, and since he had, while still alive, made answer in writing. Remembering also that these three had driven out the archbishop of York,[7] and thinking that with this archbishop of Canterbury he would never have peace, the king also made parliament bring charges against the archbishop of Canterbury. However, when the speaker began the proceedings against the archbishop, the king said to him, 'Do not proceed against my kinsman. You may leave in safety, father.' When the archbishop had duly left, however, a messenger was sent after him ordering him not to reappear in parliament, and he was then sentenced to perpetual exile and to loss of all his goods, on the grounds that he had procured his own appointment to the Commission (*of 1386*), and that he had enforced and authenticated it with his seal when he was chancellor ...

The archbishop declared that he had no wish to go into exile: he had been born here, and he intended to die here. The king, accompanied by the duke of Lancaster, went into the chamber where he was sitting,

6 In fact Warwick's trial took place a week later, on 28 September.

7 Alexander Nevill, archbishop of York 1373-88, was one of those appealed of treason in 1387-88, whereupon he fled abroad. He was translated by the Roman pope to the bishopric of St Andrews in April 1388, but could not go there because Scotland adhered to the Avignon papacy; he died in exile in May 1392.

downcast, with several of the earls, and said to him, 'Do not be so depressed, and do not refuse to go into exile, for I assure you that within a short time you will be recalled, and that for as long as we two are both alive no one but you will be archbishop of Canterbury.' 'Before I go, there are certain things that I want to say to you,' replied the archbishop, and he then delivered a lengthy sermon to the king denouncing the extravagance which ruled the lives of those about him, and the greed and arrogance that was everywhere about the court, through which they were corrupting the whole realm. Then, on the day assigned to him, namely the vigil of Michaelmas (*28 September*), he left the port of Dover and went into exile ... [8]

After this, on solemn festivals when, by custom, (*Richard II*) performed kingly rituals, he would order a throne to be prepared for him in his chamber on which he liked to sit ostentatiously from after dinner until vespers, talking to no one but watching everyone; and when his eye fell on anyone, regardless of rank, that person had to bend his knee towards the king ...

In the year of Our Lord 1398, the twenty-first year of King Richard's reign, the duke of Norfolk – the former earl of Nottingham – secretly and in total confidence said to Henry the son of the duke of Lancaster, who was then duke of Hereford, 'The king has ordered you and me to be killed, because we rode with the duke of Gloucester. You had better decide what you are going to do about it, and I shall do the same.' 'But the king pardoned us for that,' said Hereford. To which Norfolk replied, 'But the king is faithless, as you can see from his treatment of the duke of Gloucester and the earls.' The duke of Hereford reported this conversation to his father, and his father reported it to the king. When questioned about it, the duke of Norfolk denied it, but the duke of Hereford appealed him both for what he had said and for the murder of the duke of Gloucester, so they threw down their gloves against each other, and a day was assigned for them to do battle at Coventry. Having arrived there, they were just about to join battle when the king, present in person, decided to take their cause into his own hands. He exiled the duke of Hereford for ten years; the duke of Norfolk, like Thomas Arundel archbishop of Canterbury, he exiled for life. The duke of Norfolk later died at Venice.[9] The king also granted the duke

---

8 This date is too early; Archbishop Arundel probably left England between 19 and 24 October: M. Aston, *Thomas Arundel* (1967), 373.

9 Mowbray died at Venice, following his return from a pilgrimage to the Holy Land, on 22 September 1399.

of Hereford a certain sum of money which he was to receive each year
from the English crown,[10] but he forbade him to make contact with
Thomas Arundel; indeed he was obliged to swear not to do so, for the
king feared (*Arundel's*) shrewdness and judgement ...

10 Richard granted Bolingbroke an annuity of £2,000 from the exchequer (P.R.O.
   E403/562, 20 June).

3. Thomas Walsingham on the tyranny of King Richard

Source: Annales Ricardi Secundi, 199-239.

Language: Latin

Walsingham's famous comment that in the summer of 1397 the king 'began to tyrannise and burden his people' sets the tone for his account of Richard's later years, which is characterised by the chronicler's willingness – his desire, even – to believe the king capable of almost any evil. Some of the accusations which he made against Richard were copied virtually verbatim, although without acknowledgement, from the 'Record and Process' (below, Doc. 17), and cannot therefore be treated as confirming the accusations made by Bolingbroke in 1399, although they are certainly evidence of the success with which the usurper and his supporters disseminated their propaganda. Although this detracts somewhat from the value of Walsingham's account, the extent of his knowledge and the circumstantial detail which he provides makes his chronicle the classic 'Lancastrian' account of Richard's fall.

About the time of the feast of St John the Baptist (*24 June 1397*), messengers arrived from Germany, including the dean of Cologne, who, knowing the rashness and ambition of the king, intimated to him that he either had been or was about to be elected emperor.[1] The king, immediately believing this, gave the dean and his companions an extraordinary number of gifts, and sent ambassadors abroad to find out if what they had said was true, in other words, whether he had been or was likely to be elected. On their return, they reported that a

---

1 There was much dissatisfaction at this time with the German Emperor Wenzel, who was eventually to be deposed in 1400. For the background to Richard's imperial aspirations, see D. M. Bueno de Mesquita, 'The Foreign Policy of Richard II in 1397: Some Italian Letters', *EHR* (1941), 628-37. Master Hugh de Hervorst, ambassador of the archbishop of Cologne, was in England in the summer of 1397 (*CCR, 1396-9*, 148), and in April 1399 the dean of Cologne, Tilmann de Smalenborg, was granted £40 a year by Richard after doing homage to the king (*CPR, 1396-9*, 577). Walsingham's story is also supported by the fact that on 21 July 1397 the bishop of Carlisle, Sir Roger Siglem and Janico Dartasso were dispatched by Richard on an embassy to Cologne (P.R.O. E403/555, 21 July).

majority of the electors were indeed favourable to him; only two or three were withholding their consent, on the grounds that if the king could not deal with his subjects in his own country, how could he be expected to govern all his subjects throughout the length and breadth of the empire? They suggested that those who dissented ought to be bribed and won over with gifts from the king. Whether they invented this in order to stir up the king's wrath against the lords – the duke of Gloucester, the earls of Arundel and Warwick, and others – or whether they spoke the truth, is not known; but one thing is known for sure, that from that time onwards he began to tyrannise and burden his people with great loans, so that no prelate, no town, no citizen, indeed no one anywhere throughout the whole of England who was known to have any wealth, could find a place to hide, but was forced to loan his money to the king. His agents in this business carried with them letters sealed with the royal seal, on which was written the amount which they wanted to borrow, but they were not endorsed until they found the people from whom they wanted to borrow it. Then, when these agents arrived in towns or cities, they would make secret inquiries to find out who were the richest people there, and, having been given a name, would endorse the letters to make it look as if it had actually been agreed by them. Thus did the wily royal agents acquire untold sums for the royal treasury ...

Shortly after the feast of St John the Baptist, at the beginning of King Richard II's twenty-first year, England seemed to be basking in peace and the future looked entirely favourable: the country had an impressive-looking king who had just married the daughter of the king of France and had thereby acquired not only great riches but a truce to last for thirty years, and it had more, as well as more talented, lords than any other kingdom could boast. It was at this time, however, that through the rashness, cunning, and pride of the king, the entire kingdom was suddenly and unexpectedly thrown into confusion.

On the sixth day after the Ides of July (*10 July*), the king decided to hold a feast ... to which he invited the duke of Gloucester, the earls of Arundel and Warwick, and various other people whom he hated, in the hope that with so many people present at such an occasion it would be easy for him to seize them without any great commotion or disturbance. The duke, however, who was gravely ill, excused himself. The earl of Arundel, who because of the experiences which he had already undergone was well aware of the king's wicked machinations, declined to attend the feast, waiting instead at his well-fortified castle of

Reigate. Of all those who had been invited only the earl of Warwick came to the feast, and when the day came, the king, who was the most practised of dissimulators, smiled at him and spoke to him so kindly before the meal that nothing was further from the earl's mind than that the king was planning to ensnare him. Taking the earl's hand, the king confided that he would be a good friend to him, and that he should not grieve for the loss of his lordship of Gower, promising him that although he had lost those lands, he would provide him with other lands of the same value.[2] As soon as the meal was over, however, he had the earl arrested and sent to (*blank*) to be kept under guard until the time came for the parliament which, since he was planning the destruction of many people, he had decided to summon.

On that same night he asked the archbishop to persuade his brother, the earl of Arundel, to give himself up voluntarily to the king, swearing by his usual oath – St John the Baptist – that no bodily harm would befall him if he was willing to hand himself over peacefully. But when the archbishop passed this message on to his brother the earl, the earl refused to take his advice, for, he claimed, he was only too well aware of the king's deceits and evil designs, and in fact the king was merely trying by all possible means to capture him and put him to death. The archbishop, however, believing the king's promises, continually begged the earl to yield himself up ..., saying that if he did not it was quite likely that he and his heirs would be disinherited. Many people said, and they were widely believed, that the only reason why the king wanted to hold these lords under arrest was in order to demonstrate to the ambassadors from Germany that he was capable of keeping his lords under control, for they had originally said to him that the only thing standing in the way of his election was the belief that he lacked authority over his magnates, and that when he had held them for a sufficient time, and their detention had been made known to the Germans and other foreigners, he intended to restore them to their former dignity. At the prompting of the archbishop, therefore, the earl unfortunately gave himself up, and was sent off to prison on the Isle of Wight to await his appearance in the coming parliament ...

(*The duke of Gloucester was also arrested, at his castle of Pleshey.*) When the news of the arrest and imprisonment of these lords got around, there

---

2 The Marcher lordship of Gower had been disputed between the Beauchamp and Mowbray families throughout the fourteenth century. It was 'restored' to Thomas Mowbray by judgement of the king in 1396-97: see G. A. Holmes, *The Estates of the Higher Nobility in Fourteenth-Century England* (1957) 39.

was such public grief among all the people of the realm that one would have thought that the kingdom had been destroyed by enemies; for such hope had been placed in them, and especially in the duke of Gloucester, by all the people, that it was possible to believe that with him alive and well the kingdom might be not only governed well internally but also saved from its enemies abroad. Seeing this outpouring of popular affection for the lords, and fearing that, since feelings were running so high, there might be an uprising of the people, the king issued a proclamation throughout the realm that he had ordered the lords' arrest not for any crimes which they had committed in the past, but for recent offences which they had committed against the king, since the time when they had obtained from him their charters of pardon for those earlier misdeeds, as would be publicly demonstrated to all in the forthcoming parliament.[3] But, as events were to prove, this proclamation was totally false ...

With his long-cherished hope to revenge himself upon the lords now approaching fulfilment, the king summoned all the estates of the realm to a parliament at London after the Octaves of the Nativity of the Blessed Virgin (17 September). He also ordered all his supporters among the lords to be there, and to bring with them archers and men-at-arms as if they were setting out to do battle with the enemy.[4] In order to facilitate further his evil designs, the king also commanded a great number of evildoers from the county of Chester to come and form his bodyguard, and committed himself entirely to their protection. By nature bestial, these Cheshiremen were ready to commit every sort of crime, and their shamelessness soon increased to the point where they regarded only the king as their equal, treating everybody else, however powerful or noble he was, with contempt. Yet they themselves were by no means gentle-born, but rustics, or shoemakers and suchlike, people who in their own localities were scarcely regarded as worthy to pull off their masters' boots; here, however, they thought themselves to be the peers and equals of lords. And so greatly did their unwarranted pride, disdain, and cruel insolence grow, that before long,

---

3 On 15 July the king issued a writ ordering proclamation to be made that the three lords had been arrested 'not for their assemblies and ridings, but for extortions and oppressions against the king's majesty, such as would be declared more fully in the coming parliament ...' (*Calendar of Letter-Books of the City of London*, ed. R. R. Sharpe, Letter-Book H (1907), 437).

4 The king summoned his retainers on 20 August, to join him at Kingston upon Thames 'at high morn' on 15 September, 'to ride with the king to Westminster palace, and there abide on his service as long as need shall be ...' (*CCR, 1396-9*, 210).

when travelling through the realm with the king, either within the royal household or apart from it, they began to beat and wound with impunity the king's faithful subjects; some indeed, with extraordinary cruelty, they even killed. They also seized people's goods, paying nothing for their provisions, and raped and ravished both married and unmarried women, for no one dared to stand up to them ...

(*Parliament met. Gloucester, Arundel and Warwick were convicted of treason, and Archbishop Arundel was banished.*) Wishing to expedite further his evil designs in this parliament, the king did not wish to dissolve it yet, but because Christmas was approaching he shrewdly ordered the magnates and prelates to return to their homes and convene again after the festivities at Shrewsbury, where the parliament would be brought to a conclusion.[5] When they met again, the king, artful and deceitful as ever, cleverly made them concede that, with the consent of all the estates of the realm, parliament's power should be delegated to certain persons, six or eight in number, who, once parliament had been dissolved, would have the power to decide various petitions which had been presented to the parliament but which had not yet been properly dealt with.[6] Under the guise of this concession, however, those persons later proceeded to deal with other more general matters concerning the parliament; this was done by the king's will, in derogation of the estates of parliament, and to the great prejudice of the whole realm, a pernicious example. Moreover, in order that it should look as if he had proper authority for doing this, the king ordered the rolls of parliament to be altered and deleted, contrary to the intention of the original concession. And because the king, and those lords who danced attendance upon him, had spent so much money on what they termed the reform of the realm, it was also agreed in this parliament, at the king's demand, that he be granted one and a half tenths from the clergy and one and a half fifteenths from the (*lay*) community ...

(*Richard created five new dukes, a duchess, a marquis, and four earls.*) Wishing to aggrandise further those persons whom he had just dignified with the titles of duke, marquis, or earl – whom the common people nicknamed in derision, not 'dukes', but 'duketti', that is, 'the little dukes' – the king granted to them most of the lands of the duke

---

5 In fact the parliament was prorogued on 30 September.

6 Walsingham's discussion of the 'parliamentary committee' of 1398 is lifted directly from the 'Record and Process' (below, Doc. 17). On this subject, see J. G. Edwards, 'The Parliamentary Committee of 1398', *EHR* (1925), 321-33. In fact the committee numbered eighteen, of whom nine were required to form a quorum.

of Gloucester and the earls of Arundel and Warwick, thereby
disinheriting all their children from the inheritances which they
should have received from their fathers. And now nobody dared to
stand for the truth, or to say openly what they believed, because of the
tyranny and malice of the king; nor, since they were so struck with
fear, did anyone dare to speak the truth in public, especially when they
saw two well-known friars and doctors of theology, John Paris and
(*blank*), being thrown into prison and made to pay enormous fines,
more than even wealthy men could have paid, because they went about
preaching of the evils of the king's government and the wickedness of
his advisers.[7] Those who were foremost among his counsellors were,
according to common opinion, the worst of men: the duke of Aumale,
the duke of Norfolk, the duke of Exeter, the earl of Wiltshire, and
Lords John Bussy, William Bagot, and (*Henry*) Green, all of whom
were held in the greatest odium by the common people of the realm ...

The year of grace 1399, and the twenty-second year of King Richard's
reign: in this year the laurel trees throughout almost the whole of
England suddenly withered, and then shortly afterwards many of
them revived again; which seemed to presage the fact that, although
some of the lords had been humiliated and imprisoned, and others had
been sent into exile, they would soon be restored to their former
dignity ...

Not long ago, on the morrow of the Purification of the Blessed Virgin
(*2 February*), died Duke John of Lancaster, whose funeral, which the
king attended, was held with great solemnity at St Paul's church in
London. His death gave the king a further opportunity to display his
ill-will towards Henry duke of Hereford, the duke of Lancaster's son
and heir, whom he had already banished for ten years. The king now
decreed that he should be banished for ever, and at the same time
revoked the letters patent which he had earlier granted to him,
whereby his general attorneys were to be allowed during his absence
in exile to sue for livery to be granted to him of any inheritances or
successions which fell in to him, and his homage for them would be
respited in return for a reasonable fine. By revoking these letters the
king showed manifestly how much he hated the duke, and that the
reason why he had originally banished. him was not, as he had

---

7 The additional name omitted by Walsingham may be that of Thomas Prestbury,
M.Theol., not a friar but a monk of Shrewsbury abbey, who, according to Adam
Usk, was imprisoned by Richard because 'he had righteously preached certain
things against his follies' (below, Doc. 15). See also *CPR, 1396-9*, 321.

dishonestly pretended, because of the quarrels or disturbances which might have broken out between his servants and retainers and those of the duke of Norfolk, but in the hope that, when the chance came, he would be able to extend his banishment for life, and thus get his hands upon the duke's very considerable possessions and appropriate them for himself ...

Shortly after Easter there arose yet further opportunities, astonishing to relate, for the king to impose even heavier burdens upon his subjects by demanding from them, under threat of death, still larger sums of money. For he charged seventeen of the counties of the realm that they had sided with the duke of Gloucester, etc., against him, and that because of this he was preparing to ride against them as if they were public enemies. Firstly he made each of these counties give him surety, for he claimed that he dared not enter any of these counties without an army unless he had received a prior assurance that they would not attempt in any way to injure him or his followers. Then he sent certain bishops and other men of standing into those counties to persuade the lords, spiritual as well as temporal, and all the lesser people there, to submit themselves to the king and acknowledge, by letters drawn up under their seals, that they had acted as traitors towards him, whereas in fact they had never done him any injury by word or deed. As a consequence of this the clergy, the common people, and the lords were all forced to hand over enormous sums of money to recover the king's goodwill. The sums thus raised from these counties were called 'Le Pleasaunce', because they were levied at the king's pleasure, and went into his pockets. Later on, when he was about to set out for Ireland and wished to curry favour with the people of these counties, he ordered these letters obligatory – or rather submissory – to be returned to them. This did not mean, however, that he had released them from their obligations to him, for instead he forced their representatives, to whom the county communities had granted full power for this purpose, to bind themselves and their heirs to him under their own seals, in the name of, and with the authority of, the people whom they represented. Thus was the king continually scheming to entrap and grind down his subjects, lest at any time in the future an opportunity might arise for them to regain their former liberty ...

The king also compelled his liegemen to affix their seals to blank charters;[8] some people said that he did this so that whenever he wanted

8 For Richard's infamous 'blank charters', see C. Barron, 'The tyranny of Richard II',
   BIHR (1968), 1-18.

to move against his people he would have the means – albeit unlawful – to crush whomsoever he wished. Others, however, said that he planned to use them to demonstrate to the king of France that the entire population of England had agreed to the sale of Calais and the other overseas territories which, so it was rumoured, the king of France wished to acquire – though only as long as it was clear to him that the English would not under any circumstances attempt to challenge him in the future for lands which he had acquired with their agreement ...

The king, realising that his iniquities were alienating him from his people, now entrusted his personal safety to the Cheshiremen, who, swarming around him in great numbers, assured him that as long as he retained enough of them to guard him, he need fear no man; if he had faith in their strength and reliability, they declared, he could prevail against the whole of England, the whole world even. Because of their pride and arrogance, however, these Cheshiremen were hated by all the king's other household servants ...

About the feast of Pentecost (*18 May*), the king sailed to Ireland with his Cheshiremen and many other lords, notably the dukes of Aumale and Exeter. It was rumoured, however, that he was so afraid that all these lords, even those setting out with him, would have so many soldiers with them that they would outnumber his own troops – with the result that, should he wish to, he would not be able to control them – that those who had been used to commanding five hundred men were now, so it was said, allowed to bring scarcely twenty with them ...

4. Extracts from the Rolls of Parliament, 1397-99

Source: RP, iii, 347-72

Language: French

The following extracts from the official parliamentary record may be taken as representative of the 'royalist' view of the events they describe. They cover the announcement of Gloucester's death; the final proceedings of the September 1397 session of parliament; the principal items of business at the January 1398 session; and the course of the Bolingbroke-Mowbray dispute.

Gloucester's 'confession', read out in parliament on 25 September following the announcement of his death, consists of a preamble and nine articles, which may well have been drawn up in response to specific questions sent to him by the king. Parts of the confession were apparently left out when it was read in parliament, partly in order to disguise the true date of Gloucester's death, and partly in order to omit his pleas for mercy. On this question see J. Tait, 'Did Richard II Murder the Duke of Gloucester?', Historical Essays by Members of the Owens College Manchester, ed. T. F. Tout and J. Tait *(1902), 193-216. Those parts which were left out are given below in square brackets.*

The second (Shrewsbury) session of the parliament lasted only four days, 28-31 January 1398. Its chief purpose was probably to secure a grant of taxation, for no grant had been made at Westminster. In the event, a generous lay subsidy was granted, and the wool custom was granted to the king for life – the first time that it had been granted to any king for a period of more than three years.

It may have been the outbreak of the dispute between Bolingbroke and Mowbray which brought the session to a rapid close. This dispute was now committed to the consideration of the 'parliamentary committee' appointed on the final day of the Shrewsbury session. Because the committee acted during the next year or so with the authority of parliament, its proceedings were recorded on the Rolls of Parliament. It considered the dispute on several occasions, culminating with its infamous decision on 18 March 1399, following the death of John of Gaunt, to revoke Bolingbroke's licence to receive his inheritance while in exile.

(a) 24-25 September: the death of the Duke of Gloucester

Order was then given to Thomas earl marshal, captain of Calais, by writ of the king, to bring forward in this present parliament, before the king and the lords of parliament, the person of Thomas duke of Gloucester, that he should respond to the said appellants respecting their appeal ...

On Monday 24 September, the said captain returned his writ to the said parliament as follows:

THE RESPONSE OF THOMAS EARL MARSHAL

I am unable to bring forward into your presence and that of your council in this present parliament that Thomas duke of Gloucester who is named in the writ addressed to me, so that he may do as is requested in the writ, because the said duke is dead. By order of my most excellent lord the king, I held this duke in my custody in the lord king's prison in the town of Calais; and there, in that same prison, he died.

To our lord the king and his council in this present parliament, from Thomas earl marshal, captain of the town of Calais.

When the said writ and response had been read and heard in parliament, the aforesaid appellants prayed the king, in their own persons, that the said duke of Gloucester should be adjudged a traitor and an enemy to the realm, seeing as, contrary to his allegiance, he had levied war against the person of the king in his own realm, of which crime they had appealed him ... (*The same request was made by the commons*). Whereupon all the aforesaid lords temporal, and the said Sir Thomas Percy exercising his authority in the aforesaid manner, with the assent of the king, adjudged the said duke guilty of levying war in the said manner, and thus of being a traitor ...

Following this, on Tuesday 25 September, the said appellants, present in person in full parliament, requested the king that, if there was any further matter on record concerning their appeal and declarations, be it a confession from any of those appealed, or from some other person, it should be made known and publicly recited in full parliament. Whereupon, at the king's order, and by advice of all the aforesaid lords temporal, a commission was read out in parliament, addressed to Sir

D

William Rickhill, one of the king's justices of his common bench, together with a confession, consequent upon this commission, made in his presence by the said duke of Gloucester, and the response to the commission ...

(*Rickhill's commission from the king, ordering him to go to Calais and speak with Gloucester, was dated 17 August, at Woodstock. Gloucester's confession is in English.*)

THIS IS THE ANSWER OF WILLIAM RICKHILL TO THE COMMISSION OF HIS LIEGE LORD

Thomas duke of Gloucester, by name Thomas of Woodstock, [on the eighth day of September] in the twenty-first year of King Richard, in the castle of Calais, by virtue of a commission of the king, as is more plainly set out in the same commission directed to William Rickhill justice, has acknowledged and confessed before the same William all the matters and points written in the great roll annexed to this schedule, which schedule and great roll are sealed under the seal of the aforesaid William. [On the same day of September], all the aforesaid matters and points having been acknowledged and confessed by the aforesaid duke in the castle of Calais, the aforesaid duke by his own hand fully and plainly wrote it down and delivered it to the same William Rickhill, in the presence of John Lancaster and John Lovetot.[1] And whatever the aforesaid William Rickhill did concerning this affair was done in the presence of the aforesaid John and John, and in no other manner.

> I, Thomas of Woodstock, [on the eighth day of September] in the twenty-first year of my lord the king, by virtue of a commission of my lord the king of the same year directed to William Rickhill justice, which is set out more fully in the aforesaid commission, acknowledge that I was one of those, along with other men, who instigated and assented to the making of a Commission; in which Commission I, amongst others, restrained my lord's freedom, and, along with others, took upon myself royal powers – though truly I did not know or realise at that time that I was acting contrary to his estate or his regality, as I did afterwards, and do now. And forasmuch as I realised afterwards that I had done wrong, and had taken upon myself more than I should have, I submitted myself to my lord, and cried him mercy and grace, and still do, as humbly and as meekly as any man may, and I place myself fully in his mercy and in his grace, as one that always has been full of mercy and of grace to all others.

---

1 Lancaster and Lovetot acted as witnesses at Rickhill's request: see below, Doc. 20(b).

Also, at the time that I came armed into my lord's presence, and into his palace,[2] albeit that I did it out of fear for my life, I acknowledge for certain that I did evil, and acted against his regality and his estate: wherefore I submit myself humbly and meekly to his mercy and his grace.

Also, in that I took my lord's letters from his messengers, and opened them against his leave, I acknowledge that I did evil; wherefore I submit myself humbly to his grace.

Also, in that I slandered my lord, I acknowledge that I acted evilly and wickedly, inasmuch as I said things of a slanderous nature to him in the presence of other persons. But I swear, upon pain of my soul, that I meant no evil thereby. Nevertheless I realise and acknowledge that I acted evilly and foolishly, wherefore I submit myself in all things to his grace.

Also, inasmuch as I, along with others, discussed, [out of fear for my life, the question of surrendering my homage to my lord, I fully admit that I and others did indeed discuss this,] and we asked certain clerks whether we could, out of fear of our lives, surrender our homage, or not; whether we agreed to do it or not, truly I cannot remember, but I believe that we did: wherefore I submit myself fully and for evermore to his grace.

Also inasmuch as I was present when the question of the deposition of my lord was discussed, I acknowledge in truth that we did, for two or three days, agree to do this; but then we performed our homage and our oaths to him, and restored him to as high estate as he had been in previously.[3] Nevertheless I acknowledge that I acted disloyally and unkindly to him that is my liege lord, who has been such a good and kind lord to me. Wherefore I beseech him, as humbly as any creature may beseech his liege lord, that, notwithstanding my unkindness, he may be merciful and graceful towards me.

[As to any new matter or agreement that I might be aware of, or have ordained or assented to, whether secretly or openly, that is directed against my lord's estate, or his power, or any of those about his person, I swear, by the oath that I swore to him upon God's body at Langley that, ever since the day that I took that oath to him, I have not been aware of any gathering directed against either him or any others about his person.[4]

Concerning all these points that I have confessed to William Rickhill

---

2 A reference to the events of 30 December 1387, when the Lords Appellant entered the Tower with 500 men-at-arms (*Westminster Chronicle*, 227).

3 This passage provides further evidence for the idea that the Lords Appellant did actually agree to depose Richard for a few days at the end of December 1387: see M. V. Clarke and V. H. Galbraith, 'The deposition of Richard II', *BJRL* (1930), 157-61.

4 This incident at Langley occurred in 1388 (below, p. 182). The inclusion of this article suggests that Richard was hoping to uncover some evidence for those 'recent offences' with which, according to Walsingham, he planned to charge his opponents (see above, Doc. 3); its omission in the parliament must have followed from his failure to discover any such evidence.

justice, through which I readily acknowledge that I have, by my disloyalty and unkindness, offended my lord and, as I have said before, acted against him; yet truly, and as I will answer before God, it was my intention and my wish to do the best that I could for his person and his estate. Nevertheless I am well aware now that my actions and deeds did not fulfil my intentions. But, upon pain of my soul, in relation both to these points and to any other foolish or negligent deeds which I have committed, I declare that it never was my intention, or my desire, or in my thoughts, to do anything that might have been distressful or harmful to the salvation of my liege lord's person – and so will I answer before God at the day of judgement.

I beseech my liege and sovereign lord the king, therefore, that he will, of his high grace and bounty, grant to me his mercy and his grace, for I put my life, my body, and my goods wholly at his will, as humbly and as meekly as any creature can or may do to his liege lord. And I beseech his high lordship that he will, for the passion that God suffered for all mankind, and the compassion that he had of his mother on the cross, and the pity that he had of Mary Magdalen, vouchsafe me his compassion and pity, and grant his mercy and his grace to me, for he has always been full of mercy and grace to all his lieges, and to all others that have not been so close to him as I have been, even though I am unworthy.]

The appellants then prayed that the said William Rickhill, a man of great loyalty and proven integrity, should be ordered by the king upon his allegiance to tell the truth concerning the aforesaid confession. Whereupon the said William Rickhill, in the presence of the king and of all the lords spiritual and temporal, and of the commons of the realm then gathered in parliament, announced and declared that at about eight o'clock in the morning he arrived in Calais Castle and came to the said duke of Gloucester, whose memory was then good, and who was not under duress in prison, and, in the presence of John Lancaster and John Lovetot, he showed him his commission and explained why he had come, and said to him that if there was anything which he wished to say, he should put it all down in writing. And then the said William Rickhill left the duke of Gloucester, returning to him at about nine o'clock in the evening of the same day, when the duke of Gloucester read out, in person, the confession which he had written, and then, with his own hand, gave the written confession to the said William Rickhill. Following this, William Rickhill said to the duke of Gloucester that if there was anything that he wished to add concerning the same business, he would communicate it personally to the king, for the king was well aware of the full truth of these matters; whereupon the duke of Gloucester said that there was one matter which he had only remembered after writing the confession, namely, that he had said to the king that, if he wished to be a king, he should stop begging to save the life of Simon Burley. And he asked the said William Rickhill to explain this to the king by word of mouth ...

(b) 29-30 September: pardon granted to the earls of Derby and Nottingham; the lords swear to uphold the decisions of parliament

Item: on the Saturday following (*29 September*), the commons reminded the king that, since he had graciously declared certain great persons named in the aforesaid Commission drawn up in the tenth year to be innocent of malice, and had for his own part pardoned them and testified to their good behaviour and bearing towards him on that occasion;[5] so might he also be pleased to consider how, at the time that Thomas duke of Gloucester, Richard earl of Arundel, and Thomas earl of Warwick had risen up and ridden, contrary to their allegiance, against our lord the king, the said duke and earls had wanted to pursue and search out our lord the king wherever he might be found in the kingdom, and to kill a great number of the king's liege subjects, in order to accomplish their wicked designs and intentions, and were only prevented from doing so by those honourable kinsmen of the king, Henry of Lancaster earl of Derby, and Thomas Mowbray earl of Nottingham, whose belief it was that the actions of the said duke and the earls of Arundel and Warwick were notoriously contrary to their allegiance and to the estate of our lord the king; whereupon the said earls of Derby and Nottingham, wishing to do their duty to our liege lord, forsook the company of the said duke and the earls of Arundel and Warwick, and came into the honourable presence of our lord the king. And since it is to the king's honour to reward good and worthy persons according to their merits and deserts, it might please our lord the king to commend especially the said earls of Derby and Notting-ham, and to make public declaration in this present parliament of their estate, name, good conduct, and loyal bearing. To which our lord the king, sitting in his royal dignity in parliament, replied that this matter was known better to him than to any other person, and he publicly

5 Those members of the 1386 Commission who were still alive in 1397 and were then pardoned by the king were Edmund duke of York, William Wykeham bishop of Winchester, and Richard Lord le Scrope (*RP*, iii, 353).

declared, recorded, and bore witness to the loyal bearing and good name of the said earls of Derby and Nottingham, adding that it was indeed well known to him that the said earls of Derby and Nottingham had done their duty loyally to the king, and had, like loyal liegemen, forsaken the company of the said duke and the earls of Arundel and Warwick, and had come to him, and thereafter remained with him, and borne themselves well and truly, like good and loyal liegemen, and for loyal liegemen he held them. He wishes and grants, therefore, that not only they but also those who were in their company at the time when the said duke and the earls of Arundel and Warwick rose up, should, in reputation, name and honour, be known as, held for, and publicly declared among all his liege subjects throughout the realm to be, loyal liegemen; and that they should be entirely excused on this matter, and never, at any time in the future, be impeached, molested, or harmed on account of their conduct in these affairs. Moreover our lord the king, with the assent and advice of all the lords in parliament, and at the petition of the commons, has decreed and ordained that this declaration and grant should have the force and virtue of a statute, and should be regarded as a statute ...

Item: be it remembered that, at the request of the commons, made to the king in parliament on the 26th day of September, concerning the oaths which the lords spiritual and temporal were to take before the shrine of St Edward (*the Confessor*) to uphold and maintain all the statutes, establishments, ordinances and judgements made or given in the said parliament, as set out below; on Sunday the feast of St Jerome (*30 September*), after the celebration of mass in the church of Westminster Abbey, the lords spiritual and temporal approached the shrine of St Edward in the honourable presence of our lord the king, namely ...(*the names of fourteen bishops and four other prelates follow*), and there all the prelates severally, upon the altar of St Edward's shrine, took their oaths according to the form of a schedule there read to them, inasmuch as it pertained to them, saving the integrity of their estate ...

And following this, the lords temporal then, in the same place, and in the presence of the king, namely ...(*seven dukes, the marquis of Dorset, eight earls, and twenty-four barons are named*), took their oaths upon the same altar, agreeing expressly to the form of a schedule there read to them, the tenor of which oath was:

> You swear that you will faithfully and truly preserve, maintain and uphold, without deceit or evil design, all the statutes, establishments, ordinances and judgements made or given in this present parliament, without ever

doing or attempting anything contrary to them, to any part of them, or to anything arising from them; nor will you ever repeal, revoke, overthrow, undermine, reverse or annul them, nor allow them to be repealed, revoked, overthrown, undermined, reversed or annulled, as you live and die.

You swear that you will never, at any time to come, allow any living person to do or attempt anything contrary to any of the statutes, establishments, ordinances and judgements made or given in this present parliament, nor to any part of them, nor to anything arising from them. And if any person should do so, and should be duly convicted of doing so, you will do everything in your power, without deceit or evil intention, to assist the king and his heirs as kings of England to have such a person executed, as a false and high traitor to the king and kingdom of England; saving to the king his regality and his liberty, and the rights of his crown.

Furthermore, the knights of the shires of England, who were present there for the parliament, were asked by the king if they wished to take the same oath? To which these knights replied, their voices loud in unison, that they promised to keep this same oath, collectively raising high their right hands in token of their agreement to the aforesaid oath.

(c) 29-30 January: the Shrewsbury session

Item: on the following Tuesday (*29 January*), Sir John Bussy explained to the king in parliament how the chancellor and treasurer had demonstrated to him and his companions the needs and necessary charges of the king and the kingdom, and said that although the commons were in great poverty, nevertheless they were and would be ready, like loyal liegemen, to do their duty to the best of their ability. Whereupon they prayed the king that, seeing as great riots, disturbances, and crimes offensive to his royal majesty had been committed in the past, as a result of which his people were in great peril from the law, it should please the king, for the comfort of his people, graciously to grant and issue a general grace and pardon to all his people. To which the chancellor replied, at the king's command, that the king understood their request, but that he wished first to know how they for their part intended to aid him; and, once he had been given to understand from their deeds and wishes that he could be beholden to them, he would be minded for his part to grant such a grace and pardon as would give them reason to be beholden to him ...

Be it remembered that on the same Wednesday (*30 January*), Henry duke of Hereford came before our lord the king in parliament carrying in his hand a schedule, and said to the king that he had, as ordered by the king, come into his honourable presence at Heywood,[6] where the king had said to him that he had been given to understand that the duke of Norfolk had made a number of incriminating remarks to the slander of our lord the king's person, which remarks, so the king had been led to believe, had been made to the duke of Hereford. Whereupon the king had ordered the duke of Hereford upon his allegiance to repeat those remarks to the king, faithfully and exactly as they had been spoken to him. Upon this the said duke of Hereford, at the king's command, not out of malice or enmity nor for any other reason, but solely in order to obey and comply with the king's order, as he was bound to do, wrote down what the duke of Norfolk had said to him, inasmuch as he had understood it and retained it in his memory, and committed the substance of these remarks to the aforesaid schedule. The duke of Hereford then gave the schedule to the king, together with his protestation concerning these matters, the tenor of which was as follows:

Made upon the understanding that I may enlarge upon or abridge any of the following at any time that it should please me or seem necessary to do so, saving always the substance of my accusation: My lord, in the month of December in the twenty-first year of your reign (*1397*), while the duke of Hereford was riding between Brentford and London, the duke of Norfolk approached him in great haste and spoke to him of various matters, saying to him, among other things, 'We are on the point of being undone.' 'Why?' asked the duke of Hereford. 'For what was done at Radcot Bridge,' came the reply. 'How can that be?' said the duke of Hereford, 'for the king has pardoned us and made a declaration on our behalf in parliament, saying that we acted well and loyally towards him.' But the duke of Norfolk replied that despite this, he would deal with us as he had dealt with others in the past, for he intended to annul that pardon. It would be a strange thing indeed, said the duke of Hereford, if after having announced it to the people, the king were afterwards to have it annulled. To which the duke of Norfolk replied that it was a strange and a fickle world: 'for I know well,' he said, 'that had it not been for certain people, your father the lord of Lancaster and you would have been either seized or killed when you came to Windsor after the parliament'.[7] For, he added, the dukes of Aumale and Exeter, the earl of Worcester, and himself, had sworn together that they

6 Heywood in Cheswardine, Shropshire; letters patent were dated there between 18 and 23 January 1398 (*CPR, 1396-9*, 182, 280, 317, 352).

7 Letters patent were dated at Windsor between 6 and 8 October 1397 (*CPR, 1396-9*, 207, 210-2).

would never assent to the ruin of any lord without just and reasonable cause. It was the duke of Surrey, the earl of Wiltshire, and the earl of Salisbury, drawing in also the earl of Gloucester, whose evil designs underlay this plot, for they had sworn to effect the ruin of six other lords, namely, the dukes of Lancaster, Hereford, Aumale and Exeter, the marquis (*of Dorset*), and himself. The duke of Norfolk also said that they planned to reverse the judgement concerning Earl Thomas of Lancaster,[8] 'which will result in the disinheritance of us and of several others.' 'God forbid!' replied the duke of Hereford, adding that it would be extraordinary if the king were to agree to that, since he had been so gracious towards him, or so it seemed to him, and had promised to be a good lord to him. Moreover, as he well remembered, the king had sworn by St Edward to be a good lord to all the others as well as to him. Indeed, replied the duke of Norfolk, and he had sworn the same to him by God's body on several occasions, but he placed no greater trust in the king just because of that. He also told the duke of Hereford that the king planned to lure the earl of March and others into agreement with the plans of the said four lords, in order to achieve the ruin of these lords. 'If that is the case,' replied the duke of Hereford, 'then we can never trust them.' 'Indeed we cannot,' said the duke of Norfolk, 'for even if they do not succeed with their present plans, they will still be plotting to destroy us in our homes ten years from now.'

Then on the next Thursday, 31 January, in order to bring the parliament to a conclusion, it was ordained by the king, with the assent of all the estates of parliament, that the matters contained in this said accusation should be discussed and decided by the good advice and discretion of our lord the king, with the counsel and guidance of certain commissioners appointed to deal with such business by the authority of parliament: namely, the duke of Lancaster, the duke of York, the duke of Aumale, the duke of Surrey, the duke of Exeter, the marquis of Dorset, the earl of March, the earl of Salisbury, the earl of Northumberland, and the earl of Gloucester, or any six of them; the earl of Worcester and the earl of Wiltshire as proctors for the clergy, or one of them; John Bussy, Henry Green, John Russell, Richard Chelmswick, Robert Teye, and John Golafre, knights attending parliament, or any four or three of them ...[9]

---

8 Thomas earl of Lancaster, first cousin to King Edward II, was executed for treason by the king in March 1322, but the judgement against him was reversed in 1327; for discussion of these accusations by Mowbray see above, pp. 17-22.

9 Bussy, Green and Russell were king's knights and members of the royal council. Chelmswick was a king's esquire, JP in Shropshire and steward of Cornwall; Teye was a king's esquire, JP in Essex, and constable of Colchester castle; Golafre was the son of a former chamber knight of the same name, an esquire of the royal household and sheriff of Oxford and Berkshire (*CPR, 1396-9*, 1, 46, 82, 228, 235, 330, 486).

Item: on Thursday ..., the duke of Hereford knelt humbly in full parliament before the king and said to him, 'My liege lord, I am well aware that various riots, troubles and misdeeds, injurious to yourself and to your royal estate, have occurred in your kingdom, at some of which I was present, among others, although without evil intention, or desire to cause you offence, or realisation at the time that I was committing any crime or offence against you. But, my lord, inasmuch as I now acknowledge and confess my offences and misdeeds in these matters, I cry you mercy, my lord, and beg you to pardon me for them.' Whereupon our lord the king, gratefully accepting this humble prayer and confession from the duke, graciously and in full parliament pardoned him all his conduct in the aforesaid matters, and anything arising out of them that might pertain to him; moreover, he granted him good lordship. In addition the king bore witness, announcing this whole business to all the estates of parliament, that he had granted him a full pardon ...

Item: on the same day, the commons of the realm, with the assent of the lords spiritual and temporal, granted to the king the subsidy on wools, hides, and wool-fells for the term of his life, together with one fifteenth and tenth, and one half-fifteenth and half-tenth ...

Item: on the same Thursday, our lord the king issued his grace, remission, and pardon to all his liegemen of the kingdom of England ... (*The form of the general pardon follows*) ... Provided always that no person may claim the benefit of this pardon for treason or felony unless he sue out a charter of pardon. And provided always that none of those who rose up forcibly and rode against the king, in the company of the lords who have now been adjudged and convicted, in the eleventh year of his reign, may claim pardon for that deed done at that time unless they sue out charters of pardon for it between now and the feast of St John the Baptist next (*24 June*).

Following the grant of this grace and pardon issued to his liegemen on this occasion, our lord the king publicly declared, in his own words, that if the lords or commons of the realm who should come to parliaments in times to come should attempt to impede or undermine the grant of the said subsidy of wools, hides, and wool-fells made for the term of his life, then the said grace and pardon would be quite void, and would be annulled in its entirety.

After this declaration had been made by our lord the king, the chancellor, at the king's command, and on behalf of the king, thanked the lords spiritual and temporal, the knights of the shires, citizens, and burgesses, for their good bearing and the diligence which they had shown in accomplishing the business of the parliament. And, having ordered the knights, citizens and burgesses to sue out writs for their wages, he gave them leave to depart.

(d) March 1398–March 1399: Records of the parliamentary committee

On the sixteenth day of September (*1398*), therefore, proclamation was made to the said Henry duke of Hereford and Thomas duke of Norfolk, by command of the king, that whereas on the Wednesday after the quinzaine of St Hilary in our lord the king's twenty-first year (*30 January*), in the said parliament at Shrewsbury, Henry had handed to our lord the king a bill the tenor of which was as follows: 'My lord, in the month of December in the twenty-first year of your reign, while the duke of Hereford was riding between Brentford and London, etc. ...' verbatim as above; and afterwards the said Henry of Lancaster and Thomas Mowbray appeared at Oswestry, on the 23rd day of February, as is stated in the record of that day, at which time a day was assigned to them, to be at Windsor on Sunday 28 April in our lord the king's twenty-first year; on which day both parties appeared, and a day was assigned to them until the morrow, which was Monday 29 April. In the meantime our lord the king, at his council at Bristol (*on 19 March*), bearing in mind the decision made at Oswestry by advice of those exercising authority on behalf of parliament, ordered that a trial by battle be held between the said dukes of Hereford and Norfolk unless sufficient proof could be found to decide the issue otherwise. And the said dukes of Hereford and Norfolk appeared at Windsor, as mentioned above, on the Sunday and the Monday; on which Monday, because in the meantime no proof had been found by which the issue could be decided, as had been required in accordance with the decision of that meeting, it was decided, by the advice of the dukes, earls, barons, bannerets, and a great number of knights of England, gathered together for this cause, and of those who exercised authority on behalf of parliament, that battle should be waged between the said dukes of Hereford and Norfolk. Whereupon a day was assigned to the said dukes of Hereford and Norfolk to be at Shrewsbury, there to be given their day, their place, and their lances.

On the day assigned, therefore, the 16th day of September, the said
dukes were ready at the town of Coventry to do their duty. Our lord
the king, however, considering how great was the issue at stake in the
battle, in that, as declared in parliament, it involved treason, and
considering how closely related to the king the two dukes are in both
blood and arms; and desiring as always to promote the welfare and
honour of all those who are of his blood and arms, and, like a good and
gracious lord, grieving in his heart at them above all others even
though they did not merit it – for each of them was more to blame than
any other; and wishing to avoid the great dishonour which would
befall one or other of these dukes who are so closely related to the
king; decided, like a rightful, natural and sovereign lord, of his special
grace, to take the issue into his own hands. Our lord the king
therefore, by the full advice, authority, and assent of parliament,
declared to Henry duke of Hereford that he wished, decreed and
adjudged, for the peace and tranquillity of himself, his realm, and his
subjects, and in order to avoid quarrels and disagreements, particularly between the said dukes of Hereford and Norfolk and their allies
and supporters, that the said Henry of Lancaster duke of Hereford
should quit this realm for the space of ten years; to comply with which
order he should have left the realm by the time of the coming octaves
of St Edward the Confessor (*20 October*), under pain of treason, as
authorised by parliament. He also decreed, by the same authority and
under the same penalty, that the said duke of Hereford should not
under any circumstances travel in the company of the said duke of
Norfolk, nor of Thomas Arundel, nor should he in any way communicate with either of them, either by sending or by receiving messages,
or by causing messages to be sent or received. It is to be understood,
however, that this sentence is not given on account of any misdemeanour committed by the said duke of Hereford in matters concerning his
appeal, or any part of it, for he clearly fulfilled his duty concerning his
said appeal up to the moment when the battle was taken into the king's
hands.

Thomas Mowbray duke of Norfolk was then informed that since on
Monday 29 April, in the king's twenty-first year, at Windsor, he had
confessed to certain civil points contained in the aforesaid Appeal,
which he had formerly denied on 23 February at Oswestry, which
points, once admitted, might be the cause of great trouble in the realm;
our lord the king, wishing, like a rightful lord, to punish those whose
desire it is to breed such trouble and disturbance, and wishing to

remove any likelihood of such trouble arising, has ordained and adjudged, with the same advice, authority, and assent of parliament, that the said Thomas Mowbray duke of Norfolk should quit the realm for the term of his life; that he should have left the realm by the time of the coming octaves of St Edward the Confessor, and should either live in Germany, Bohemia and Hungary, or cross the Great Sea (*the Mediterranean*) on pilgrimage, but that he should not enter or live in any other part of Christendom, under pain of treason, by the aforesaid authority. Nor should he under any circumstances travel in the company of the said Henry duke of Hereford, or of Thomas Arundel, nor communicate with either of them, either by sending or receiving messages, or by causing messages to be received or sent, under pain of treason, by the same authority. This is not done, however, because of any wrongdoing on the said duke of Norfolk's part in his defence, for since the aforesaid 29th day of April until the moment when the battle was taken into our lord the king's hands, he has done his duty.

Furthermore, seeing that, despite the fact that it appeared necessary, honourable and expedient to our lord the king and to all those of his council, as well as to the appellants and others in the said parliament, that the wrongful and misnamed parliament held in the eleventh year should, since it was contrary to the estate and person of our lord the king and enfeebled the liberties of the crown, be entirely revoked, cancelled and annulled – otherwise, as the king was plainly advised, the proceedings of the last parliament, which strengthened our lord the king and his crown, would have come to nothing and had no force, since the one was entirely contrary to his interests, while the other was and is entirely in his interests – nevertheless the said duke of Norfolk both privately and publicly opposed the said annulment in so far as he was able to do so, and maintained the validity of the wicked and unlawful appeals passed in the aforesaid misnamed parliament of the eleventh year;[10] for which action our lord the king declined at that time to pronounce upon the extent of his guilt because the said duke of Norfolk is of the blood and arms of the king; seeing moreover that our lord the king, in his parliament held at Westminster, gave to the said duke of Norfolk, as he did to the other appellants, as a reward for the appeal that was then brought, certain lordships, lands and tenements, yet the said duke of Norfolk did not fully and lawfully support that appeal as the other appellants did, in that he failed, without any reasonable or lawful excuse, to appear on the day that the

10 That is, the 'Merciless' Parliament of 1388.

said appeal was to be decided; our lord the king, for these reasons, has adjudged, by the said authority of parliament, that the said duke of Norfolk and his heirs should forfeit to him and to his heirs in perpetuity the said lordships, lands and tenements, together with all the offices which he holds for life, and anything which the ancestors of our lord the king had bound themselves to confer upon the ancestors of the said duke of Norfolk. In addition, because of his bad governance of our lord king's town of Calais, his failure to make due payments there, and the consequent peril in which he placed the town, the king, by the same authority as above, has adjudged that all the lands of the said duke of Norfolk's inheritance should be taken into his hands, with the exception of £1,000 a year to be granted to the duke of Norfolk; the remainder is to go to the king until such time as he is fully satisfied for those sums upon which the duke of Norfolk defaulted.

It was also ordained by the aforesaid authority of parliament that if either the duke of Hereford or the duke of Norfolk, or any other person, should in any way attempt to overturn any of the decisions, or any part of them, made on the said 16th day of September, even to the smallest point in this ordinance, he should incur sentence of treason to the same extent as if it were a part of the ordinance made in the parliament which began at Westminster and continued at Shrewsbury. It was also ordained by the same authority that if either the duke of Hereford or the duke of Norfolk, or any person or persons acting in their name or on their behalf, should in any way attempt to secure a pardon, or a licence to return to this land, or in any other way act contrary to this ordinance or any part of it, he or they should also incur sentence of treason. The king also wishes and ordains, by the same authority, that all the penalties declared in the said parliament should extend to the ordinances and judgement on these two, as well as to the ordinances made in the aforesaid parliament ...

Be it remembered that on Tuesday 18 March in the twenty-second year of the king's reign (*1399*), in the king's presence at Westminster, the chancellor of England explained to various lords spiritual and temporal who had assembled there at the king's order that, following the judgement given against him at Coventry by authority of parliament, Henry duke of Hereford had submitted to our lord the king a petition dealing with various matters which had been read out to our said lord the king and the lords: among other things, he especially requested that, if any succession or inheritance for which he ought to perform homage were to descend or escheat to him during his absence, he should be permitted, through his attornies, to petition for and be granted livery of them, his homage and fealty being respited, as is more fully explained in the letters patent relating to this;[11] which letters were inadvertently, and without advice or full deliberation, so it is said, granted to the said duke. Since then, however, these letters, the circumstances surrounding them, and the consequences following from them, have been scrutinised and diligently examined, and it has been found that they are blatantly contrary to the aforesaid judgements given at Coventry, since the said duke, once that judgement had been given, was no longer in a position to claim or receive any benefit from such letters. Our lord the king therefore, together with Edmund duke of York, Edward duke of Aumale, John duke of Exeter, John marquis of Dorset, John earl of Salisbury, Henry earl of Northumberland, Thomas earl of Gloucester, Thomas earl of Worcester, William earl of Wiltshire, and John Bussy, Henry Green, John Russell, and Robert Teye, knights representing parliament, has adjudged, with the assent of the said lords spiritual and temporal − since he has by authority of parliament sufficient power to do this − that the said letters patent, and all matters arising out of them or dependent upon them, should be entirely revoked, annulled, overturned and repealed, and that their enrolment in chancery be cancelled; and that the said letters patent and their enrolment be for ever regarded as void and of no force.

Item: on the same day, declaration was made publicly before the king and the same lords that Thomas duke of Norfolk had similar letters patent concerning any succession or inheritance that should fall in to him,[12] so that his homage too could be respited in his absence in the same way as had been allowed to the duke of Hereford; whereupon it was requested that these letters should be similarly repealed, to which the king was pleased to agree ...

11 *CPR, 1396-9*, 425.
12 *CPR, 1396-9*, 487.

5. Two Cistercian views of Richard

Despite its brevity, the Kirkstall chronicler's description of the 1397 parliament is valuable for the fact that it is the only chronicle account of the parliament to have been written before the revolution, and thus without either knowledge of the king's failure or the influence of Lancastrian disinformation. No doubt this helps to explain its benevolent attitude to the king. Richard found considerable support in the chronicles written in Cistercian abbeys in the years around 1399, and in none more so than the first part of the Dieulacres chronicle, the author of which was the most fervently Ricardian of the English chroniclers of the time – even to the point of denying the king's responsibility for the death of the duke of Gloucester. The Kirkstall chronicler was more circumspect on this point, hinting at Richard's involvement but not actually accusing him of the deed.

(a) The parliament of 1397 according to the Kirkstall Chronicle

Source: Short Kirkstall Chronicle, 118-20.

Language: Latin

In the year of grace 1397, and the twenty-first year of his reign, King Richard, remembering and again recalling to mind the injustices which had been inflicted upon himself and his kingdom by a number of English lords in the year of Christ 1388, determined to right those injustices, and set out to bring the kingdom of England under his control. About the feast of St John the Baptist (*24 June*), therefore, just after nine o'clock, at his manor of Kennington, a proclamation was issued on the king's behalf that all who were at court should prepare themselves at once and as best they could to set out with the king; where they were going, however, or why, they had not the least idea. Once the king and his whole court, together with a large company of men who had come to join him, had passed through London, and he had entrusted the security of

the city to the mayor and sheriffs,[1] he immediately set off and,
riding through the night, arrived at daybreak at Pleshey manor,
which belonged to Lord Thomas Woodstock duke of Gloucester;
the latter, having just been forewarned of his king's imminent
arrival, came out with his lady the duchess, all his children, and the
staff of his chapel, all of whom solemnly knelt before the king and
in various other ways displayed the sort of respect that was due to
him. The king greeted them in turn and respectfully raised the
duchess from the ground; he then arrested the aforesaid Thomas
duke of Gloucester and handed him over to the earl marshal of
England, who, having taken custody of him, took him across to
Calais, where, so it is commonly said, he was secretly murdered.
Straight after this, Lords Richard earl of Arundel and Thomas earl
of Warwick were also arrested and placed in safe custody. The lord
king then summoned his formal council to meet at Nottingham on
23 July, where the duke of Gloucester and the earls of Arundel and
Warwick were appealed of high treason against king and kingdom
by six earls present there in person.[2] Later, on 16 September, the
king held his parliament at London, where, on the first day of the
lords' trial, Thomas Arundel archbishop of Canterbury, the brother
of the earl of Arundel, got up to make answer, but hardly had he
begun when he was told to keep quiet, for, as he was also told, it
might prejudice his ability to reply more fully to the charges
against him at some time in the future. On the second day, in full
and open parliament, Lord Thomas Arundel was publicly proclaimed a traitor to king and kingdom, and sentenced by judgement
of parliament to be exiled from England within forty days following. It was alleged against him that, at the time when he had first
been appointed as the king's chief councillor, he had consistently
revealed all the king's secret deliberations to someone who was
opposed to the king, namely his brother the earl of Arundel; and it
was because of this, as well as other things imputed to him, that he
was exiled from England.

Next day the aforesaid lords, namely the duke of Gloucester and the
earls of Arundel and Warwick, were called to stand trial. When the
earls had been brought in – the duke of Gloucester appeared in a
higher court, before the Supreme Judge – and when the charges
against them, so grave as to comprise treason towards the king, had

1 The mayor of London from June 1397 was Richard ('Dick') Whittington.
2 The appeals were in fact presented at Nottingham on 5 August.

been read out, they were condemned to death, and all their goods were judicially declared to be forfeited to the lord king. At length, however, heeding the pleas for mercy of Lady Isabelle, queen of England, the king relented and granted Lord Thomas earl of Warwick his life; thus, tempering the wine of justice with the oil of clemency, he banished him to the Isle of Man, granting him also a fixed annuity for the term of his life. The earl of Arundel, however, was beheaded that same day – that is Friday, the feast of St Matthew the apostle (*21 September*) – on the same spot hard by the Tower of London where Lord Simon de Burley had been executed. How admirable and long-suffering is the king's forbearance! Previously the sun was hidden behind a cloud – in other words, the royal majesty was obscured by a hostile force – but now, soaring in arms above the mountains, and bounding over the hills with his might, he has dispersed the clouds with his sun, whose light shines ever more brightly ...

(b) The Dieulacres chronicler on a much-maligned king

Source: Dieulacres Chronicle, 164-70.

Language: Latin

For a servant or a subject to rebel against his lord is ridiculous. In order therefore that no crime should remain unpunished, God directed the king's heart towards finding a way to punish these rebels, whereupon the rightful king came secretly with his followers at dawn one day in the year of Our Lord 1395 (*recte 1397*) to Thomas duke of Gloucester's manor of Pleshey in Essex, and arrested him and sent him to be imprisoned at Calais, where he died. How he died, God knows, but it was not by the king's will, although a lot of liars and evildoers, either from their own malice or at the prompting of the devil, maliciously accused the innocent king of the death and exile of these lords. On the contrary, the source of this problem will be fully and clearly revealed in what follows, and it will become obvious who was the real cause of these deaths and exiles. In addition, the earl of Warwick was banished to the Isle of Man, and various others were sent off to be incarcerated here and there in different prisons.

In the year of Our Lord 1396 (*recte 1397*), in the new great hall which had been built at Westminster, Richard earl of Arundel was sentenced by John duke of Lancaster to have his head cut off. He is buried in London, in the church of the Augustinian friars. Stories were told among the common people that his head had reattached itself to his body, so the king ordered the duke of Surrey to make a formal proclamation that this was untrue ...[3]

In the year of Our Lord 1397, the twentieth year of King Richard's reign, a major dispute broke out between Henry duke of Hereford and Thomas Mowbray duke of Norfolk, arising out of certain agreements made between them. Thomas publicly repudiated these agreements, so Henry challenged him to a duel. This was held at Coventry on the feast of St Euphemia the Virgin (*16 September*), but just as they began to do battle, the king suddenly proclaimed his peace and ordered them to retire without shedding blood. Then sentence was passed upon them: duke Henry was to be banished from England for ten years, duke Thomas in perpetuity. A little later therefore, on the feast of the Translation of St Edward the Confessor (*13 October*), Henry accompanied by a few followers crossed to France carrying intercessory letters from the king to the king of France – whose daughter Isabelle King Richard had married after the death of his first wife Anne.

In the same year, about the time of the feast of the Purification of the Blessed Mary (*2 February*), following the death of John duke of Lancaster, father of the above-mentioned Henry, and his burial at Leicester in the college called 'le Newerke' – which he had founded for the good memory of Henry former duke of Lancaster, the father of Blanche, who was the mother of this Henry duke of Hereford[4] – rumour had it that he (*Hereford*), while still in exile, sent a diplomatic mission bearing conciliatory letters to King Richard, asking the king if he would be gracious enough to allow him to receive the issues of his patrimony during his exile. But the king, who had already apportioned out all his lands and movable goods, even down to the beasts in the four forests of Lancashire, decided on the advice of his council not to help him at all. The king was at this time on the point of leading a large fleet to Ireland. Finally, and apparently with the support of his council, he proscribed and banned in perpetuity both the deceased duke John as well as his son Henry, and had this proclaimed

---

3 Walsingham, *Annales Ricardi Secundi*, 216-19, relates this story in greater detail.

4 Henry of Grosmont, first duke of Lancaster (d. 1361). Gaunt married his daughter, Blanche, in 1359; the College of the Annunciation of St Mary in the Newarke at Leicester was founded by Grosmont in 1356, and its endowment completed, with Gaunt's consent, under the terms of his will.

throughout the whole kingdom.[5] Blank charters were also drawn up, which were to be sealed by both the churchmen and the laymen of each county in the realm, and all the people were made to swear faithfully to acquiesce in whatever was written on them. As a result of this, evil rumours began to spread through the whole community, because of the harsh bondage to which they were subjecting themselves.

The king's preoccupation with Ireland did him little good, however, for while he was away various enemies of his, and of the country, made their way stealthily and craftily into England. They killed his ministers and, although they pretended to talk smoothly of peace, overthrew even the innocent king himself ...

---

5 '... rex suo consilio fulcitus tam Iohannem ducem mortuum quam Henricum eius filium in exilio positum imperpetuum relegavit et bannivit ...' The effect of proscribing a deceased person is difficult to understand, but this seems clearly to be the chronicler's meaning. He may have been referring to arrangements made by Gaunt before his death for the inheritance by Henry of his property.

6. The St Albans conspiracy and the Bolingbroke-Mowbray dispute according to a French source

Source: Traison et Mort (trans. B. Williams), 117-27, 146-9

Language: French

The Traison et Mort, *written by a French author who probably accompanied Queen Isabelle to England in 1397, sought to provide a justification for Richard's coup against Gloucester, Arundel and Warwick by asserting that they had been planning a new insurrection against the king. The so-called 'St Albans Conspiracy' has, however, found few believers among recent historians: its chronology as described here is impossible to reconcile with known events, and it is surprising – if such a conspiracy did indeed exist – that Richard did not use it as evidence against his opponents in parliament. In fact what we seem to have here is a garbled and melodramatic version of events which took place ten years earlier, in 1387. For a detailed rebuttal of the chronicler's story, see J. J. N. Palmer, 'The authorship, date and historical value of the French chronicles on the Lancastrian Revolution', BJRL (1978-79), 400-5, where it is described as 'sheer fantasy'.*

The author's account of the Bolingbroke-Mowbray dispute has, however, rather more to recommend it. He was probably present at Windsor on 29 April 1398, and provides valuable details concerning the new charges which Bolingbroke brought against Mowbray on that occasion. Certainly his picture of a king anxious to reconcile the two warring lords should not be too lightly dismissed.

(a) The 'St Albans Conspiracy'

King Richard restored the city and castle of Brest to the duke of Brittany in the year thirteen hundred fourscore and sixteen; and when the duke had received the said city, he turned out and dismissed all the soldiers who were therein: and upon the arrival of the garrison in England, then began the divisions between the king and his uncle the duke of Gloucester, the earl of Arundel, and many other lords.

It is to be observed that King Richard held a feast at Westminster, when he declared his intention of going to Bristol. And straightaway at this feast arrived the said soldiers who had held Brest for the king, who were received at dinner in the king's hall. When the dinner was over and the king had taken wine and comfits, the duke of Gloucester said to the king, 'My lord, have you not remarked at dinner our companions which are here?' The king replied, 'Good uncle, what companions do you mean?' 'My lord,' said the duke, 'they are your people who have come from Brest, who have faithfully served you, but have been badly paid, and know not what to take to.' And the king said that they should be paid in full; and, in fact, commanded that four good villages near London should be given up to them, that they might live there at his expense until they received their due. Then replied the duke of Gloucester very proudly, 'Sire, you ought first to hazard your life in capturing a city from your enemies, by feat of arms or by force, before you think of giving up or selling any city which your ancestors, the kings of England, have gained or conquered.' To which the king answered very scornfully, 'What is that you say?' The duke, his uncle, then repeated what he had said before. Upon which the king was very wroth, and said to the duke, 'Do you think that I am a merchant or a traitor, that I wish to sell my land? By St John the Baptist, no, no; but it is a fact that our cousin of Brittany has restored, and well and truly paid us the sum which our ancestors had lent him on the city of Brest; and since he has honestly paid us, it is only just he should have his pledge back again'.[1] Thus began the quarrel between the king and the duke of Gloucester ...

Now there was an abbot of St Albans, twenty miles distant from London, in England, who was godfather to the duke of Gloucester, and had held him over the font in baptism after his birth, which took place at Woodstock, beyond Oxford.[2] There was also a prior at Westminster, near London, who was a great friend of the duke's, and of the said abbot of St Albans.[3] The abbot of St Albans, godfather of the said duke,

---

1 Brest had been leased from the duke of Brittany in 1378. It was returned to him in April 1397, under the terms of the Anglo-French truce of 1396, in return for which Richard received 120,000 francs (about £20,000). Gloucester's assertion - if indeed it was ever made - that the garrison had not been paid, was apparently untrue: M. Jones, *Ducal Brittany 1364-99* (1970), 138-9.

2 Thomas of Woodstock was born in 1355. His godparents are unknown, but if any abbot of St Albans acted as his godfather it must have been Thomas de la Mare, abbot 1349-96.

3 John de Wratting was prior of Westminster 1382-1407.

sent to seek the great prior of Westminster, and requested him, by message, to come and speak to him without delay, for it would be greatly to his interest. And when the prior arrived at St Albans, he was received at a great feast held in the chambers of the abbot, where he found the duke of Gloucester seated at dinner; and the abbot and prior seated themselves at the bottom of the duke's table. After dinner, at the collation, the abbot began and said to the prior, 'So may God and St George aid you! Tell us, did you not last night have a vision of anything in the world?' 'Yes,' said the prior. 'Then tell us now, prior,' said the duke, 'the truth of your vision ...' The prior then said, 'By St George, my lords, it was revealed to me last night – forgive me – that the kingdom would be lost by our lord the King Richard.' Then said the abbot, 'By the Virgin Mary, the same was revealed to me also, and I will give you, my lord and godson, a reason why I beg that you will not be displeased, because we have told our visions at your request; for you can see how matters go when a king begins to give away his cities, which his ancestors have acquired by war, for gold or silver, as the king our lord has begun to do; that is to say, he has restored two fortresses into the hands of his enemies, which were useful and profitable to the kingdom of England; for you know very well that he has restored Brest to the duke of Brittany, and Cherbourg to the king of Navarre, which were useful and profitable for our kingdom of England in making war'.[4] Then answered the duke to the abbot and the prior that it should be effectually remedied, and that shortly; afterwards he added, 'I beg, between yourselves, that you will not fail to be at Arundel this day fortnight to dinner, and there we will dine together.'

After the duke of Gloucester had left St Albans, he returned to his house in London and sent a sealed letter to the earl of Derby, begging him to come to speak to him at Arundel on the day that the said abbot and prior would be there. Afterwards he sent to the earl marshal, who was captain of Calais, to the earl of Warwick, and to the archbishop of Canterbury, and desired that they would come to Arundel on a certain day; and he also sent to the earl of Arundel to say that he would come to dine with him there, and that he would bring with him all the other lords. The earl of Arundel returned him answer that he would be right welcome, and all the lords it would please him to bring with him in his company. It is true that the duke of Gloucester arrived at Arundel the

4 Cherbourg had been leased from the king of Navarre in 1378; it was returned in 1393.

eighth day before the month of August in the year thirteen hundred fourscore and sixteen, as well as the earl of Derby, the earl marshal, the archbishop of Canterbury, the abbot of St Albans, and the prior of Westminster. As these lords were seated at dinner, there arrived the earl of Warwick; and when he joined the company of the lords, the duke of Gloucester said to him, 'My brave man, you must take the same oath as we have taken.' And the earl replied, 'My lord, what do you wish me to swear?' The duke said, 'You will swear as we have done, if you please, to be true and faithful to the realm, and also to be true and faithful to each other.'

That night all the lords rested at Arundel, and on the morrow they heard mass, and the archbishop of Canterbury chanted the mass and gave the sacrament to the duke of Gloucester, then to the earl of Derby, to the earl of Arundel his brother, and to the earl marshal, who had married the daughter of the earl of Arundel,[5] and afterwards to the earl of Warwick. And when all the lords had been to mass, they retired to a council chamber, and there were of accord to seize the noble King Richard, the duke of Lancaster, and the duke of York, and that they should be put in prison for ever; and that all the other lords of the council of King Richard should be drawn and hanged. Such was their counsel and their oath, and such their determination, and it was to be put into execution in the month of August thirteen hundred fourscore and sixteen. It is true that the earl marshal, who was captain of Calais, revealed to King Richard all their counsel, and informed him of the day when they were to begin to put it into execution. And when the king heard the news from the earl marshal, who was of their accord and undertaking in appearance but not in fact, he said to the earl, 'Take care what you say, for if I find it true, I will pardon you; but if I find it otherwise, assuredly you shall repent it.' To which the earl marshal replied, 'If you find it otherwise, let me be quartered and sent to the four ends of England: and be upon your guard, I beseech you.' And, shortly after, these very words were plainly declared in open parliament, when the earl of Arundel was condemned to death ...'[6]

---

5 Mowbray married Elizabeth, daughter of the earl of Arundel executed in 1397, in July 1384.

6 None of the surviving accounts of the 1397-98 parliament contain any mention of this supposed conspiracy.

(b) The king tries to reconcile Bolingbroke and Mowbray

(*29 April 1398: the king had summoned the two lords to appear before him at Windsor.*) Then a herald cried on the part of the king that the duke of Hereford and the duke of Norfolk should come forward before the king, to tell each his reason why they would not make peace together. And when they were come before the king and his council, the king said to them himself, 'My lords, make matters up; it will be much better.' 'Saving your favour, my dear sovereign,' said the duke of Norfolk, 'it cannot be, my honour is too deeply concerned.' Then the king said to the duke of Hereford, 'Henry, say what it is you have to say to the duke of Norfolk, or why you will not be reconciled.' The duke of Hereford had a knight, who, having asked and obtained permission from the king and the council to speak on behalf of the duke, said, 'Dear and sovereign lord, here is Henry of Lancaster, duke of Hereford and earl of Derby, who declares, and I also for him, that Thomas, duke of Norfolk, has received from you eight hundred thousand nobles to pay your men-at-arms to guard your city of Calais, whom he has not paid as he ought to have done; I say this is great treason, and calculated to cause the loss of your city of Calais: and I also say that he has been at the bottom of all the treasons committed in your kingdom these last eighteen years, and has, by his false counsel and malice, caused to be put to death my dear and beloved uncle, the duke of Glouces-ter, son of King Edward, whom God absolve, and who was brother of my dearly beloved father the duke of Lancaster. The duke of Hereford says, and I on his part, that he will prove the truth of this by his body between any sunrise and sunset ...'

Then the king asked the duke of Norfolk ... if he wished to say anything more. The duke of Norfolk, in person, answered the king: 'My dear lord, it is true I have received so much gold from you to pay your people of your good city of Calais, which I have done. I say that the city of Calais is as well guarded and as much at your command now as it ever was, and also that no person of Calais has lodged any complaint to you against me. My dear and sovereign lord, for the journeys that I have performed in France on account of your noble marriage, and for the journey that the duke of Aumale and I took in Germany, where we expended much treasure, I never

received from you either gold or silver.[7] It is true, and I acknowledge, that I once laid an ambush to kill my lord of Lancaster, who
is there seated; and it is true that my lord forgave me, and peace
was made between us, for which I thank him.[8] This is what I wish
to say and to reply, and to support it I will defend myself against
him. I beseech you to grant me justice, and trial of battle in
tournament.' The two parties were then withdrawn, and the king
consulted with his council. Afterwards the two lords were summoned to hear the decision. Again the king desired them to be
asked if they would be reconciled or not. They both replied they
would not; and the duke of Hereford threw down his pledge, which
the duke of Norfolk received. Then swore the king by St John the
Baptist that he would never more endeavour to reconcile those two;
and Sir John Bussy, on the part of the king and council, announced
that they should have trial of battle at Coventry, on a Monday in
the month of August, and that there they should have their day and
their lists ...

7 Mowbray had made a number of journeys to France in connection with the king's
  marriage negotiations (P.R.O. E403/554, 7 February and passim), and he accompanied Rutland on an embassy to Germany between 4 March and 11 July 1397
  (Palmer, 'French chronicles', 404).

8 For this incident, see above, pp. 21-2.

7. Bolingbroke's exile in Paris, 1398-99

Source: *Chronique de Saint-Denys*, ii, 674-6

Language: Latin

Bolingbroke arrived in Paris in mid-October. The chronicler of Saint-Denys, near Paris, was in a good position to observe the favourable treatment accorded to him, and his account is confirmed by other sources. The fact that a man who had been exiled from the kingdom of Charles VI's son-in-law was treated with such honour indicates the extent to which Anglo-French governmental relations had cooled during the previous eighteen months or so.

Having left England, Henry went to France, where he was counting on a warm welcome from the king and the princes of the fleurs-de-lis. He was indeed received by them with all the respect due to a favoured kinsman: for as long as he remained in the kingdom, the king accommodated not only him but all his followers in royal residences, entertained them, and plied them with gifts.[1] The king of England, annoyed that so much respect was being shown to them, wrote to his beloved father (-*in-law*) the king of France and to his dear cousins the dukes explaining that he had exiled from his realm several persons guilty of treason, and requesting them not to show too much favour to these traitors, nor to offer them any support. This message, which was somewhat different from what he had said in his letters patent, was but one example of the implacable hatred which he felt towards Henry: for when the young duke's father – a valiant lord – died in the same year, the king, making a mockery of his own promises, did not hesitate to help himself to his treasure, nor to reunite the duchy of Lancaster to the royal domain.

Hearing that he had thus been deprived, the young duke, at the limits of his patience, complained to the king and princes of France about the cruelty of such a deed, accusing King Richard of perjury and declaring that he knew not what to do, nor what course of action to take. Meanwhile, he had already begun to think in terms of hostile action

1 Henry was given the Hotel de Clisson in Paris as his residence.

against the English king and his kingdom. The duke of Berry, in whom he placed special trust, had noticed his mood, and, whenever he heard him complaining, endeavoured to sympathise with him.[2] He told him that brave souls do not allow themselves to be downhearted by reversals of fortune, but resign themselves to waiting for better times. He reminded him in eulogistic terms of the valour and loyalty of his father, and whenever the young duke showed him letters from his partisans in England urging him to return, he advised him to eschew any dishonourable action which might sully the reputation bequeathed to him by so great a prince. Henry thanked the duke of Berry for his words of consolation; he feigned indifference, and pretended to be cheerful. This, however, was but one of those ruses which are familiar to the English, a way of concealing more effectively the plan which he had to avenge his injuries, as will be seen later ...

2 John duke of Berry (1340-1416), uncle of King Charles VI.

Part two: June to September 1399

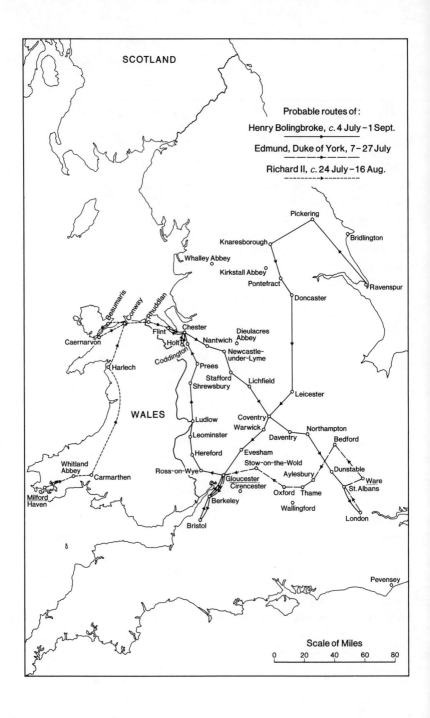

SCOTLAND

Probable routes of:

Henry Bolingbroke, c. 4 July – 1 Sept.

Edmund, Duke of York, 7 – 27 July

Richard II, c. 24 July – 16 Aug.

Pickering

Knaresborough

Bridlington

Whalley Abbey

Kirkstall Abbey

Pontefract

Ravenspur

Doncaster

Beaumaris

Conway

Rhuddlan

Chester

Dieulacres Abbey

Caernarvon

Flint

Holt

Nantwich

Newcastle-under-Lyme

Coddington

Harlech

Prees

Stafford

Shrewsbury

Lichfield

Leicester

WALES

Ludlow

Coventry

Warwick

Northampton

Leominster

Daventry

Bedford

Hereford

Evesham

Whitland Abbey

Carmarthen

Ross-on-Wye

Stow-on-the-Wold

Dunstable

Aylesbury

Ware

St. Albans

Milford Haven

Gloucester

Cirencester

Oxford

Thame

Berkeley

Wallingford

London

Bristol

Pevensey

Scale of Miles

0   20   40   60   80

8. Bolingbroke's departure from France

Source: *Chronique de Saint-Denys*, ii, 697-708

Language: Latin

To what extent Bolingbroke received active French assistance on his departure from Boulogne in 1399 was a matter of debate among contemporaries, and remains so. Suspicions were certainly aroused in some Englishmen,[1] as they were among many Frenchmen. The chronicler of Saint-Denys, who reflects growing French impatience with Richard, noted that several people 'expressed disapproval' of Orléans' alliance with Bolingbroke, and added somewhat ambiguously that Henry acted 'in accordance with the advice given to him by the duke of Berry.' Other members of the French government may well have been duped by Henry's claim that he was planning a journey to Spain. Since Henry passed through Saint-Denys, the author should have been in a good position to hear whatever story he was putting around about his intentions.

The king of England sent a letter to his beloved father-in-law the king of France to inform him of his plans (*to go to Ireland*). When Duke Henry, who was in exile at the French court, heard of this, he decided that the moment had come to avenge the wrongs done to him. Searching around for friends to help him in his designs, he concluded a secret alliance with the duke of Orleans. Later, a number of people expressed disapproval of this alliance, and reproached the duke of Orleans for it. In fact, however, its principal terms were simply that the two princes promised sincere and lasting friendship towards each other, that they would support the same friends and oppose the same enemies, and that, whatever the circumstances, they would, in so far as they could, protect, guard and defend each other's life and honour by both word and deed ... This treaty was sworn on 17 June and sealed by both princes.[2]

---

1 See, for example, the marginal note in a fifteenth-century manuscript from Cheshire asserting that the French gave him help: N. R. Ker, *Medieval Manuscripts in British Libraries*, iii (1969), 439.

2 See below, Doc. 9, for the text of the alliance.

Duke Henry remained at Paris until the departure of the king of England ...

(*King Richard*), who thought of himself as one of the most powerful of western kings, was irritated because that part of Ireland which had submitted to his lordship had now rebelled against him, so he had decided at the beginning of the year to go across there with a large army and a good deal of treasure. In an attempt to forestall any problems which might arise in England, he entrusted the direction of affairs during his absence to a council composed of his uncle the duke of York and the knights William le Scrope, (*John*) Bussy, (*William*) Bagot and John Russell, in whose loyalty and ability he had the utmost confidence. He also entrusted to them the care of the young queen, his beloved wife, the daughter of the king of France. Out of hatred for the French, however – so it is said – they soon began to treat her in the most dreadful way. They drove out of England all the lords and ladies in her following, whose company she had relied upon for frequent comfort and consolation at a time when she was so far away from her country and her family, leaving her with only one lady-in-waiting and her confessor. They cut back her normal living expenses, restricted her household to a few English servants, and confined her to Wallingford (*castle*), where she led an almost solitary existence and was forbidden either to receive any French visitors in private or to converse with them in public.[3]

The king and queen of France, and all the princes of the blood, were incensed at this behaviour. May it serve as an example to strike fear into the hearts of any French noblewoman intending to marry an Englishman! These perfidious foreigners have always distrusted the French, no doubt because they fear some attempt by them against England. Little did they know, however, what danger threatened them from a different quarter.

As soon as Duke Henry of Lancaster heard that the king had left England, he decided that the time had come to recover his duchy. He therefore wrote letters to the English complaining of the tedium and length of his exile, reproaching the king for his harshness, and accusing him of perjury. He declared that he had been unjustly disinherited, and requested support for his cause. The English, who are naturally fickle and given to sudden enthusiasms, agreed to what he asked and made a secret alliance with him. A sizeable fleet therefore

3 For the treatment accorded to Queen Isabella in 1399, see above, p. 30

left the shores of England and awaited the duke's arrival for nearly three weeks between Calais and Boulogne.[4]

Philip duke of Burgundy,[5] having been informed that a large number of boats was at sea in this area, and being ignorant as to their objective, wrote to the people of Boulogne warning them to be on their guard. Henry, who knew exactly what was going on, obtained permission from the king and lords of France to depart, and, thanking them for their expressions of goodwill towards him, set off to join the fleet. With typical English duplicity, he dissimulated as to his real intentions, saying that he was planning to travel to Spain. After leaving Paris he first visited the church of Saint-Denys, in accordance with the advice given to him by the duke of Berry. There he was given a warm welcome; among other matters, the venerable abbot raised with him the question of the priory of Deerhurst in England, which belonged to the abbey but was at that time in lay possession. The duke promised to do what he could to have it restored to him; and, once he became king, he faithfully kept his word.[6] From there he went on to Boulogne, where he embarked on the fleet which awaited him with a force of men-at-arms, and, helped by a favourable wind, soon reached the duchy of Lancaster; here he was greeted in triumph by his subjects, amidst scenes of inexpressible joy. His uncle the duke of York, who had been made regent of England, was unaware of his landing. He was told of it by William le Scrope, whom he had sent to inform the king of France that the English in Guyenne, who were continuing to exact an annual tribute from the local French inhabitants, had recently sworn, in accordance with his orders, to observe the treaty agreed between the kings. Arriving at Dover, however, Scrope found no boats there, and, learning that they had been commandeered for Henry's use, he postponed his mission and returned to the duke of York to tell him how he had been tricked ...

---

4 Whether the ships which carried Henry to England were French or English is not known. Walsingham (below, Doc. 10) states that Henry met up with a group of English merchants at Boulogne and returned with them, but he also comments that the French offered him military support, which he rejected.

5 Philip the Bold (1342-1404), duke of Burgundy, the uncle of King Charles VI.

6 On 22 August 1399, on the advice of Bolingbroke, Archbishop Arundel, and other members of the royal council, the custody of Deerhurst priory (Gloucestershire) was taken out of the hands of Sir John Russell and given to Master Richard Wyche, clerk: *CPR, 1396-9*, 589.

E

9. The alliance between Bolingbroke and Orleans, 17 June 1399

Source: *Choix de Pièces Inédites Relatives au Regne de Charles VI*, ed. L. Douet-D'Arcq (Societé de l'Histoire de France, 119, Paris 1863), 157-60

Language: Latin

Two texts of this agreement survive: the one given below was printed by Douet-D'Arcq from a manuscript in the Archives Nationales in Paris, and was the text given by Bolingbroke to Orléans; the other, preserved in La Chronique d'Enguerran de Monstrelet, *ed. L. Douet-D'Arcq (Societé de l'Histoire de France, 91, Paris 1857), 49-52, is a copy of the text given by Orléans to Bolingbroke, and was appended by Bolingbroke to a letter which he wrote to Orléans on 5 December 1402, replying to Orléans' claim that he had betrayed Orléans' trust in deposing Richard in 1399. Bolingbroke later expressed astonishment at Orléans' claim, stating that 'we apprised you openly and fully of (our plans) before our departure from overseas, at which time you approved our plans and promised aid against our dear lord and cousin King Richard ...' Orléans' part in abetting Henry in 1399 caused considerable debate in France: following his assassination on 23 November 1407 by agents of the duke of Burgundy, he was publicly accused by Burgundy of having plotted with Bolingbroke to secure Richard's downfall, a charge which his own supporters decisively rejected. For these accusations and the replies to them, see* Chronique d'Enguerran de Monstrelet, *i, 43-67, 234-6, 328-9.*

The two surviving texts of the treaty are broadly similar in their wording except in one respect, that is, the list of those excluded from it by name. Since this was a question over which Bolingbroke and Orléans exchanged angry words in 1402-3, the differences are worth noting. Of those listed in the text below, only the kings of France, Bohemia, Hungary and Castile appear in the copy of the alliance sealed by the duke of Orléans, but the following are also included in it: the queen of France, the Dauphin and all other children of the king of France, the dukes of Berry, Burgundy and Bourbon, the marquis of Moravia, the duke of Milan (Orléans' father-in-law), the king of Scotland, the duke of Lorraine, the count of Cleves, and Lord Clisson.

TREATY OF ALLIANCE BETWEEN HENRY DUKE OF LANCASTER AND
LOUIS DUKE OF ORLÉANS, PARIS, 17 JUNE 1399

Henry, duke of Lancaster and Hereford, earl of Derby, Lincoln,
Leicester and Northampton, lord of Brecon and Steward of England,
to all who shall see these letters, greetings and good health. Be it
known by these letters that, although promises of love and friendship
have already been agreed between us and the magnificent and
illustrious prince Louis, son of the late king of France, duke of Orléans
and count of Valois, Blois and Beaumont, nevertheless we two, wishing
sincerely to strengthen and maintain the friendship and alliance
between us – for nothing in the world could be more pleasing and
profitable to us – have agreed, in the name of the Almighty and the
most holy Trinity, which is a splendid example and perfect guide in the
ways of love and friendship, and without the support of whose grace
and favour nothing can be brought to a fitting and happy conclusion,
and in order too that this friendship between us should be regarded by
each of us as just, honourable and praiseworthy, to draw up a treaty
and alliance in the following form:

> Firstly, it seems to us right to exclude from this treaty and alliance all
> those whom each of us thinks ought properly to be excluded, and thus
> we have jointly decided to exclude from it the following: to begin with,
> the most high and illustrious prince, my lord the king of England,
> together with all his causes and quarrels, the queen of England, and the
> heirs of the same king; our kinsman the most high and illustrious
> prince, Charles king of France; the duke of York, our uncle; the most
> high prince and our dear kinsman, the king of the Romans and of
> Bohemia;[1] the king of Hungary, our brother;[2] the king of Portugal, our
> brother;[3] the duke of Guelders, our kinsman;[4] all others who are allied
> or bound to the aforesaid lord king of England, and to whom, along
> with the same lord my king, we are rightly obliged to be faithful; the
> most illustrious prince the king of Castile, our brother, whose welfare
> and honour, on account of our affinity with him, it is right that we
> should seek to uphold;[5] and the most illustrious prince the king of
> Cyprus, to whom we are, by a long-standing and binding oath, joined in

1 Wenzel, German emperor 1378-1400.

2 Sigismund, brother of Wenzel, king of Hungary 1387-1437, and German emperor
1410-37.

3 Joao I, king of Portugal 1383-1433; he was married to Bolingbroke's sister Philippa.

4 William I, duke of Guelders 1371-1402.

5 Henry III, king of Castile 1390-1406; he was married to Bolingbroke's half-sister
Katherine.

alliance.[6] We also exclude our children, born or yet to be born, and all
those close in blood to us or of our stock, of either sex, born or yet to
be born; and all our other vassals and those who are bound to us by
oath or fealty, whom we regard ourselves as bound to protect from
harm or evil; and any others who are bound to us by alliances, which it
is only right that we should uphold and preserve towards each other.

Item: between the duke of Orléans and us there will without fail always
be pure and sincere love and affection, as there should be between true and
honest friends.

Item: each of us will at all times be the friend of the other's friends and
well-wishers, and the enemy of the other's enemies, as is right and proper.

Item: each of us will at all times, in all places, and in all matters, make
every possible effort to help the other to uphold his honour, estate, health
and well-being, whether by word or deed, in the most honourable manner
possible.

Item, in times of unrest or war, we shall come to each other's help in any
possible way and with every means in our power – with counsel, men,
arms, subsidies, engines of war, or in any other way which might prove
effective – against any prince, lord or magnate, or indeed against any other
individual, corporation or community, regardless of their rank, status, or
authority, and shall willingly exert ourselves to the greatest possible
degree and in any way against each other's enemies; always excepting
those named above.

Item: we will firmly and unfailingly observe all the above agreements for
as long as the present truce between my lord the king of England and the
aforesaid king of France shall endure – and, should a more lasting peace be
agreed between them, for as long as that peace lasts; in testimony of which
we have caused these letters to be drawn up and have attached our seal
thereto. Given at Paris, on the 17th day of June, in the year of Our Lord
1399.

---

6 Janus, king of Cyprus, Jerusalem and Armenia 1398-1432; but the alliance referred
  to had probably been made between Henry and the previous king, James I (1382-
  98), on the occasion of Henry's visit to the island in 1392 (G. Hill, *A History of
  Cyprus*, ii (1948), 442).

10. Thomas Walsingham's account of the revolution

Source: Annales Ricardi Secundi, 240-52

Language: Latin

Walsingham's narrative of Richard's downfall is characteristically moralising, but it also includes many details which are useful in trying to piece together a comprehensive picture of the events of June to September 1399: for example, his description of Bolingbroke sailing up and down the English coastline testing the coastal defences, or his comment that the duke of York declared publicly that he had no intention of using his forces to attack Henry. Since it was at St Albans that York initially mustered his troops, Walsingham should have been in a good position to gather information about both the conduct of those who answered the summons and the intentions of their leader. For events in North Wales, however, he was much less well-informed, and his account of events at Conway and Flint is remarkable chiefly for its brevity.

While the king remained in Ireland attacking the Irish, imagining that he was achieving great things, God suddenly decided to humble his pride and bring succour to the people of England, who were now so miserably oppressed that they had lost all hope of deliverance and relief unless God were to reach forth and help them. He therefore implanted into the heart of Lord Henry, duke of Hereford – and now, since the death of his father, duke of Lancaster – who had firstly been exiled for ten years and then most unjustly disinherited, the idea that he should return to his native land and demand the restoration of his ancestral rights, namely the duchy of Lancaster and all that pertained to it; and if the king were to put obstacles in his path by refusing to return his rightful lands to him, then he should summon help to recover them by force. He was well aware how much the king was hated, and with good reason, by all the English people, so that he hoped that if he, or indeed some other person, made a landing in England, the common people would rally to him in order to regain their liberty and throw off this insupportable yoke. He was also encouraged by the presence of Lord Thomas Arundel, archbishop of Canterbury, who had spent the last two years in undeserved exile at Utrecht,[1] and by the arrival of Arundel's nephew, the son and heir of Lord Richard, earl of Arundel, who had recently fled from 'the heat of the house of Rechab', that is from the household of the duke of Exeter, to whom this young man's custody had been entrusted, and where he had been shamelessly humiliated by one of the duke's knights called John Schevele, to whom the duke had committed him, and who had treated him like some menial servant, forcing him to wait upon him like a prisoner rather than as a free man.[2]

The people of France, where (Henry) was residing, also encouraged him to demand the return of those rightful possessions which had been denied to him, promising him military support if he needed it. He told them that he was very grateful for their goodwill, but that he preferred not to call upon military support from abroad, for he had sufficient faith in the loyalty and support of his own countrymen to make French help unnecessary for the present. However, should things turn out worse for him than he expected, in other words if he received little support from his own people, he told them that he hoped that they would still be prepared to honour their commitment to him. Having been given permission to return, therefore, he arrived by the sea at Boulogne along with Thomas, the former archbishop of Canterbury, and the son and heir of the earl of Arundel; also with him were Lord Thomas Erpingham, a famous and excellent knight, and John Norbury, an esquire of great worth and wisdom ...[3] A number of English merchants whom he had met in those parts preparing to return home also came with him, but, even including the rest of his household, the number of fighting men accompanying him did not

1 Archbishop Arundel spent time during his exile at Ghent and at or near Rome as well as at Utrecht: *Diplomatic Correspondence of Richard II*, ed. E. Perroy (Camden 3rd Series 1933), 238, 240; *Literae Cantuariensis*, ed. J. B. Sheppard, iii (Rolls Series 1889), 70-2; Pierre Salmon, *Memoires*, ed J. A. C. Buchon (Collection des Chroniques Nationales Françaises, xxiv, 1826), 21-2.

2 The biblical allusion is to Joshua 2.i. The two sons of the earl of Arundel had been committed on 12 October 1397 to the custody of the dukes of Exeter and Norfolk (*CPR, 1396-9*, 214). John Schevele, a retainer of the duke of Exeter's, was to die along with his master in the aftermath of the 'Epiphany Rising' (below, Doc. 21).

3 Sir Thomas Erpingham, a knight from Norfolk, served as chamberlain and then steward of the royal household after Henry became king. John Norbury, an esquire from Cheshire, was treasurer of England from 3 September 1399 to 31 May 1401. Both were among that small band of dedicated supporters who had gone into exile with Bolingbroke in 1398.

amount, so it was said, to more than fifteen, and they had only ten or twelve ships with them. With such a small force, it is a wonder that he even dared to invade the kingdom of England, but even more astonishing is the fact that within such a short time, as we shall see below, he was able to pacify the entire realm.

He put to sea at Boulogne and headed towards England, but decided not to make directly or immediately for the English coast, instead taking his ships back and forth along the coastline, approaching different parts of the kingdom in turn, trying to discover whether the coastal defences had been put in a state of readiness to resist him. When rumours began to circulate through England that the duke of Lancaster had put to sea and was getting ready to return, there was great joy amongst the people, who now truly believed that God had sent him in order to release them from their dreadful yoke of servitude. Nobody was prepared to declare openly for the duke, however, until they were sure of the outcome, for they feared that if the king were to return from Ireland and succeed in overcoming the duke, he would come down with great severity on anybody who had supported the duke in the least degree, whether openly or secretly. They also feared that even if the king did initially pretend to submit to the duke, he might later, as was his custom, go back on his word and punish not only the duke but also those who supported him. There was, therefore, great hope among the people that this enterprise upon which the duke had embarked would end happily.

The duke of York, who had been appointed keeper of the realm in the king's absence, was in London with the chancellor, Master Edmund de Stafford bishop of (*Exeter*), the treasurer, Lord William le Scrope earl of Wiltshire, and the knights of the king's council, including John Bussy, William Bagot, (*Henry*) Green and John Russell, among others, when the news was brought to him that the duke of Lancaster was on the seas and was preparing to land in England. He therefore called together these royal councillors, who had been left behind by the king so that they could give him advice on any major issue that might arise, and asked them what could be done. But they, confused and panic-stricken like men with guilty consciences – I speak here of the aforesaid knights, not of the bishop, who was blameless in these matters – were quite unable to offer any sensible advice as to how the duke might be repulsed and prevented from entering the realm. Accordingly they advised him to make his way to St Albans and there await the arrival of forces with which to resist the duke's advance.

Once he had arrived at St Albans the duke of York sent out letters patent in King Richard's name to all the shires of England ordering the sheriffs to summon as many men-at-arms and archers as they could and bring them to him as soon as possible, whereupon he would most willingly and generously reward them with the king's treasure. As a result of this many worthy lords joined him with their retinues, although none of them was in favour of attacking the duke of Lancaster apart from the bishop of Norwich, who had brought with him as powerful a troop of soldiers as he could muster.[4] The rest of the lords and commons simply regarded this as a diversion, however, for they declared openly that they had no wish whatsoever to move against the duke of Lancaster. Even the duke of York stated publicly that the duke of Lancaster had been wrongfully disinherited, and that he had no intention of attacking someone who came in a just cause and to ask for the restoration of his rightful inheritance.

Meanwhile, on about the feast of the Translation of St Martin (*4 July*), the duke of Lancaster and his followers landed unopposed near the place where the town of Ravenspur had once stood; soon so many of those who had served his father, and of his own retainers, had flocked to join him, that within a short time he was in command of an almost invincible army. When the king's councillors, that is, William le Scrope, John Bussy, (*Henry*) Green, William Bagot and John Russell, heard this, they were seized with fear and seemed to lose heart entirely. Seeing this, the bishop of Norwich declared, 'These men are doomed to die. There is no point in hoping for any resistance from men who give up so easily.' But they, having given up hope of any support from the villeins of St Albans, persuaded the duke of York to take all the troops who had answered his summons to Oxford. They also issued a public proclamation to the effect that the men-at-arms and archers should accompany them thither without delay, for which they would receive, in ready cash, enormous payments from the royal treasury, which was overflowing with riches and contained quite enough to reward all those who were prepared to stand firm with the king against his enemies. It was these same men, now extolling the king's wealth, who a short while earlier had been devoting their energies to accumulating that wealth for him, ruining rich and poor alike in the process. There were many therefore who, having taken payment for their troops on the understanding that they would raise

---

4 Henry Despenser, bishop of Norwich 1370-1406, the leader of the 'Flemish Crusade' of 1383. For York's army see Appendix A.

forces in their localities, set off, as soon as they had gathered in any numbers, to find the duke of Lancaster and to fight for him at the wages of King Richard.

Having reached Oxford, the aforesaid royal councillors began to realise what a sizeable military force the duke had collected, and what little hope there was that the common people would remain loyal to them, and they became thoroughly alarmed. The duke of York had already sent messengers to the duke of Lancaster to ask him why he had been so bold as to invade the land; these messengers now returned and reported back that the duke of Lancaster did not intend to speak to them, but to approach the duke of York in person and explain to him the reasons for his landing.[5] They knew too that Lord Henry Percy, earl of Northumberland, and his son of the same name – whom the Scots used to call 'Henry Hotspur' because he pursued them so hotly – and several other lords, all of whom feared the guile and deceit of the king, had also joined Lancaster, so that his army was now estimated to be sixty thousand strong. They immediately sent letters to the king in Ireland, therefore, warning him that if he did not want to be driven out of his kingdom, he should drop everything and hurry back to England as rapidly as he could. They also wrote to say that they expected to meet him, with an army of twenty thousand men, near the sea at (blank), to be with him and help him as he advanced.[6]

Having done this, these knights – that is, William le Scrope and the others – realising how hated they were throughout the land, and fearing that if they stayed any longer with the duke of York they were likely to be forcibly seized by the populace, fled in great haste to Bristol, where they provisioned the castle and fortified it strongly with about five hundred men whom they had brought there.

When news was brought to the duke of Lancaster that these knights, whom the common people regarded as public enemies, had taken refuge in the castle there, he promptly turned his army towards Bristol, planning to besiege the castle – assuming, that is, that there was anyone there who was unwilling simply to yield it up along with the knights whom he was pursuing. The regent, the duke of York, had already joined him, and many other nobles had come with him and

5 On 12 July, three valets received payment from the exchequer for 'bringing news to the lord treasurer and others of the king's council concerning the position and organisation of the duke of Lancaster' (P.R.O. E403/562, 12 July).

6 Messengers had been sent to Ireland by 4 July at the latest (P.R.O. E403/562, 4 July).

pledged their forces to his service, and were now willingly riding with him. The only people who tried to attack him were the bishop of Norwich and William Elmham, a knight, who seemed unaware of the fact that the whole world was now supporting the duke of Lancaster, and fondly hoped to discourage those others who, as already mentioned, had taken his side. These two were easily captured, however, and, once they had been despoiled of all the goods which they had brought with them, were sent off to prison, where they stayed until the duke, taking pity on them, ordered them to be released.[7]

When the duke of Lancaster arrived at Bristol with his uncle the duke of York, the earl of Northumberland and his son Henry, and an innumerable number of other lords and commons, he sent a message to the keeper of the castle, Lord Peter Courtenay – whom the duke of York had, a short time earlier, appointed to that post – asking him to hand over the castle together with those persons mentioned above.[8] At first Courtenay did what he could to resist this demand, but the duke of York, acting on the authority of his commission, insisted that the castle be surrendered. Surrendered it was, therefore, everyone being allowed to go free apart from three people, namely William le Scrope, John Bussy, and (Henry) Green, who were taken into custody. They were kept under strict guard overnight, and in the morning beheaded. In carrying out such swift retribution against them, the lords were influenced partly by the vociferous urgings of the commons, who, given the chance, would have broken them into little pieces, and partly by the news which arrived that day that the king had brought a large army across from Ireland and landed in Wales. With such danger threatening, it was not thought safe to carry them around alive, and it was for this reason, and at the insistence of the common people, that they suffered such a harsh judgement. Yet it was a judgement which was greeted with great joy by all the ordinary people of the kingdom, since it seemed to them that they had thus swiftly and opportunely been delivered from the enemies whom they most dreaded.

While these things were happening, the king in Ireland began to hear most unwelcome rumours of the duke's landing and his march through

---

7 William Elmham, a Suffolk knight, had been a royal retainer since the 1380s; after the revolution he was given back the 'horses and harness which were taken from him at Berkeley or elsewhere' (*CPR, 1399-1401*, 39).

8 Sir Peter Courtenay (d. 1405) was the uncle of the earl of Devon; on 12 July, he had been given £1,133 with which to buy provisions and weaponry for the garrison at Bristol castle (P.R.O. E403/562, 12 July).

England, and of the support which he was gaining from the lords and commons of the realm. His first reaction was to summon to his presence the eldest son of the duke of Lancaster, who was scarcely even an adolescent,[9] and, putting on a great show of melancholy, said to him, 'Look, Henry, at what your own father is doing to me. He has invaded my country and is marching through it in arms as if he were at war, seizing and killing my liegemen without mercy or compassion. It is you I fear for, though, because as a result of your father's unfortunate behaviour you are the one who is likely to be deprived of his patrimony.' To which Henry, although but a boy, replied in most unchildlike fashion, 'My gracious king and lord, I too am much grieved by what I hear. Yet it is surely apparent to you, as it is to me, that I am innocent of my father's deeds.' 'Indeed,' said the king, 'I am well aware that no guilt attaches to you for what your father has done, and I regard you as blameless on that account.' The king therefore ordered the boy to be confined, together with the son of the duke of Gloucester,[10] in Trim castle. The reason why the king had brought him, and indeed the sons of many other nobles, to Ireland with him, was so that if their fathers or friends or supporters had been tempted to conspire against the king while he was abroad, they would, out of consideration for their children, at least think twice about it, and might well desist from such schemes.

Having appointed a governor in Ireland, therefore, the king gave orders for ships to be got ready for him to cross to Wales as soon as possible, in the hope that he could prevent the duke of Lancaster's advance through his country. It so happened, however, by God's will, that just at the moment when everything was ready for departure, a different plan occurred to the king, and he gave orders for the horses and other provisions, which had already been loaded on to the boats, to be unloaded again and taken to a different port. The result of this was that it was another seven days before the horses and all the other apparatus could once more be assembled on board ship.[11] It was as if God had ordained that the duke of Lancaster should be allowed to gather his strength and prepare himself to the extent that the king would be unable to challenge him. At length, however, the king, the

9 The future King Henry V; he was born in 1387.

10 Humphrey, the son of the duke of Gloucester, aged about seventeen, died within two months or so of this, either on his way back to England or shortly after his arrival there.

11 This corroborates the more circumstantial account given by Creton of a delay: below, Doc. 13.

dukes of Exeter, Aumale, and Surrey – whom he had created – and many other magnates whom he had brought with him, together with the bishops of London, Lincoln, and Carlisle and various other bishops and prelates, including the abbot of Westminster, all boarded ship and crossed to the port of (*blank*).[12] Here, despite receiving news of the size of the duke of Lancaster's following, the king at first proposed to give him battle; being cautious and timid, however, he soon changed his plan, believing that the common people, who had sworn to oppose him, hated him so much that they would rather die than give in to him. Thus, having committed the charge of his household to the steward, Lord Thomas Percy, he took flight with a few supporters to the castle of (*blank*). Lord Thomas Percy, having summoned the household to gather in the hall at (*blank*), informed them that the king had fled, but that before going he had commended himself to them, thanked them for their good and long service, and said that he intended, when God and kinder fortune smiled upon him, to reward each and every one of them according to his merits. Percy then advised them all to leave this place for the moment and save themselves as best, or in any way that, they could; and, breaking his rod of office, he wept bitterly, for he had never wished to perform such an unwelcome task.

Thus was the household disbanded, a reversal of fortunes which a short time earlier would have been thought impossible. The king's treasure, which – without consultation – he had taken out of the country with him, fell into the duke's hands along with his horses and valuables and all his household furnishings; while the king's followers – magnates, lords, or lesser men, regardless of their status – were harassed by Welshmen or men from Northumberland and Westmorland. Of those who had been with or followed the king, scarcely one escaped unless he was prepared to hand over not only his arms but whatever was in his purse as well.

Meanwhile the king betook himself hither and thither, fleeing at one time or another to Anglesey, to Conway castle, and to the castles of Beaumaris, Flint, and Holt – in the last of which much of his treasure was stored.[13] At length, however, when all hope of escape had

12 Robert Braybrooke, bishop of London 1382-1404; Henry Beaufort, bishop of Lincoln 1398-1404; Thomas Merks, bishop of Carlisle (but see also Creton's account, below, Doc. 13). The abbot of Westminster was William Colchester, a noted supporter of Richard's who was to be arrested for his involvement in the 'Epiphany Rising' (*CCR, 1399-1402*, 41, 157).

13 For Richard's use of Holt castle as a treasury see Given-Wilson, *Royal Household*, 90.

vanished, he decided to send his brother the duke of Exeter to request
an interview with the earl of Northumberland and the archbishop of
Canterbury – or rather, the former archbishop, for he himself had
deprived him of his see, as already mentioned. These two, who had
been sent by the duke, held a parley with the king at Conway in North
Wales, at which the king made a proposal to them, namely that he was
prepared to resign and lay down the cares of government provided
that he would not be put to death, but would be provided for in
honourable fashion, and that promises would be given in good faith
guaranteeing the lives of himself and eight of his followers; apparently
these were the dukes of Exeter, Aumale, and Surrey, the earls of
Salisbury and Gloucester, Thomas Merks bishop of Carlisle, (*Richard*)
Maudeleyn clerk, and another.[14]

When these assurances, earnestly solicited by the king, had been
given, he had another parley with the duke of Lancaster at Flint castle,
though only a brief one, following which they were soon upon their
horses again and making their way towards Chester castle, both
apparently in good spirits. That night was spent by the king at
Chester, where, for his comfort, the aforementioned persons whom he
had singled out were allowed both to dine with him and to pass the
night with him. He had asked the duke of Lancaster, his cousin, to keep
the general public away from him and to stop them all disrespectfully
crowding in and insulting him, which the duke was more than happy
to allow; indeed he treated the king with entirely proper decency and
respect, allowing no one to insult him either publicly or privately.
After this the king and the duke, with the earl of Northumberland and
his son Henry, and those who had been captured with the king, left
Chester castle and journeyed on by day towards London. With them
too were several lords who had taken part in the campaign, and a
selected band of knights, esquires and valets numbering about fifteen
thousand, the rest of the army having been sent back to their homes
now that the king had given himself up, lest they ravage the areas
through which they would have to travel. It was on the twentieth of
August that the king gave himself up, which was the forty-sixth or
forty-seventh day after the duke had landed in the country. It was a
remarkable feat, in so short a time, to have brought such peace and
stability to the whole realm, so much so, indeed, that the sole and
universal desire of the inhabitants was now that King Richard should

14 Maudeleyn, a favourite clerk of the king's, was to lose his life following the
'Epiphany Rising'; for his career, see Given-Wilson, *Royal Household*, 180-1.

be set aside and Henry duke of Lancaster become their king – all except the Cheshiremen, that is, who continued to launch furtive attacks on the duke, assaulting his baggage-train and plundering the local residents, until, through the valour of the younger Henry Percy, their presumption was punished and their boldness repaid in kind.

After several days' journeying from Chester, the king was brought with his entourage to St Albans on the last day of August. He stayed here from the Saturday until after dinner on the Monday,[15] completely surrounded each night by an enormous number of guards, about a thousand men, as he had been elsewhere. Then on the Monday he was taken on towards London, where he was lodged in Westminster palace, for he had asked not to be exhibited to the citizens of London since he had been led to believe that they were taking great pleasure in his downfall. On the following day he was taken along the Thames to the Tower, where he was to be kept until the meeting of parliament which had been summoned in his name.

The duke of Lancaster, who accompanied the king from Chester to London, ordered solemn processions to be held in each place where there was a religious house, and made sure that they showed due kingly respect for the king in the same way as they would to a man enjoying full regal status; at the same time he refused to allow any incense-burning or any other sort of ceremony to be performed in his own honour by the religious who took part in these processions, but always deferred to the king, standing behind him, resplendent in his armour, waiting until due worship had been done to the king.

Soon after this writs were sent out, in the name of King Richard, to all those estates of the realm who were meant to attend parliaments, summoning them to a parliament to be held in London on the morrow of Michaelmas (*30 September*), which they must be sure to attend because matters of great importance to the kingdom were to be dealt with there. Letters were also sent out to all the abbeys and major churches of the kingdom instructing the heads of these religious houses to make available for examination all of their chronicles which touched upon the state and governance of the kingdom of England from the time of William the Conqueror up until the present; also that they should send certain persons who were knowledgeable about chronicles, who were to bring these chronicles with them, authorised

---

15 Walsingham's chronology is wrong here: Saturday was the 30th, not the 31st of
   August.

under the common seals of the religious houses; these people should also be competent to answer for and expound upon their chronicles.[16] These letters were sent in the name of King Richard, and under his privy seal ...

16 Presumably the chronicles were sent for so that they could be searched for evidence of Henry's claim to the throne (see for example Adam Usk's remarks, below, Doc. 15); also, perhaps, for precedents relating to deposition.

11. Bolingbroke's campaign and his meeting with Richard according to the monk of Evesham

Source: *Vita Ricardi Secundi*, 151-60

Language: Latin

Well-placed to acquire news about the later stages of Bolingbroke's march from the north, the monk of Evesham adds significant details to our knowledge of events in late July and early August 1399. He is, for example, our chief source for the crucial meeting between York and Bolingbroke at Berkeley on 27 July, and he provides an apparently accurate account of Bolingbroke's subsequent itinerary along the Welsh border to Chester. As with Walsingham, however, he was less well-informed about events in North Wales, even to the extent of confusing Conway and Flint.

In that same year, on about the feast of St John the Baptist (*24 June*), as already noted above, Duke Henry, the son and heir of the duke of Lancaster, arrived in England with sixty followers, including Thomas the former archbishop of Canterbury, Thomas the son and heir of the convicted earl of Arundel, the king's confessor, Lord Cobham, Thomas Erpingham and Thomas Rempston knights, John Norbury, Robert Waterton and Francis Court esquires, and various others.[1] He landed in the north of England, between Hull and Bridlington in Yorkshire, where nobody – or at least hardly anybody – had been able to land previously, and was enthusiastically welcomed by the lords and great

---

1 The 'king's confessor' must refer to Philip Repingdon, abbot of Leicester, whose presence with Bolingbroke is confirmed later in this extract and by Catesby's chronicle (below, Doc. 12[b]). However, Repingdon did not become Henry's confessor until 1404, which suggests that the *Vita* was not completed until after that date. Whether Repingdon did in fact return from France with Bolingbroke is doubtful: he is more likely to have joined him, presumably at Leicester, on his march southwards. Nor, it seems, did John Lord Cobham or Robert Waterton cross from France: Cobham was in exile on Jersey, while Waterton was acting as one of Bolingbroke's attorneys in England during his exile. According to Adam Usk (p. 174), Waterton was the first to join Henry after his landing. Rempston and Court were, like Erpingham and Norbury (for whom see above, Doc. 10), trusted followers of Bolingbroke who had gone into exile with him. Rempston became Henry's first steward of the royal household, and Court became a knight of the king's chamber.

men of the region. Thus gathering together a mighty army he hastened southwards, passing in great strength through Evesham on his way to Berkeley, with the result that within three days all the king's castles, or at least most of them, had been handed over to him. And this was a wonder to behold.

Then Edmund of Langley, duke of York, the king's uncle, whom the king had appointed as regent for the time being, hearing of the approach of the duke and his army, gathered together a large force of men-at-arms and archers to try to oppose him. Yet not a single one of them, so I believe, was willing to fire so much as one arrow at the duke of Lancaster or his followers, or indeed to launch any sort of attack against him or his men. The duke of York therefore led his army across towards Wales to await the king's return from Ireland, and, being admitted to Berkeley, decided to remain there. It was here that the duke of Lancaster with his enormous following eventually caught up with him, and, since the duke of York did not have the strength to resist him, the two of them eventually, on the Sunday (*27 July*) after the feast of St James, spoke together in a church outside Berkeley castle and came to an agreement. The duke of York had with him at the time the bishop of Norwich, Lords Berkeley and Seymour,[2] and a number of knights and other men. On the duke of Lancaster's side were Lord Thomas Arundel the exiled archbishop of Canterbury, the abbot of Leicester, the earls of Northumberland and Westmorland, the earl of Arundel – the son and heir of the deceased Earl Richard – Baron Greystoke, Lord Willoughby and Lord Roos,[3] along with many other lords, knights and common people who had been joining him daily from every part of the kingdom. Those who refused to join him, or were too slow to do so, were despoiled of all or a large part of their goods, which, for the most part, were never subsequently restored to them. Thus, in order to protect both themselves and their goods, great numbers of men joined the duke each day from this time onwards.

On the same day and at the same place the bishop of Norwich, Lord William Elmham and Walter Burley, knights, and Laurence Dru and John Golafre, esquires, were arrested and ordered to be placed in custody.[4] On the following day the aforesaid dukes with their crowds

2 Thomas Lord Berkeley (1368-1417), and Richard Lord Saint Maur (1361-1401).

3 Ralph Lord Greystoke (1359-1418), William Lord Willoughby (1396-1409), and William Lord Roos of Helmsley (1394-1414); all three were northern lords.

4 By 'Walter Burley', the chronicler probably meant Walter Bytterley, a knight from Shropshire who had been retained by Richard II in 1395. Dru was a lawyer who had

of followers went on to Bristol where, with about 100,000 fighting
men in all, they made a splendid display of themselves and their arms
and weaponry in front of the town and castle.

In the castle at that time were Lord William le Scrope, earl of
Wiltshire and treasurer of England, and the knights Lord Henry
(*Green*), and Sir John Bussy, the speaker in the last parliament, who
had been foremost in counselling King Richard to commit the sort of
crimes which have been mentioned above. After a while they were
captured and, much against their will, taken out of the castle to meet
the duke of Lancaster. They were immediately arrested, and then, on
the following day (*29 July*), they were brought before the justices, that
is the constable and marshal,[5] to stand trial, and having been convicted
of treason and of evil government of both the king and the kingdom,
they were condemned to death and beheaded. Also captured there at
the same time was Lord John Russell, knight, who was so terror-
struck that he pretended to be insane, and thus for the moment
avoided the same penalty.[6]

Next day the duke of Lancaster returned with his men to Berkeley,
while the duke of York stayed at Bristol. Then, on the second day
after these events, the duke of Lancaster and his men travelled on
to Gloucester, and from there to Ross, and then on to Hereford,
where he was joined by the bishop of Hereford and Lord Edmund
de Mortimer, knight.[7] On the following Sunday (*3 August*) he
arrived at Leominster, where he was joined by Lord Charlton.[8]
Next day he moved on to Ludlow, and from there on the following
day to Shrewsbury, where he rested for a day. While he was there
he received a visit from Lord Robert a Leigh and Lord John a

been a member of the king's council since 1393; Golafre was an esquire of the royal
household and sheriff of Oxford and Berkshire: Given-Wilson, *Royal Household*, 185,
249, 288.

5 The earls of Northumberland and Westmorland respectively, formally appointed to
these posts at Henry's coronation (below, Doc. 16).

6 Although at first sight improbable, this story is confirmed by Catesby's chronicle
(below, Doc. 12[b]). An official record of this time speaks of Russell's 'infirmities'
(*CPR, 1396-9*, 589).

7 John Trefnant, bishop of Hereford 1389-1404. Sir Edmund Mortimer (1376-1409)
was the uncle of the seven-year-old heir to the earldom of March, also called
Edmund; he was later, in alliance with the Percies and Owen Glendower, to rebel
against Henry.

8 John Lord Charlton of Powys (1374-1401).

Leigh, knights,[9] and several other people who had been sent from Chester to treat with the duke on behalf of the community of Cheshire and to submit to his authority in all matters. He was also joined there by Lord Scales and Lord Bardolf, who had come from Ireland and had been robbed while passing through Wales.[10]

Next day he left Shrewsbury and took his men to Prees in Wales, and on the following day (*8 August*) he arrived at the town of Chester, where he remained for several days displaying himself and his military might in splendid fashion to the people of the town ...

Meanwhile the king, who as already mentioned was staying at Flint castle,[11] hearing that practically the whole kingdom was now supporting the duke of Lancaster, was overcome with fear and decided to send Lord John Holand, duke of Exeter, to treat with him for peace. Also here (*at Chester*) Piers de Leigh was beheaded and his head set up above the highest of the town gates. At this time the duke was also joined here by the dukes of Aumale and Surrey, Lord Thomas Percy earl of Worcester, Lord Lovel and Lord John Stanley, who put themselves at his mercy.[12] Then on the Sunday (*17 August*) following the Assumption of the Blessed Virgin, Thomas the former archbishop of Canterbury, the earls of Northumberland and Westmorland, and Lord Henry Percy went off to seek the king, who was still in the aforesaid castle, taking with them the duke's reply to him. When they had given him the reply and discussed many other things, they brought him to the mighty castle of Conway, where he waited for the duke of Lancaster to arrive.

On the third day after this, which was a Tuesday (*19 August*), the duke of Lancaster arrived with his large and powerful army, which he drew up in awe-inspiring manner in full view of the king, who had remained inside the castle. Then he dismounted, walked up to the castle, and crossed the bridge into the outer ward, where he waited for the king to emerge from the interior of the castle.

9 The Leighs were one of the most powerful gentry families in Cheshire under Richard II. Robert had been retained by the king in 1397; their relative Perkin, or Peter, was (as the monk states later) to be beheaded by Bolingbroke a week or so after this (see also Adam Usk, 177).

10 Robert Lord Scales (1387-1402) and Thomas Lord Bardolf (1386-1408); the latter was to die rebelling with the earl of Northumberland against Henry.

11 The author has confused Conway with Flint and vice versa in this paragraph.

12 According to Creton (below, Doc. 13), Surrey was sent by Richard, along with his brother Exeter, to negotiate with Bolingbroke; John Lord Lovel (1361-1408); Sir John Stanley was controller of the royal household.

Then the king approached, accompanied by the bishop of Carlisle, the earl of Salisbury, Lord Stephen le Scrope,[13] who bore the royal sword, and a few more members of his household. He remained where he was, in the place which had been got ready for him for the occasion. The duke, as soon as he saw the king, paid his respects to him; then, moving closer to him, he again paid his respects by bowing to him; and when he had come right up to him he paid his respects for the third time by kneeling before him.

The king took him by the hand and raised him up, saying, 'Welcome, dear cousin.' The duke replied by thanking him and saying, 'My esteemed lord and king, the reason for my coming here is, saving your dignity, to reclaim, with your royal permission, my life, my lands and my inheritance.' To which the king replied, 'My dear cousin, I am quite prepared to grant that. You may have back all that is yours in peace and without any difficulty.' With these words they passed through the gate and out of the castle, and the king called for wine.

Then, when they had drunk together, and horses had been got ready, they rode rapidly on to Chester that same day, and on the next day to Leicester,[14] the next day to Nantwich, and the next day to Newcastle-under-Lyme, where they were met by a cheerful Thomas earl of Warwick, who, as noted above, had earlier been exiled to the Isle of Man, but who had now been recalled by the duke of Lancaster. On the following day they rode on to Stafford, and the day after that to Lichfield, where they rested that day, which was a Sunday, the feast of St Bartholomew the Apostle (*24 August*). From there they rode day by day to Coventry, then to Daventry, then to Northampton, then to Dunstable, then to St Albans, and then on to London. Not once during this time was the king allowed to change his clothes; during all the time that he rode through these towns he was dressed in the same simple set of garments.

Yet it was rumoured that among his other worldly riches the king had on his own orders had a robe made for himself, of gold and pearls and other precious stones, which was reckoned to be worth 30,000 marks. O good Jesus! surely your seamless robe of which we read in the Gospels was not valued at such a price? Yet that was both more precious and more honourable.

13 Sir Stephen le Scrope was the younger brother of William, earl of Wiltshire, whom he replaced as chamberlain of the royal household in 1398.
14 'Leicester' must be an error on the chronicler's part; for the journey from Chester to London see above, p. 40.

The king was taken straight to Westminster, while the duke made a splendid entrance into London and was received with great joy at the bishop of London's palace. On the following day the king was taken to the Tower and placed under close watch ...

12. Two accounts of Bolingbroke's progress through England

Taken together, the Kirkstall Short Chronicle and the 'chronicle' of John Catesby enable a fairly detailed picture to be drawn up of Bolingbroke's itinerary from his landing at Ravenspur until his meeting with the duke of York at Berkeley on 27 July. Kirkstall Abbey, near Leeds in Yorkshire, was under the patronage of the dukes of Lancaster, and Bolingbroke must have passed within a few miles of it on his journey southwards. The chronicler's account is thus likely to be based on first-hand information: it is of interest to note that Bolingbroke apparently spent some time moving around Yorkshire – awaiting news, no doubt, and testing the strength of his support – before deciding to go south. There is also – for a northern chronicle – a surprisingly circumstantial description of the siege of Bristol.

The second passage given below is found in an account compiled by John Catesby, a lawyer, of his protracted legal defence of the manor of Ladbroke in Warwickshire against his relatives, the Cardians, who claimed title against him. The dispute also involved the earl of Warwick, before whose council the case was heard, and the duke of Surrey, who had been granted many of Warwick's lands after the latter's exile in 1397, and who, along with his brother the duke of Exeter, was appointed in 1398-99 to arbitrate between the parties. It was presumably the deaths of Surrey and Exeter in the 'Epiphany Rising', before their decision could be awarded, that induced Catesby to write his own version of the revolution, as evidence of the difficulties he had encountered in tracking them down during these months.

(a) According to the Kirkstall chronicler

Source: Short Kirkstall Chronicle, 121-5

Language: Latin

Knowing that the king was in Ireland, the aforesaid Lord Henry of Lancaster, duke of Hereford, returning from France to England in order to claim his hereditary right, landed on 4 July near Ravenspur

on the Humber – in a certain boat near Bridlington in Holderness[1] –
bringing with him the noble archbishop of Canterbury, the recently
exiled Lord Thomas Arundel, the son and heir of the earl of Arundel,
and about a hundred soldiers, all of whom set off peacefully across the
country and after three days arrived at Pickering castle, the custody of
which had been committed by the lord king to Lord William le Scrope
earl of Wiltshire; as soon as the lord duke arrived there, the sub-
custodian of the castle delivered it up to him, and after spending two
days there he moved on to Knaresburgh castle, which was likewise
handed over to him, though not quite so easily. Leaving his own
garrisons in these castles, he then moved on to Pontefract castle,
where crowds of gentlemen, knights and esquires from Yorkshire and
Lancashire flocked to join him with their retinues, some of whom came
willingly and others out of fear of what the future might hold.
However, the aforesaid Lord Henry duke of Lancaster found it easy to
win the goodwill of the lords: thus the noble earl of Northumberland,
together with his son Lord Henry Percy and their powerful and large
retinue, Lord Ralph de Nevill earl of Westmorland, and Lord
Willoughby, both with their retinues, came to help and serve him, so
that by the time he reached Doncaster he had about 30,000 fighting
men with him. By the advice of the lords they divided themselves into
companies, some advancing on the right and others on the left, in
order to gather and preserve the corn and other provisions they
needed; thus did they march along with the duke, and wherever he
went the number of people joining him kept on increasing, so that by
the time he approached Gloucester it had reached 100,000 men. From
the Gloucester area they crossed over to Bristol, for it was to Bristol
castle, so the lord duke had been informed, that the above-mentioned
justices (*William le Scrope, John Bussy, Henry Green and William Bagot*)
had fled for protection.

Then the lord earl of Northumberland had it proclaimed outside the
walls of Bristol castle to all those within that anyone who wished to
leave the castle and come out to where he was would be permitted to
go his way without bodily harm, but that anyone who refused to do so

---

1 This phrase is inserted as a footnote in the manuscript. Ravenspur - modern Spurn
Head - is some thirty miles south of Bridlington, which suggests some confusion on
the part of the chronicler over the location of Bolingbroke's landing. It is worth
noting that the chronicler of Whalley Abbey (below, Doc. 14[b]) used exactly the
same words to describe Bolingbroke's landing, i.e. 'cum quadam nave in Holdernes
iuxta Bridlyngton' (Short Kirkstall Chronicle, 121; British Library Harleian Ms.
3600, f. 232v). Both chronicles were written at Cistercian houses, and it is likely that
they were in some way interdependent.

would be beheaded. On hearing this, some came out to join the earl by lowering ropes from the castle walls, others through the windows, and others by the gate. The only people left in the castle were Lords William le Scrope, John Bussy, and Henry Green, along with a few friends who had come to their assistance at that time. When the earl of Northumberland had arrested them he brought them before the duke of Lancaster, and on the following day, 29 July, by definitive judgement of the lords, they were condemned to capital punishment. For their greater shame, their heads were then distributed as follows: that of William le Scrope earl of Wiltshire was placed above London bridge, that of Lord John Bussy above the bridge at York, and that of Lord Henry Green above the bridge at Bristol. Lord William Bagot, however, had already managed to escape secretly to Ireland, so that he was not taken with the king's other councillors; nevertheless he was captured later in Ireland and led publicly to parliament in London by that worthy knight Lord Peter Bukton.[2] He gave such eloquent answers, however, to the questions put to him in the parliament, that he escaped death for the time being, although he was put under constant supervision by the bailiffs.[3] With King Richard's council thus utterly deprived of leadership, the duke of Lancaster and his army marched towards and against the county of Chester, trampling down with their horses' hooves the corn and the meadows throughout most of the county; thus having captured the town of Chester and other castles, and having killed many of the local inhabitants and confiscated numerous goods from them, the duke accomplished what he had set out to do. Meanwhile all King Richard's English castles were taken, the keepers whom he had appointed turned out, and new keepers and captains appointed ...

Meanwhile King Richard, hearing rumours of the duke of Lancaster's landing in England, and of his rapid progress, crossed from Ireland to Wales with 10,000 armed men; together with the army he collected in Wales, this figure increased to twenty thousand fighting men who had gathered to assist their king. However, fear of the duke of Lancaster and his army, now approaching the area, caused the king's army to dwindle, and so the king moved off with a small group of intimates to

2 Sir Peter Bukton was a staunch Lancastrian, having been steward of Bolingbroke's household before his exile; he also came from Yorkshire, which helps to explain his favourable treatment in this chronicle.

3 For Bagot's trial in the October 1399 parliament, see below, Doc. 20[a]. He was still imprisoned in the Tower in September 1400, but seems to have been released soon afterwards (CPR, 1399-1401, 78, 204).

the powerful – indeed almost unassailable – castle of Conway. He did this so secretly, however, that many of his followers, and even some of his privy council, were unaware that he had left them, and thus, having been divided, the king's household was totally dispersed. When the duke of Lancaster knew for certain that the king was in Wales, he too hastened thither, and, having come to within a short distance of where the king was, he sent the earl of Northumberland to him; the king gave his assent to the various arguments put forward by the earl, and on the following day the king and the duke of Lancaster met. By definitive injunction of the duke and the other lords, the king was led to the city of London and there held in the Tower under the close guard of the lords. They sent the other dukes and earls who had initially supported the king, and had advised him in his schemes, to a number of different castles and fortified houses in the north; a few days later, however, they were all brought back to the city of London to await the feast of Michaelmas, when they could expect to hear either the judgement or the clemency of the duke of Lancaster and the other lords who had gathered there for parliament ...

(b) According to John Catesby

Source: J. B. Post, 'Courts, councils and arbitrators in the Ladbroke Manor dispute, 1382-1400', in *Medieval Legal Records Edited in Memory of C. A. F. Meekings*, ed. R. F. Hunnisett and J. B. Post (London 1978), 323-4

Language: French

Then afterwards, about the quinzaine of the Nativity of St John, Henry duke of Lancaster and Hereford landed at Ravenspur in the county of York and began his march. In his company were the earl of Northumberland, the earl of Westmorland, Sir Henry Percy the son and heir of the said earl of Northumberland, Lord Willoughby, the son and heir of the earl of Arundel, Thomas Arundel archbishop of York, Philip abbot of Leicester,[4] and many other knights and esquires. They advanced towards Pontefract, then on to Leicester, and from there, two days before the feast of St James, to Coventry, and on the vigil of St James (*24 July*) to Warwick; there, because Thomas Holand, earl of Kent – and, by creation of King Richard in his twenty-first year, duke

---

4 Philip Repingdon: see above, Doc. 11, n.1.

of Surrey – had placed above the gates of Warwick castle a crowned
hart of stone, which at that time was the said King Richard's livery,
and a white hind, which was at that time the said duke's livery, the
duke of Lancaster ordered them to be knocked down, which was done.[5]
From there they marched on to Bristol, where Sir William le Scrope
earl of Wiltshire and treasurer of England, Sir John Bussy, and Sir
Henry Green were beheaded; Sir John Russell escaped, for he had lost
his mind. From there they marched on to Flint castle, where King
Richard was, having landed at Milford and made his way to Conway
castle; and there, through the mediation of the aforesaid archbishop
and the earl of Northumberland, King Richard surrendered to the duke
of Lancaster, whereupon the duke of Surrey and John earl of Salisbury
were sent to the north in the custody of the earl of Westmorland,
where the said John Catesby was unable to follow them ...

5 This action of Bolingbroke's has been interpreted by some historians as early
evidence of his intention to usurp the throne (see for example Post, 'Courts, councils
and arbitrators', 323, n. 357). Warwick castle had been seized and fortified by
former retainers of the earl of Warwick as early as 4 July (R. Mott, 'Richard II and
the crisis of 1397', in *Church and Chronicle in the Middle Ages: Essays Presented to John
Taylor*, ed. I. Wood and G. A. Loud (1991), 176).

The plates

The accompanying illustrations are from a series of sixteen miniatures in an early fifteenth-century French manuscript of Jean Creton's 'Metrical History' of Richard's deposition. The manuscript in question is now in the British Library (Harleian MS. 1319).

At least some of these illustrations were probably copied from originals which may have been made by Creton himself, for on a number of occasions in his poem he refers the reader to such 'visual aids'. In his account of Richard and Bolingbroke's meeting at Flint, for example, he describes Bolingbroke's armour 'comme vous povez veoir en ceste ystoire' ('as you can see in this picture'). The portraits, although presumably not lifelike in any genuine sense, do not seem to be merely stylised. Richard, for instance, is distinguished by the forked beard which can also be seen on his effigy in Westminster abbey; he is easily identifiable by the hood which he wears, just as Bolingbroke is identifiable by his tall black hat.

The use of illustrations to accompany the text demonstrates the importance of the image as well as the written word in medieval literary works. The illustrations are intended to reinforce key points in Creton's story, such as Northumberland's oath upon the host at Conway, followed by his seizure of the king later that day.

For more detailed discussion of the illustrations see E. M. Thompson, 'A contemporary account of the fall of Richard the Second', *Burlington Magazine* (1904), 160-72 and 267-77

The author and publishers wish to express their gratitude to the British Library for permission to reproduce the plates.

The arrival of the Earl of Salisbury at Conway

Henry receives the Dukes of Exeter and Surrey at Chester

The Earl of Northumberland received by Richard at Conway

The Earl of Northumberland swears that he means no treachery to Richard

Richard II captured

Henry Bolingbroke (Henry IV) claims the crown before parliament

13. The betrayal and capture of the king according to Jean Creton

Sources: 'Metrical History', ed. and trans. Webb, 55-176; *Collection des Chroniques Nationales Françaises*, ed. J. A. Buchon, xxiii (Paris 1826), 341-415.

Language: French

Jean Creton, a Frenchman and a valet-de-chambre to King Charles VI (and probably also a servant of the duke of Burgundy) provides the most circumstantial account of the crucial meetings at Conway and Flint which determined the success of Bolingbroke's revolution. He was, as he tells us, an eye-witness to these events, having crossed to Ireland with Richard II in May, whence he was sent back to North Wales with the earl of Salisbury in July; here he was joined by the king and his small band of followers early in August, and witnessed the visit of the earl of North-umberland to Conway and the interview between Richard and Henry at Flint. Although strongly partisan towards Richard, he was prepared to give credit to Bolingbroke for, for example, his considerate treatment of the captured king, and his kindness towards Creton himself and his (unnamed) companion. Although doubts have been quite rightly raised about Creton's chronology and about some of the details of his story, there is now a widespread measure of agreement that he provides, in its essentials, a credible account of these events.

Creton wrote most of his chronicle in verse. The following translation is based upon that made by Webb, but substantially modernised and at times corrected from the text printed by Buchon. The extracts which follow begin at Dublin, at the moment when news was brought to the king that Bolingbroke had landed in England.

It seemed to me that the king's face turned pale with anger at this news. 'Come hither, friends,' he said. 'Good Lord, this man plans to deprive me of my country.' And he ordered both the young and old of his council to assemble, to consider what had best be done. Now they agreed on a Saturday, to put to sea on the next Monday, without

waiting longer than a day and a half.[1] But when the duke of Aumale
heard of the plan to depart, he slyly decided on a trick, thinking that,
if he could, he would undermine it. He went with great secrecy to the
king, therefore, to try to dissuade him from what they had all agreed
upon, saying, 'My lord, do not vex yourself, for I have never heard of
so ill-conceived a plan. Do not be in such a hurry to set out; it would
be much better to take your time and send first for the whole of the
navy; for we have less than a hundred barges; how can we go, seeing
that around here there are many huge rocks in the water, and the sea-
bed is dangerous? Take my advice: it would be much better to send the
earl of Salisbury across, who can hold the field against the duke and
make sufficient war on him: he will have all the Welsh to help him to
subdue the duke. Meanwhile we will go by land to Waterford, where
you can send to all the ports for your navy, so that your whole army,
the weak as well as the strong, can then cross over. Then will you soon
see your enemies captured, killed, or discomfited: this, I assure you, is
the best plan to follow.' The king put more trust in him than any of his
friends: by his advice the entire plan agreed by the others was set aside ...

(*Creton accompanied the earl of Salisbury to North Wales, where they landed
at Conway; here they were told of Bolingbroke's progress through England.*)
The earl then promptly sent his summons throughout Wales and
Chester, ordering all gentlemen, archers, and other persons to come to
him without delay, upon pain of death, to take King Richard's side,
assuring them that the king bore no grudge against them. They were
eager to do so, for they believed for certain that the king had arrived
at Conway: I am certain that forty thousand of them were marshalled
and mustered in the field within four days, each of them keen to fight
against anyone who opposed the ever-honourable and valiant King
Richard. Then the earl, at great effort and trouble to himself, went to
meet them, and swore to them by Jesus who died on the cross that
before three days had passed he would deal so harshly with the duke
and his supporters that they would be unable for the moment to
advance any further, or to devastate the land. Soon after this he came
upon all his supporters gathered together in the fields, and prudently
addressed them as follows: 'My good gentlemen, let us all make haste
to avenge King Richard in his absence, so that he will be satisfied with
us in time to come: for my own part I intend neither to stop nor to take

1 Assuming Creton's memory was correct, this would probably have been Saturday
  12 July. The writ appointing the earl of Salisbury as governor of Chester and North
  Wales was enrolled at Chester on 19 July (Davies, 'Richard II and the principality
  of Chester', 275).

rest until such time as I have made my attempt against those who are acting so cruelly and treacherously towards him. Let us go on from here and march straight towards them. If we are determined to assault them, then God will help us; for according to our law, it is the duty of every man to support a just cause unto death, indeed in a situation such as this God expressly commands us to do so.'

But when the Welshmen realised that the king was not there, they became downcast, and began to murmur among themselves in groups, for they thought that the king must have died of grief, and they were full of alarm and dread at the terrible cruelty of the duke of Lancaster and his followers. They became displeased with the earl, saying, 'We must tell you, sir, that for the moment we shall advance no further, since the king is not here; and we will tell you why: look at the duke, he is subduing every thing to his authority, and it strikes great fear into our hearts. Indeed we believe that the king is dead, for he did not accompany you at your landing: were he here, whether his cause were right or wrong, we would all be eager to assail his enemies. But for now we will not go with you ...' Some made their way straight to the duke, and the rest returned into Wales, leaving the earl alone in the middle of the fields with only his own men, who amounted, I think, to less than a hundred. He was greatly saddened by this, and declared, 'Let us make our retreat, for our enterprise goes very badly ...'

Now I must tell you of the arrival of King Richard, though he was too late, for he delayed for eighteen days after our departure from Ireland.[2] This was a great act of folly. May the curse of Jesus Christ be upon the body and the life of the man who caused this to happen. Thus did he show his love for the king, who so loved him. Throughout his host he gave orders for the loading of barges and ships, and for those who could bear arms to embark. King Richard took only a short time to cross the sea, for the weather was fair and bright, and the wind good, so that within two days he had arrived at Milford. He did not stop there, because of his concern for the distress, complaints and lamentations of the poor people, and the mortal fear which gripped them. He decided instead that, without saying a word, he would set out at midnight from his host, accompanied by only a few persons, for he was determined not to be discovered. So he disguised himself in the garb of a poor priest, because of his fear that he might be recognised by his

2 Creton was probably reckoning from the time that he and Salisbury left Ireland to the time that Richard rejoined them at Conway, which would place the king's arrival in North Wales in the first week of August.

F

enemies. Alas, he thought that the earl was still holding the field with his troops, so he rode hard towards him, in sad and pensive mood.

I must now tell you the names of those friends who accompanied him through the countryside. I saw the duke of Exeter there, and with him the good duke of Surrey, who was loyal and true unto death; the brave earl of Gloucester was also with them, and three bishops, two of whom, as you shall hear, did not behave like men of honour. But first I shall tell you their names. One was the bishop of St Davids, another was my lord of Carlisle: he was the best of them, for he would never desert the good king, nor did he ever change his mind about it, whatever they might say to him. The third was the bishop of Lincoln, who cared nothing for what they did, for he was the duke's half-brother, and thought he would easily be able to make his peace with him when he wished to.[3] Of the laymen, there were two knights, both worthy in arms, honourable and bold. The first was called Stephen Scrope, the second Ferriby: he was strong and agile. Also with them was Janico, who was reputed to be a good fighter; it was said of him that he had performed great feats of arms.[4]

Thus did they set out that very night, just fourteen of them including the king, travelling hard in the hope of soon joining up with the earl of Salisbury ... The king rode on without any interruption until he arrived at Conway, where the houses are covered with tiles, at break of dawn ...

Now I will tell you how the constable,[5] who commanded the king's following, shamelessly went off without waiting for him, and led away all his men, for which action he has earned nothing but contempt ... On that night when the good king set out from the sea-port at midnight, a rumour began to spread through the army that the king had fled without saying a word. The constable was delighted at this, for he had been unable to find an excuse to depart; so when he saw the alarm in the host, he called out loudly so that all could hear him, 'Let us be gone! If our lord is so careful to ensure his own safety, we are all lost.'

3 Walsingham said that the bishops of Carlisle, London and Lincoln were among those who returned from Ireland with Richard. Braybrooke apparently returned to London from South Wales (Barron, 'Deposition of Richard II', 148 n. 75). Creton is probably correct in saying that Guy Mone (bishop of St Davids 1397-1407) was with the king (Johnston, 'Richard II's departure from Ireland', 801-2).

4 William Ferriby was not in fact a knight but a clerk, and a member of the king's council. Janico Dartasso came from Gascony and was an esquire of the royal chamber: Given-Wilson, *Royal Household*, 174, 180-1, 312.

5 The duke of Aumale.

He promptly ordered the trumpets to sound, and commanded them all
to prepare immediately for departure, for he did not know when the
king would return ... The king's steward, whose name was Sir Thomas
Percy, was in charge of all the loading and packing. He had long been
in the king's service; he was, as the French would say, the chief grand
maître d'hôtel. He and the constable spoke together: shortly afterwards they set out, making their way straight through Wales; but the
Welsh, who saw their treason for what it was, attacked them in
strength, in groups of one or two thousand, saying to them, 'Wretched
traitors, you shall go no further this way, so God help us. And you
shall surrender all the stolen jewels you are carrying away, for the
king did not give them to you.' Thus were the English despoiled by the
Welsh ...

I will tell you now about the king, who remained, downcast and
miserable, at Conway. 'Sirs,' he said, 'In God's name I beg you to
advise me, for in his hour of need a man must turn to his friends.' The
duke of Exeter spoke first, for he was the king's brother: 'It would be
best to send immediately to the duke,' he said, 'to find out what he
means to do, and what he hopes to gain, and why it is that he is trying
to seize your kingdom, your person and your goods; and whether he
wants to be king and sovereign lord of England, prince of Wales, and
rightful lord of Chester.' Thus did the noble duke of Exeter speak to
his brother the king. 'Let him be told that he was banished by consent
of his own father; let him also think carefully about what he is doing,
for it would be a terrible disgrace upon him for ever if it came to pass
that by him or his deeds his lawful king was undone ... Let him be told
also that he may have back all his land again, but that he must at least
come and do you the honour of suing for mercy. If he does not deign
to come, then some other person will have to suggest some better plan
...' And so they all agreed to send someone to Duke Henry, and it
happened that the duke of Exeter was chosen by them; indeed they
could not have chosen a man who was wiser in his speech or more
skilled in presenting a matter of such importance. The good king also
ordered his worthy cousin the duke of Surrey to go with him. They left
the king in the morning; he earnestly exhorted them to make haste, to
perform their task well, and to explain clearly to the duke all the
aforesaid matters, in the hope that they would secure from him some
agreement or pact ...

(*King Richard planned to send for his troops at Milford to join him, but a
messenger arrived at Conway to tell him that they had dispersed.*) Then they

agreed to remain no longer at Conway, for they were in great fear and dread, and with good reason. They went straight to Beaumaris, which was ten miles from Conway. This is a castle that could not be taken in two years, as long as it was victualled for that time, and garrisoned with good defenders. On one side of it were the open fields, and the other rose straight from the sea. St Edward had it built, or so I have heard the English say.[6] The king stopped here, but he would not stay long, for he thought that he and his people would be more secure at Caernarvon; the town and castle there are very fine and strong. On one side there are great stretches of woods for the chase, and the other side is washed by the high tide. The king was there, his face often pale, as he lamented his hard fate and condemned the hour and the day that he had ever crossed the salt sea into Ireland ... What was worse, in his castles, to which he retired, there was no furniture, nor did he have anything but straw to lie upon; thus did he sleep for four or six nights, for there was, in truth, not a farthing's worth of victuals or of anything else to be found in them. I hardly dare speak of the king's misery. He did not remain long at Caernarvon, for he had little rest there on account of his misfortune and great poverty. He returned to Conway, where he began fervently to bewail his wife ...

The two dukes (*Surrey and Exeter*) travelled morning and night until they came to Chester, which the duke for his part had already taken by skill and cunning, without an assault. They both entered: when they first arrived, many of those present thought that they were abandoning the king and coming to sue for mercy to Henry Duke of Lancaster: but this was great folly on their part, for they would not have crouched to him for all the gold in England. They were led straight to Duke Henry in the castle, which is a regular building; he was delighted when he saw them, and gave every appearance of making them most welcome. Then he said to the duke of Exeter, 'Come, brother-in-law, tell us, I pray you, without further ado, what news do you bring?' 'None, brother-in-law, that is very good for my lord, but only such as brings shame and evil to him, which causes me great sorrow and distress.' And he went on to tell him very carefully what you have already heard at the time when they left the king ... He also told him that he could have his land and his goods, but that he must henceforth do his duty; and that the king would gladly and freely pardon him entirely for the outrage he had committed against him. Thus did the duke of Exeter faithfully and eloquently tell him what had happened;

6 It was Edward I, not Edward the Confessor, who built Beaumaris.

and he spoke quite boldly to him too, for he had married his own sister, and was thus his kinsman.[7] The duke of Exeter concluded by saying to him, 'I beseech you, brother-in-law, to give us your answer as soon as possible, in so far as you are able to, for my lord is waiting for us to return, and is in a poor frame of mind.'

(*Henry replied that he proposed to detain both of them at Chester for the time being.*) Thus were the two dukes detained, and they were greatly distressed at it, fearing that Duke Henry's heart was set against them, and lamenting the fate of the king, who remained alone, without a soul to aid or support him. Each of the two dukes often wept; but, regardless of their feelings, they were obliged to endure it all. Duke Henry separated them: he kept his brother-in-law the duke of Exeter close to him, but had the good duke of Surrey shut up in the castle of Chester ... Six miles from the city was another fortress, built high upon a rock, called Holt, and during this time the duke marched against it with all his army. Those who were in it were so afraid that they did not know what to do, although they knew well that the duke could not harm them in the least at any time: for the castle is so strong and sound that, in my opinion, considering the height upon which it is constructed, it could not have been taken by force in ten years. It was also well garrisoned with good troops: there were a hundred elite men-at-arms in it, carefully provisioned on the part of the king. They were not, however, careful about guarding the entrance or the pass, which is narrow, and must be ascended on foot, step by step. So, faint-hearted and cowardly as they were, they gave it up to the duke, who lost no time in entering it, more delighted than ever; for it contained a hundred thousand marks sterling in gold, or more, which King Richard had ordered to be stored there, as well as a great number of other precious jewels ... Thus, as I have told you, was Holt surrendered, and all the wealth of King Richard seized ... [8]

He did not stop there, but returned straight to Chester, where he summoned all his councillors and asked each of them to tell him what he thought ought to be done. The archbishop of Canterbury answered first, saying, 'My lords, King Richard has taken refuge in Wales, where there are many dangerous mountains, over which neither wagons nor

---

7 John Holand duke of Exeter married Elizabeth, Bolingbroke's sister, in 1386, apparently having first seduced her.

8 Holt had belonged to the earl of Arundel before his forfeiture in 1397. Richard II strengthened its defences and used it as his chief treasury in the Cheshire region, depositing over £40,000 there: Given-Wilson, *Royal Household*, 90, 181.

baggage can pass; on the other side is the sea, where an abundance of fish is available; your army could not get close to him. Instead we must send a messenger to him, and make promises to him: you must make an agreement with him to the effect that the two of you will be at peace forever, on condition that he will swear to summon a parliament in which those evil men by whom his uncles were put to death shall be punished; and that henceforth you will be good friends. You must also humbly beg his pardon, and tell him to name whatever day seems appropriate to him for the parliament, and that it shall be held in such a place that every one, clerk or layman, knight, priest, or monk, may get to it; for you cannot take him by any other means, since he has the power, in spite of us, to put to sea at any time and be gone. For I have heard it said that he has ordered ships to be detained at Conway. I think you ought to consider this question well. Now tell me what you think of it, my lords and friends.' Every one then said, 'By God, this is the best advice I ever heard.' Then Duke Henry said, 'It is a good plan, and will suit our purposes well. It is my advice that the aged earl of Northumberland, my fair cousin, should set out tomorrow early in the morning, and that he should not return until, either by agreement or by force, he brings back the king; let him also take with him two hundred men-at-arms and a thousand archers, who must be very careful; for there is nothing in the world that I desire so much as to have the king in my keeping.' Then he said to the earl, 'Fair cousin, get ready to depart, and to fulfil this plan well; for you can do me no greater service in the world. I pray you in God's name to make haste. I shall stay at Chester till you return, or until I have such news from you as will fill my heart with joy.' 'God grant it may be so,' said the earl, 'by argument or by craft, I will bring him to you ...'

(*Northumberland set out for Conway at once, receiving the surrender of Flint and Rhuddlan castles on the way. A few miles short of Conway he left his troops concealed behind some rocks with orders not to move until they saw him or the king returning. Then taking five men with him he went on to Conway, where King Richard granted him safe conduct to enter the castle.*) Then the earl went on board a vessel and crossed the water. In the castle he found King Richard, and with him the earl of Salisbury and the bishop of Carlisle. He said to the king, 'My lord, Duke Henry has sent me here to make an agreement between you, so that you will in future be good friends. With your leave, my lord, let me be heard, and I will deliver his message to you, and conceal nothing of the truth. If you will agree to be a good and true judge, and will deliver up all those whom I shall here name to you, by a certain day, to be brought to justice; and will listen to the parliament which the two of you together shall faithfully cause to be held at Westminster; and if you will restore to him the office of chief judge of England, which the duke his father, and all his ancestors have held for more than a hundred years;[9] then I will tell you the names of those who shall stand trial. For it is time that this were done, my lord, if it please you.' 'I am indeed most eager to learn who they are.' 'Know then, my lord, that the first is your brother; the second who has done wrong is the duke of Surrey, who has been imprisoned in Chester castle, though I do not know what offence he has committed against Duke Henry; also the earl of Salisbury, and the bishop of Carlisle; the fifth, so I have heard my lord say, is Maudeleyn. These are the men who most wrongfully advised you to put your uncle to death, and gave their consent to that deed; and if they deny it, they can await the judgement of your parliament, at which you shall be crowned with honour as lord and king. Duke Henry shall act as chief judge there, and those who have been guilty of criminal behaviour or of treason shall be punished without partiality. This is my lord's decision. He does not wish to do anything that is unreasonable. And there is one further thing that I wish to say to you, that is, that you must name the day soon, for there is nothing in the world that he desires more. This I know well; he wants nothing but his land, and whatever belongs to him. He desires nothing that is yours, for you are his immediate and rightful king; and he truly regrets the great mischief and wrong that he has committed against you ..., and will come before you most humbly on his knees and sue for mercy. When this is done, you shall go together to London, like devout and peaceful men; or, if you choose to go a different road, you may do so; and then the parliament will be proclaimed throughout the land. All this you must believe: I will swear upon the body of Jesus Christ, consecrated by a priest's hand, that Duke Henry will most faithfully adhere to everything that I have said, and do everything just as I have explained it to you, for he solemnly pledged it to me upon God's body when last we parted. Now, my lord, consider how you will act, for I have delayed long enough.'

Then King Richard wisely replied: 'Northumberland, withdraw: before long you shall have our answer, and then you can hurry back.' And with that they separated. They spent a long time discussing what the

---

9 A reference to the stewardship of England, held by the earls, then dukes, of Lancaster since the time of Edmund, earl of Lancaster 1267-96.

earl had said to them, until eventually the king said, 'My lords, we will go along with him, for I see no alternative. You perceive, as I do, that all is lost. But I swear to you, that whatever assurances I may give him, he shall surely be put to a bitter death for this outrage and injury that he has done to us. Doubt it not, there shall be no parliament held at Westminster on this matter, for I love you truly, and would not allow you to be brought to parliament to die for the fulfilment of the duke's pleasure ... I tell you, moreover, that I shall summon men from throughout Wales, and secretly muster them to be ready for us on a certain day. First we shall speak with Duke Henry, and then we will make our way through Wales; and if he asks us why we do so, we will tell him that there are no victuals – not a penny's worth – the other way, since his people and his army have wasted everything, and that we are going that way lest provisions fail us. Thus shall we speak to him, if it seems good to you; and I believe that he will readily agree to it, for the earl has told us so. And when we have found our people mustered, we will hoist our banners in the wind, and suddenly march with vigour against him. For I am as sure of it as of my death, that when they behold my arms, they will be so sorry at heart for the wrong that they have done me, that half of those who have gone along with him will desert him and come over to us ...'

Thus did the king speak to them, and they all agreed to it, saying, 'My lord, let the earl of Northumberland be sent for, and let him be made to take the oath at once, as he has declared that he will as long as we agree to all that he proposes.' Then, without further discussion, the earl was sent for, and the king said to him, 'Northumberland, the duke has sent you here to reconcile us two; if you will swear upon the body of our Lord, which we will have consecrated, that everything which you have said is true; that you have no hidden design of any kind whatsoever; but that like a worthy lord you will indeed keep the agreement; then we will perform it. For I know well that you are an honourable man, and would not perjure yourself for any robes, jewels, or other gifts. For the man who perjures himself knows that he must live forever in shame and disgrace, and, in the end, die in great sorrow.' Then the earl replied, 'My lord, let the body of our Lord be consecrated. I will swear that there is no deceit in this affair, and that the duke will observe everything that you have heard me relate here.' Each of them devoutly heard mass: then the earl without further hesitation took the oath upon the body of our Lord. Alas, his blood must have run cold at it, for he knew well to the contrary; nevertheless, he took the oath, just as you have heard, in order to accomplish his desire and to fulfil his promise to the duke, who had sent him to the king. Thus was the agreement made between them ...

The earl begged the king to set out, saying, 'My lord, I pray you, let us think of our journey, for I know well that the duke is eager to learn if peace is made.' Alas, the king knew nothing of the trickery, or of the real wishes of the earl, who, as you shall shortly see, planned to deceive him. The king said to him, 'We can set out whenever you wish; but I think it right that you should go on ahead of us to Rhuddlan, so that dinner can be prepared there.' 'Just as you please,' replied the earl, and departed. King Richard soon followed him. The earl rode on until he saw all his men under the mountain; and he was pleased with them, for he saw that they remained in good order, and had taken care to guard the pass. He explained to them what had happened; that he had succeeded, and that the king was on his way to them. They all rejoiced greatly at this news, for they were very eager to get possession of their lord. The king set out after him from Conway, on the road to Rhuddlan; he passed the very broad and great water, and then rode on four miles, till he came to the rock where the earl was concealed at the descent. When he climbed the rock and saw them, he was absolutely astonished, saying, 'I am betrayed! What can this be? True God of heaven help me!' They were recognisable by their banners, which were waving in the wind. 'I think it is the earl,' he said, 'who has enticed us out upon his oath.' Then were we all in great fear. I could have wished myself in France at that time, for I saw them almost in despair; and indeed it is hardly surprising that they were all so fearful, for not one of them could flee or escape from that place without being stopped or taken. To explain what I mean, you must understand that the king had approached so close to them that it was much further to return to the town than to descend the rock, which rose directly from the sea. Nor could we get away on the other side owing to the rock. So that, no matter what, we were forced either to die or to pass on into the midst of the earl's forces. He could be seen, armed in mail. The king was so humbled and miserable that it was a pity to behold; he kept saying, 'O true God, what shame and trouble must I undergo! Now I see clearly that this man is leading me to the duke, who has no love for us. O Virgin Mary, sovereign queen, have mercy upon me; for if you deign not to look upon me, I know in truth that I am lost.' Thus spoke the king, but he was quite powerless there, for there were only twenty of us, as I remember, or perhaps twenty-two. So, to the king's great grief, we all descended the lofty rock. Salisbury, who was quite astounded, said to him frequently, 'Now I see truly that I am certain to be a dead man, for I know that Duke Henry bears a great hatred towards me. Alas, why did we trust the earl's promises? It has been the ruin of us. But it is too late. May Jesus, in whom I believe, now help us!' And while they conversed in this fashion, we drew ever nearer to them, until we were about the distance of a good bow-shot from them.

Then the earl came forward and knelt on the ground, and said to the king, 'Do not be displeased, my rightful lord. I have sought you out for your own safety; for the country, as you know, is disturbed by war.' To which the king said, 'I could easily have passed through it with fewer men than you have brought here. This is not, I think, what you promised me. You told me that you had been sent with only five others. By God in heaven, this is most shameful, considering the oath that you made. You seem to me to have acted most disloyally in setting up your guards here. Depend upon it, I shall return to Conway, which I left earlier today.' Then the earl said to him, 'My lord, you accuse me of dishonour, but I swear to you on the body of Christ, who died for all of us on the cross, that now that I have you here, I will take you to Duke Henry as soon as I can; for you must know that I promised this to him ten days ago.' Then he ordered bread and wine to be brought, and insisted on presenting it in person to the king, who, seeing the strength of his forces, did not dare to refuse whatever the earl commanded. When this was over they remounted, went straight on to Rhuddlan, and dined sumptuously in the strong castle there.

(*After the meal the whole party moved on to Flint for the night. Northumberland sent a messenger to Chester to inform Henry of his success, whereupon Henry set out immediately for Flint. At this point Creton switched from verse to prose.*) Now I shall tell you of the capture of the king, without attempting any more rhymes, so that I can relate better the whole conversation that passed between these two at their meeting; for I think I remember it well. So I will set it down in prose ...

I shall treat in this part of the afflictions and sorrows of King Richard in the castle of Flint, where he awaited the arrival of the duke of Lancaster. The duke set out from the city of Chester on Tuesday the 22nd day of August in the year of the incarnation of Our Lord 1399,[10]

---

10 22 August was a Friday in 1399. For discussion of the chronology of these events, see above, pp. 37-40.

with his entire army, the size of which I heard estimated by many knights and esquires at upwards of one hundred thousand men. Along the sea-shore they marched, all drawn up in battle array, full of joy and satisfaction, and eager to lay their hands on their rightful and natural lord King Richard ...

(*Richard and his companions, conversing on the walls of Flint castle, see Henry's army approaching.*) While they were thus lamenting their fate, they saw a large number of people leave Duke Henry's army and spur on their horses towards the castle, to find out what King Richard was doing. In this advance company were the archbishop of Canterbury, Sir Thomas Percy, and the earl of Rutland, whom Duke Henry had demoted from his office of constable of England, and from his dukedom of Aumale, which he had formerly held from King Richard.[11] It is my firm belief, however, that he had only pretended to demote him, in order to try to convince the world that he had not known anything of what had occurred, or acted in any way treacherously, rather than for any other reason. Nevertheless, I do not know for sure whether he was aware of it. Yet I am quite sure that he and Sir Thomas Percy, who had been steward to the king – that is to say in French, grand maître d'hôtel – had set off from the port of Milford taking with them the king's men and his property, as a result of which, as I told you before, they were robbed in Wales; and then, it seems, they had gone over to the duke, for they were among the first to arrive at Flint castle, wearing the livery of Duke Henry, not the hart.

The archbishop entered first, and the others after him. They went up to the keep. Then the king came down from the walls, and they greeted him most respectfully, kneeling on the ground. The king told them to rise, and took the archbishop aside; they talked together for a very long while. What they said I do not know, but the earl of Salisbury told me afterwards that he had generally comforted the king, telling him not to be alarmed, and that no harm would come to his person. The earl of Rutland said nothing at that time, but kept as good a distance as he could from the king, as though he were ashamed to be seen in his presence. Then they mounted their horses again, and returned to Duke Henry, who was now fast approaching; for between the city of Chester and the castle it is only about ten miles, which is equal to five French leagues or thereabouts ...

11 Rutland may already have been effectively, if not nominally, replaced as constable by the earl of Northumberland, but he did not lose his dukedom of Aumale until 3 November.

(*Henry's troops surrounded the castle, but he agreed not to enter until the king had eaten.*) After he had dined, the archbishop of Canterbury and the earl of Northumberland went to look for the duke of Lancaster. He left his men, who were drawn up in fine order in front of the castle, and with about ten or twelve of the greatest lords who were with him, came to the king. At the entrance to the castle, Lancaster, the herald, brought us (*Creton and his companion*) before the duke, where we knelt on the ground: and the herald told him in English that we came from France, and that the king had sent us to accompany King Richard to Ireland for our recreation, and in order to see the country; and he begged him, for the sake of God, to spare our lives. To which the duke replied to us in French, 'My young men, do not fear, nor be alarmed at anything you might see; keep close to me, and I will answer for your lives.' This reply brought us great joy. After this the duke entered the castle, fully armed except his bascinet. Then they made the king, who had dined in the keep, come down to meet Duke Henry, who, as soon as he perceived him in the distance, bowed very low to the ground; as they came closer to each other he bowed a second time, with his cap in his hand; and then the king took off his hood and spoke first, as follows: 'Fair cousin of Lancaster, you are right welcome.' To which Duke Henry replied, bowing very low to the ground, 'My Lord, I have come sooner than you sent for me, and I shall tell you why: it is commonly said among your people that you have, for the last twenty or twenty-two years, governed them very badly and far too harshly, with the result that they are most discontented. If it please our Lord, however, I shall now help you to govern them better than they have been governed in the past.' King Richard answered him, 'If it pleases you, fair cousin, it pleases us as well.' These, I assure you, are the very words that they exchanged, no more and no less; for I heard them, and understood them perfectly well ...

Thus, as you have heard, Duke Henry came to the castle and spoke with the king, and with the bishop of Carlisle and the two knights, Sir Stephen Scrope and Ferriby; to the earl of Salisbury, however, he spoke not a word, but sent a knight to him with a message, which was as follows: 'You may be sure, earl of Salisbury, that since you did not deign to speak to my lord duke of Lancaster when you and he were in Paris last Christmas, so he will not now speak to you.' This greatly disturbed the earl, and struck fear and dread into his heart, for he saw

clearly that the duke mortally hated him.[12] Then Duke Henry called
out in a stern and savage voice, 'Bring the king's horses,' and they
brought him two little horses that were not worth forty francs: the
king mounted one, and the earl of Salisbury the other. Everyone got
on horseback, and we set out from the said castle of Flint, about two
hours after midday.

It was in this way, just as you have heard, that Duke Henry captured
King Richard, his lord; and he brought him with great joy and
satisfaction to Chester which he had left that morning ... When the
duke entered the city of Chester, the common people greeted him with
great respect, praising our Lord and shouting out at their king as if in
mockery. The duke led him straight to the castle, which is a fine and
strong building, and ordered him to be lodged in the keep. Then he
handed him over to the keeping of the sons of the duke of Gloucester
and the earl of Arundel, who hated him more than anybody in the
world, because King Richard had put their fathers to death.[13] He saw
his brother the duke of Exeter there, but he neither dared nor was able
to speak to him. Soon after this the duke sat down to dinner, making
the archbishop of Canterbury sit above him, and placing at some
distance below him the duke of Exeter, brother of King Richard, the
earl of Westmorland, the earl of Rutland, the earl of Northumberland,
and Sir Thomas Percy: all these were seated at Duke Henry's table.
Meanwhile the king stayed in the tower with his good friends the earl
of Salisbury, the bishop of Carlisle, and the two knights; from this time
onwards we were never able to see him, except when we were out in
the open travelling, and we were forbidden to speak to him any more,
or to any of the others.

Duke Henry stayed for three days at Chester, where he held a great
council: they decided that now that the king was taken they had too
many people, and that thirty or forty thousand men would be sufficient
to escort the king to London, otherwise the demands made on the
countryside would be too great, for it had already been considerably
devastated during their advance. So the duke sent most of his followers

12 A reference to the earl of Salisbury's visit to the French court during the winter of
1398-99, when he was charged by Richard II with ensuring that the proposal for a
marriage between Bolingbroke and Mary, the daughter of the duke of Berry, was
abandoned. Froissart (*Chroniques*, xvi, 141-51) states that Salisbury refused to speak
to Bolingbroke at this time, even describing him as a traitor, which greatly annoyed
him.

13 Humphrey, son of the duke of Gloucester, was probably still in Ireland at this time:
see above, Doc. 10.

home. He set out from the city of Chester on the fourth day after the
capture of the king, and took the direct road to London. Soon they
came to Lichfield, a very fine little city. While they were there King
Richard tried to make his escape by letting himself down into the
garden at night from a window of the great tower in which they had
lodged him; but it was not, I think, God's will that he should escape,
for he was spotted and most cruelly forced back into the tower.[14] So
from that time onwards there were always ten or twelve armed men
guarding him throughout the night, with the result that he hardly
slept at all ...

(*Creton and his companion accompanied Henry and Richard to London, from
where, probably in early September, they returned to France.*)

14 There may have been an attempt by some of his Cheshire loyalists to rescue Richard
   at Cholmondeston, near Nantwich (Morgan, *War and Society in Medieval Cheshire*,
   204). It is not clear whether this is the same incident as that referred to here by
   Creton.

14. Two Cistercian accounts of the perjury of Henry Bolingbroke

The attention paid by the Dieulacres chronicler to events in and around Chester during the revolution reinforces the impression that this may originally have been a Chester city chronicle later copied up at Dieulacres abbey. Although the chronicler's account of the meeting at Conway is brief, it provides significant corroboration for Creton's description of the king being tricked into surrender.

The brief extract from the chronicle of Whalley abbey which follows has not been printed before, but contains a number of verbal echoes from both the Kirkstall chronicle (above, Doc. 12[a]) and the Dieulacres chronicle, suggesting that manuscripts may have been exchanged between these Cistercian houses. The Whalley chronicle also includes an interesting explanation, unmentioned elsewhere, of the king's sudden and rather puzzling desertion of his army in South Wales – namely that it was because he had been warned that he was about to be seized, though by whom is not stated.

(a) According to the Dieulacres chronicler

Source: Dieulacres Chronicle, 170-3

Language: Latin

On the vigil of the feast of St Lawrence (*9 August*) the duke (*of Lancaster*) arrived with his army at Chester; God knows in what spirit the citizens received him. Even so, he granted them his peace, and had this proclaimed at the high cross, and he made an announcement that they would not kill anyone, or burn or destroy anything, or seize anything except victuals for themselves and fodder for their beasts. But those robbers did not keep their word: both within the city and without they seized enormous riches, devastating the countryside and secretly carrying things off with them, smashing open wine-casks and emptying them, making off everywhere with treasure and all sorts of other things which had been buried in the ground. They even destroyed the corn and slaughtered the cattle – young and old alike – in the fields and meadows, leaving the carcasses to lie there; ladders, chests, harrows, and all the other implements so essential to rural life, they burned everywhere. And for this they have incurred the wrath of God, etc..[1]

At the same time, for no good reason, the duke ordered Peter de Leigh's head to be struck off and placed above the east gate of the city. May God have mercy on his soul! His body was buried in the church of the Carmelite friars at Chester, but when in the following year the people rose up against the magnates in protest at a tax, they reinterred the head together with his body.[2]

In the same year, about the time of the feast of St Peter ad Vincula (*1 August*), King Richard heard in Ireland that the duke's rebellion was gathering its treacherous pace; but acting upon foolish advice he tarried there a long while, allowing his enemy to raise the whole kingdom against him, so that by the time he crossed to Carmarthen in Wales his army had scattered and only a few remained with him. This king had seven warlike and worthy esquires from Cheshire, and each of them had about eighty locally-chosen men specially appointed to form the most secure of bodyguards for the king. Their names were John de Leigh del Bothes, Thomas Cholmely, Ralph Davenport, Adam Bostok, John Downe, Thomas Beston and Thomas Holford.[3] On their shoulders they wore the royal badge of the white hart resplendent, but among the common people there was much talk of the extortions practised by them. Because of this the innocent king was, through no fault of his own, held in fatal odium by his ordinary subjects.

When the king was told how large the duke's army was, and that almost everybody had gone over to him, rumour has it that he set off secretly in the middle of the night, accompanied by only about fifteen companions, to Harlech castle, and from there to Caernarvon, Beaumaris and Conway, passing his time between them, now in one

1 See the similar account in Adam Usk's chronicle (below, Doc. 15).

2 The chronicler is referring here to the revolt in Cheshire which accompanied the ill-fated 'Epiphany Rising' of January 1400, for which see McNiven, 'The Cheshire rising of January 1400', 375-96.

3 According to the exchequer's list of the king's Cheshire bodyguard, these seven each had between forty-four and fourty-six 'archers of the crown' in his watch (*vigilia*). The leaders of the watches are correctly named here, except that Cholmely was called Richard, not Thomas. Thomas Cholmely was a member of Richard Cholmely's watch, and had custody of the bridge at Holt (P.R.O. E101/402/10, mm.2-5).

and now in another. Next morning the steward of the king's household awoke and, finding the king gone, informed his servants that he had fled; then, deceitfully, he broke his rod of office and advised each of them to save himself as best he could. Thus were they all scattered, and the Welsh despoiled them to a man, so it was only with difficulty that they got back to their homes.

Meanwhile the duke, hearing that the king was at Conway, sent a deputation to the king asking him to agree to present himself voluntarily to the duke, in his capacity as steward of England by hereditary right, and, under safe conduct, to the commons.[4] The archbishop of Canterbury and the earl of Northumberland, acting as chief negotiators, both promised – indeed they both swore upon the sacrament of the body of Christ – that King Richard would be permitted to retain his royal power and dominion. On this understanding, therefore, as well as other undertakings that were not honoured, the king three days later, of his own free will, handed himself over to them. But once they had reached Flint castle, all these undertakings meant nothing, for here they denied their fine promises, and began to treat their lord like a prisoner, or a servant. Thus did they move off towards Chester, and through Cheshire and on to London. Then, indeed, were those royal badges both of the hart and of the crown hidden away, so that some said that the esquires of the duke of Lancaster, wearing their collars, had been pre-ordained by a prophecy to subdue like greyhounds in this year the pride of that hated beast the white hart.

This same year, on the feast of St Michael the archangel (*29 September*), serious accusations were brought against the king by both lords and commons at a parliament held in London, with the intention of securing his deposition. According to rumour he asked not to be brought into parliament in so humble a condition, but instead, simply placing his royal crown upon the ground, he resigned his rights to God.

---

4 This sentence is obscure. The latin reads: 'Interea dux regem audiens apud Conway prestolari misit legacionem ut se sponte duci tunc Anglie senescallo iure hereditario et communibus secure presentarent.' Sherborne, 'Perjury and the Lancastrian revolution', 232, thought that 'presentarent' was a copyist's error for 'presentaret', thus translating the sentence much as above. For a possible different translation, see Taylor, *English Historical Literature*, 191.

(b) According to the chronicle of Whalley abbey

Source: British Library, Harley MS. 3600, folios 232v-233

Language: Latin

Hearing that the lord king had gone to Ireland along with the great men of the realm, the aforesaid duke of Hereford, who had been sent into exile, arrived in a certain boat near Bridlington in Holderness,[5] together with Lord Thomas Arundel archbishop of Canterbury, also then an exile, and the son and heir of the earl of Arundel. Moving on from there he came to Pickering castle and then to Pontefract castle, while every day great numbers of commoners and other people came to join him. The earls of Northumberland and Westmorland and the noble Lord Henry Percy also brought a great crowd of people to join him, and once they had all assembled together they marched on to Bristol, where they struck off the heads of that trio of traitors to the realm, Lord William le Scrope earl of Wiltshire, Lord John Bussy, and Lord Henry Green. Soon after this the king, returning from Ireland, landed not far away, but, warned by some person that he was going to be seized on the following night by enemies who were lying in wait nearby, he secretly slipped away into Wales. Following this the duke with his accomplices moved on to Chester. The lord King Richard, having been promised his safety on an oath taken by Lord Thomas Arundel and the earl of Northumberland, came to Chester in order to parley, but the said duke of Hereford, contrary to the aforesaid oath, seized King Richard there and, taking him to London, put him under guard in the Tower of London until such time as he would resign to him the crown of the realm together with all the rights pertaining to it.

5 For the use of this phrase see above, Doc. 12(a).

15. An eyewitness account of the revolution: the chronicle of Adam Usk

Source: Adam Usk, 174-86

Language: Latin

Although he joined Bolingbroke's army towards the end of July, and even sat on the committee set up to determine the grounds upon which the usurpation was to be justified, Adam Usk provides an account of the revolution which is refreshingly free from the soothing platitudes of Lancastrian propaganda. Moreover, the fact that he was an eyewitness and so closely involved in the proceedings naturally gives his narrative additional value. Thus when a so-called 'Lancastrian' chronicler criticises Bolingbroke for devastating the land around Chester, or states that he had to surround Flint castle with his army because the king 'would not come forth', or rejects so decisively Bolingbroke's claim to the throne on the basis of the 'Crouchback legend', he demands to be listened to more carefully than a Ricardian supporter conveying similar information. Also included in the following extract is Usk's famous description of his visit to the Tower on 21 September, where he found the king musing disconsolately on his former glory and current misfortunes; a sight which profoundly touched Adam.

The extracts below are from the printed translation of Usk's chronicle by E. M. Thompson.

Two days before the end of July (*Bolingbroke*) arrived at Bristol, and there he struck off the heads of Sir William le Scrope, the king's treasurer, and Sir John Bussy and Sir Henry Green, knights, the king's most evil councillors and the chief fosterers of his malice. There was I, the writer of this chronicle, present with my lord of Canterbury late returned; and I, through favour, made peace between the duke and the lordship of Usk, the place of my birth, which he had determined to harry, on account of the resistance of the lady of that place, the king's niece, there ordered; and I also got Sir Edward de Charlton, then husband of that lady, to be taken into the duke's following;[1] and I caused all the people of Usk, who for the said resistance had gathered at Montstarri, to their great joy to return to their own homes.

At length the duke came to Hereford with his host, on the second day of August, and lodged in the bishop's palace; and on the morrow he moved towards Chester, and passed the night in the priory at Leominster. The next night he spent at Ludlow, in the king's castle, not sparing the wine which was therein stored. At this place, I, who am now writing, obtained from the duke and from my lord of Canterbury the release of brother Thomas Prestbury, master in theology, a man of my day at Oxford and a monk of Shrewsbury, who was kept in prison by King Richard, for that he had righteously preached certain things against his follies; and I also got him promotion to the abbacy of his house.[2] Then, passing through Shrewsbury, the duke tarried there two days; where he made proclamation that the host should march on Chester, but should spare the people and the country, because by mediation they had submitted themselves to him. Wherefore many who coveted that land for plunder departed to their homes. But little good did the proclamation do for the country, as will be seen. The reasons why the duke decided to invade that country were: because, abetting the king, as has been said, it ceased not to molest the realm for the space of two whole years with murders, adulteries, thefts, pillage, and other unbearable wrongs; and because it had risen up against the said duke and against his coming, threatening to destroy him. Another cause was on account of the right of exemption of that country, wherein the inhabitants, however criminal elsewhere, and others entangled in debt or crime, were wont to be harboured, as in a nest of wickedness; so that the whole realm cried vengeance on them.

On the ninth day of August,[3] the duke with his host entered the county of Chester, and there, in the parish of Coddington and other neighbouring parishes, taking up his camping ground and pitching his tents, nor sparing meadow nor cornfield, pillaging all the country round, and keeping strict watch against the wiles of the men of Chester, he passed the night. And I, the writer of this chronicle, spent a not uncheerful

---

1 Edward succeeded his brother John as Lord Charlton of Powys in 1401, and died in 1421; he had just married (in June 1399) Eleanor, daughter of Thomas Holand earl of Kent (d. 1397), Richard II's half-brother.

2 Thomas Prestbury had been arrested in April 1399. His election as abbot of Shrewsbury was confirmed on 17 August, at Chester (*CPR, 1396-9*, 584, 592).

3 Usk probably meant to say the eighth of August.

night in the tent of the lord of Powis. Many in neighbouring places, drinking of the poisoned cups given to them by the people of Chester, perished. There also, from divers water-cisterns, which the men probed with spears, and from other hiding-places, vessels and much other goods were drawn forth and taken for plunder, I being present with the finders ...

(*Bolingbroke reached Chester on 9 August and, according to Usk, remained there twelve days.*) On the eve of the Assumption of the Blessed Virgin (*14 August*), my lord of Canterbury and the earl of Northumberland went away to the king at the castle of Conway, to treat with him on the duke's behalf; and the king, on condition of saving his dignity, promised to surrender to the duke at the castle of Flint. And so, delivering up to them his two crowns, valued at one hundred thousand marks, with other countless treasure, he straightaway set forth to Flint. There the duke coming to him with twenty thousand chosen men – the rest of his host being left behind to guard his quarters and the country and castle and city of Chester – sought the king within the castle, for he would not come forth [girding it round with his armed men on the one side and with his archers on the other; whereby was fulfilled the prophecy: 'The white king shall array his host in form of a shield'].[4] And he led him away prisoner to Chester castle, where he delivered him into safe keeping. Thus, too, he placed in custody certain lords, taken along with the king, to be kept till the parliament which was to begin on the morrow of Michaelmas-day.

While the duke was then at Chester, three of the twenty-four aldermen of the city of London, on behalf of the same city, together with fifty other citizens, came to the duke, and recommended their city to him, under their common seal, renouncing their fealty to king Richard. They told, too, how the citizens had gathered in arms to Westminster abbey to search for the king, hearing that he had in secret fled thither; and that, not finding him there, they had ordered to be kept in custody, till parliament, Roger Walden, Nicholas Slake, and Ralph Selby, the king's special councillors, whom they did find.[5] And so the duke,

4 The words in square brackets were inserted in the margin of the manuscript in a different hand. The prophecy referred to is from the 'Propheta Aquilae' (Adam Usk, 28, 179).

5 Usk's story of a deputation to Bolingbroke from the Londoners is supported by some other chronicles, though it is not clear where the meeting took place: see C. Barron, 'The deposition of Richard II', in *Politics and Crisis in Fourteenth-Century England*, ed. J. Taylor and W. Childs (1990), 142-3. Roger Walden replaced Thomas Arundel as archbishop of Canterbury in 1397, but was deprived of his see

having gloriously, within fifty days, conquered both king and king-dom, marched to London; and there he placed the captive king in the Tower, under fitting guard.

Meanwhile the duke sent to Ireland for his eldest son Henry, and for Humphrey, son of the duke of Gloucester, who had been imprisoned in the castle of Trim by King Richard. And when they had been sent over to him, along with great treasure belonging to the king, the said Humphrey, having been poisoned in Ireland, as was said, by the lord Despenser, died, to the great grief of the land, on his coming to the island of Anglesey in Wales.[6] But the duke's son came safe to his father, and brought with him in chains Sir William Bagot, a knight of low degree, who had been raised by the king to high places ...

Next, the matter of setting aside King Richard, and of choosing Henry, duke of Lancaster, in his stead, and how it was to be done and for what reasons, was judicially committed to be debated on by certain doctors, bishops and others, of whom I, who am now noting down these things, was one. And it was found by us that perjuries, sacrileges, unnatural crimes, exactions from his subjects, reduction of his people to slavery, cowardice and weakness of rule – with all of which crimes King Richard was known to be tainted – were reasons enough for setting him aside, in accordance with the chapter: 'Ad apostolicae dignitatis,' under the title: 'De re judicata,' in the Sextus;[7] and, although he was ready himself to yield up the crown, yet for better security was it determined, for the aforesaid reasons, that he should be deposed by the authority of the clergy and people; for which purpose they were summoned.

On St Matthew's day (*21 September*), just two years after the beheading of the earl of Arundel, I, the writer of this history, was in the Tower, wherein King Richard was a prisoner, and I was present when he dined, and I marked his mood and bearing, having been taken thither for that very purpose by Sir William Beauchamp.[8] And there and then

following the revolution; he later became bishop of London (1404-6). Slake was a clerk of the household, a royal favourite of long standing, while Selby was a lawyer and a member of the royal council since 1393 (Given-Wilson, *Royal Household*, 175-80).

6 Usk appears to be reporting malicious rumour here; nowhere else is Despenser accused of poisoning Humphrey.

7 The reference is to the sentence of deposition imposed by Pope Innocent IV against the Holy Roman Emperor, Frederick II, in 1245.

8 William Beauchamp, Lord Abergavenny (1392-1411), brother of the earl of Warwick.

the king discoursed sorrowfully in these words: 'My God!, a wonderful land is this, and a fickle; which hath exiled, slain, destroyed or ruined so many kings, rulers, and great men, and is ever tainted and toileth with strife and variance and envy;' and then he recounted the histories and names of sufferers from the earliest habitation of the kingdom. Perceiving then the trouble of his mind, and how that none of his own men, nor such as were wont to serve him, but strangers who were but spies upon him, were appointed to his service, and musing on his ancient and wonted glory and on the fickle fortune of the world, I departed thence much moved at heart.

One day, in a council held by the said doctors, the point was raised by some, that by the right of descent from the person of Edmund, earl of Lancaster – they declaring that the same Edmund was the eldest son of King Henry the third, but that, on account of his mental weakness, his birthright had been set aside and his younger brother Edward preferred in his place – Richard's succession in the direct line was barred.[9] As to this, see the history in the pedigree, known throughout England, that Edward was first-born son of King Henry, and that after him, and before Edmund, Margaret, who was afterwards queen of Scotland, was born to the same king ... (*several chronicle excerpts are then given by Usk, demonstrating that Edward I was indeed the first-born son of Henry III*) ...

---

9 This is the so-called 'Crouchback legend', for which see also John Hardyng's chronicle (below, Doc. 19). In fact Edward I was born in 1239, Margaret in 1240, and Edmund in 1245.

16. The 'Manner of King Richard's Renunciation'

Source: Corpus Christi College, Cambridge, MS. 59, ff. 230v-231, printed in G. O. Sayles, 'The deposition of Richard II: three Lancastrian narratives', *Bulletin of the Institute of Historical Research* (1981), 257-70.

Language: French

This document, which describes the deposition proceedings in the Tower of London and at Westminster abbey between 28 and 30 September 1399, was first printed by Professor Sayles in 1981. Sayles described it as a 'Lancastrian narrative': in other words, he thought it to be a deliberately propagandist piece written by one of Bolingbroke's supporters and circulated by the Lancastrian regime with the express intention of justifying Henry's usurpation. As such, it would need to be treated with great caution. In fact there is much to indicate that this is not a Lancastrian propagandist tract but an independent memorandum compiled by one of those who witnessed the proceedings which it describes, possibly Thomas Chillenden, prior of Canterbury cathedral.[1] There are a number of points at which it diverges markedly from, for example, the blatantly propagandist 'Record and Process': most notably, its assertion that the king at first refused utterly to abdicate, and its statement that Henry claimed the throne as the 'nearest male heir' to Richard. As an account of both the negotiations preceding the deposition and of the ceremony of deposition itself, therefore, it deserves to be given a considerable degree of credence.

The manner of King Richard's renunciation, and of the election of King Henry the Fourth since the Conquest, etc.

Firstly, on Sunday the eve of Michaelmas (*28 September*), after dinner, the following people were, with the assent of all the great council of

---

1 C. Given-Wilson, 'The manner of King Richard's renunciation: a "Lancastrian narrative"?', *EHR* (1993).

England, sent to King Richard, who was then in the Tower of London:
the archbishop of York and the bishop of Hereford for bishops, the
earls of Northumberland and Westmorland for earls, Lord Despenser
– the former earl of Gloucester – and Lord Bergavenny for barons, Sir
Thomas Gray and Sir Thomas Erpingham for knights, Master
Thomas Stow and Master John Burbach, doctors, and Master Denis
Lopham and Master John Ferriby, notaries.[2] This was in order to
ascertain from the king, on behalf of the aforesaid council, whether he
was willing to resign all the right that he had to the crown of England
with its appurtenances, as he had previously promised to them that he
would. The king said in reply that he would prefer first of all to see in
writing the form of the resignation by which he was supposed to
resign. Whereupon they handed him a bill in which it was explained
how he had to resign all the right that he had to the crown of England
and its appurtenances, that is to say, in the kingdoms of England,
France, Ireland and Scotland, the duchies of Guyenne and Normandy,
the county of Ponthieu, and the town of Calais, and in all the other
castles, fortresses and towns which he either held at present or claimed
by right, both on this side of the sea and beyond it, and in every part
of them, for himself and his heirs in perpetuity. To which he replied by
saying that he wished to consider this until the following morning.

On the feast of Michaelmas, therefore, at nine o'clock in the morning,
the same lords came to the Tower, and with them the prior of
Christchurch Canterbury, and they asked him if he had considered
sufficiently what his reply to the aforesaid bill would be. He replied
shortly that he would not do it under any circumstances; and he was
greatly incensed, and declared that he would like to have it explained
to him how it was that he could resign the crown, and to whom. Later,
however, after various additional arguments had been put forward and
explained to him there by the aforesaid lords, he said, 'Bring my dear
cousin of Lancaster here, for I am willing, upon certain conditions
which I shall explain to him, to make my resignation to him.'

Whereupon, after dinner on that same day, the duke of Lancaster, the
earls of Northumberland and Westmorland, and a large number of
other barons, knights and esquires, rode through Cheap to the Tower,
where the archbishops of Canterbury and York, the bishop of
Hereford, the abbot of Westminster, the prior of Christchurch Canterbury, and various other spiritual clerks were at that time waiting. And

2 For details of the various deputations sent to the king, see the footnotes to the
'Record and Process' (below, Doc. 17).

there the king was asked if he was willing to resign all the right that
he had to the crown of England and its appurtenances, as set out in the
bill of resignation handed to him. To which the king replied that he
would do it willingly in the interests of his dear cousin the duke of
Lancaster, upon certain conditions which he would state. He was told
by them, however, that there was no way in which this could be done;
he must do it simply, without any conditions. Whereupon the king
picked up the aforesaid bill himself and read it out with good cheer,
loudly and clearly, thus resigning to the duke of Lancaster all the right
that he had to the crown of England and its appurtenances, together
with all other lands apart from the lands and tenements which he had
bought from Roger Walden and from Sir William Scrope, the former
treasurer of England, with which to endow a yearly anniversary for his
soul at Westminster abbey;[3] the latter having been allowed to him in
the presence of all the aforesaid lords. And upon this the names of
certain witnesses were entered as of record, namely the archbishop of
York and the bishop of Hereford, bishops, the earl of Northumberland
and the earl of Westmorland, earls, the aforesaid Lord Despenser and
Lord Bergavenny, barons, the prior of Christchurch Canterbury and
the abbot of Westminster for abbots, Sir Thomas Gray and Sir
Thomas Erpingham, knights, Master Thomas Stow and Master John
Burbach, doctors, and Master Denis Lopham and Master John
Ferriby, notaries, who were required to draw up a formal instrument
of this. Thus was the first summons to parliament withdrawn.[4]

And then on the Tuesday, at nine o'clock, the duke of Lancaster came
to Westminster. The abbot of that abbey and all his monks, fittingly
apparelled, came as far as the gate to the cemetery to meet him in
solemn procession, and began the response, 'Honor, Virtus', etc., and
then he entered the church and heard a mass of the Holy Spirit, which
was solemnly sung by all the archbishops and bishops in ceremonial
dress. And when the mass was finished he entered the great hall at
Westminster, between twelve and one o'clock, with Sir Thomas
Erpingham going ahead of him carrying his splendidly decorated and

---

3 According to the *Vita Ricardi Secundi*, Richard had acquired lands and rents to the
value of 500 marks with which to endow an obit at Westminster abbey. Another
document states that it was from Richard le Scrope, William's father, rather than
from William himself, that the king had acquired these lands, and does not mention
Walden (Sayles, 'Three Lancastrian narratives', 266).

4 Writs summoning a parliament to meet on 30 September had been sent out from
Chester on 19 August, in the king's name (*CCR, 1396-9*, 520-1), but since a
parliament could only meet at the king's request, and England no longer had a king,
they had now to be withdrawn.

bejewelled sword; at which time the crowd of people there was so great
that it filled not only the hall itself but also the adjacent courtyard
outside. In the hall there was a splendid throne, beautifully decorated
with cloth of gold as befits a king.

When the duke of Lancaster had passed through the barriers into the
area which had been designated for the parliament, he took his place
on the same parliamentary seat that his father, as duke of Lancaster,
had occupied in former parliaments, that is to say, next to the bishop
of Carlisle. Present there at that time were nearly all the bishops of
England, as well as earls and other lords of parliament – the
Appellants among them[5] – all sitting in their usual parliamentary
seats. Then the archbishop of York began a collation, taking for his
theme, 'Posuit verba sua in os meum', etc.,[6] in which he explained the
reasons for King Richard's resignation and the way in which it had
been done. When this was over Master John Burbach read out King
Richard's resignation, using the same bill that the king had used; and
when this was done, the archbishop of Canterbury addressed a general
request to all the lords, spiritual and temporal, and all the other
commons assembled there, asking them whether they agreed with this;
and they shouted out in a loud voice, 'Yes, yes, yes.' After this Master
John Ferriby, notary, read out from a list all the points which had been
given as reasons for his deposition: namely those things which he had
done which were contrary to the crown, his royal majesty, his oath,
and the law of the land; the vengeful sentences of death and exile and
other judgements passed against his lords, the peers of the realm,
without the assent of their peers or due process of law; and several
other points, including the will which he had made when he was about
to go to Ireland, by which he had planned and done great damage to
the kingdom. Then the archbishop of Canterbury asked all the people
if they were prepared to agree to the aforesaid deposition for the
reasons given, and they all cried out in a loud voice, throughout the
hall, 'Yes, yes, yes.' The same archbishop then asked all the people if
they wished to agree to the establishment of a procuracy whereby
certain people would surrender all their liege homage to the said King
Richard, and depose him; and they cried out in a loud voice throughout
the hall, 'Yes, yes, yes.' Whereupon the following were then appointed
proctors to do this: the bishop of St Asaph, the earl of Westmorland,

5 That is, the appellants of 1397, those who had appealed Gloucester, Arundel and
  Warwick.

6 Isaiah, 51:16.

the abbot of Glastonbury, the Lord Despenser, Sir Thomas Erpingham, and Master John Burbach, doctor; they were to surrender their
liege homage and depose him as aforesaid, in the name of all the estates
of the realm. The bishop of St Asaph then publicly read out the
procuracy; and thus was the crown vacant.

Then the duke of Lancaster rose from his seat, crossed himself on the
forehead and chest, and read out in a loud voice a bill which explained
the various reasons why he claimed the kingdom of England, as the
nearest male heir and worthiest blood-descendant of the good King
Henry the third, son of King John; and in the same bill he set out the
whole pedigree establishing his lineal descent from the said King
Henry right down to himself. The treasurer of England[7] then asked
each of the lords spiritual individually if he would agree to the duke of
Lancaster becoming king, and each of them, for his own part, gave his
assent. The earl of Northumberland then asked each of the lords
temporal individually if he would agree to the same request, and each
of them gave the same answer. Whereupon the duke of Lancaster, who
had remained seated all this time, said, 'My lords spiritual and
temporal assembled here, we beg you not simply to speak these words
with your mouths if they do not come from your hearts, but to agree
to them with your hearts as well as your mouths. Nevertheless, should
it happen that some of you do not in your hearts assent to this, that
would be no great surprise to me.' Whereupon they all said, 'Yes, yes,
yes.' At this the archbishops of Canterbury and York, and also the
duke of York, rose from their seats, kissed his hands, and led him up
to the throne. When he came to the throne, he went down on his knees
and said a prayer; then when he had done this, he made the sign of the
cross on the front and the back of the throne, and then, to the great joy
of all the people, who cried out loudly both inside the hall and outside,
they sat him down on the aforesaid throne as king.

Then the archbishop of Canterbury began a collation, taking as his
theme, 'Vir fortis dominabitur populo', etc.,[8] in which he expounded
upon the way in which a king ought to live and to govern his people
and kingdom, and upon what is appropriate to royal government.
When this collation was over, the chancellor of England[9] surrendered
his seal to King Henry, the treasurer surrendered his office, the
constable of England – namely the earl of Northumberland – surren-

7 John Norbury, treasurer from 3 September 1399 to 31 May 1401.

8 I Samuel, 9:17.

9 John Scarle, chancellor from 5 September 1399 to 9 March 1401.

dered his mace, and the marshal – the earl of Westmorland –
surrendered his baton; whereupon the king promptly gave back to
each of them, as his own newly-created officers, his office and his
charge. Then the archbishop of Canterbury announced that the king
would be crowned with fitting solemnity at Westminster on Monday
the feast of St Edward (*13 October*); and, at the king's command, the
same archbishop publicly summoned the parliament to reconvene on
the Monday next following (*6 October*). Thus ended the day, and the
lords then rose, at which time it was between three and four o'clock in
the afternoon.

17. 'The Record and Process'

Sources: RP, iii, 415-53; Annales Ricardi Secundi, 252-87

Language: Latin

The 'Record and Process' is the 'official' version of what occurred in the Tower of London and at Westminster abbey between 29 September and 1 October 1399. It is, as has long been recognised, a version of events which placed the need to justify the usurpation above the demands of truth: the bland tale which it tells of Richard's voluntary abdication at Conway, and of his cheerful acceptance of his fate in the Tower, is so at odds with what other sources tell us that it makes it difficult to use the descriptive passages of the 'Record and Process' with any real degree of confidence. On the other hand, the thirty-three charges against the king which form the central portion of the document have been subjected to detailed scrutiny by historians, and several of them have been found to contain a considerable element of truth. Whether they constitute a true record of the charges actually read out on 30 September is, however, a different matter. The 'Record and Process' itself states that only 'the greater part' of the charges were read out, and at least one of them (the 33rd) shows clear signs of having been added to at a later date. This naturally raises the question of how much else in the 'Record and Process' was tampered with before the Lancastrians considered it fit for circulation. For example, was Archbishop Arundel really present at Conway? And did Bolingbroke really claim the throne in the words reported here, or did he, as the 'Manner of King Richard's Renunciation' states, claim it as Richard's nearest male heir (above, Doc. 16)? If, as Professor Sayles believed, the 'Record and Process' was not drawn up in its final form until several months later, that would have allowed ample opportunity for the sort of rewriting which might have made it palatable to those who had doubts.

The existence of such doubts is indicated not only by the two documents which follow this (Docs 18 and 19), but also by comparison with the text of the 'Record and Process' given by Thomas Walsingham. Not content with enrolling it on the Rolls of Parliament, the Lancastrian regime also circulated the 'Record and Process' to certain monastic houses (though not many, it seems) for insertion in their chronicles, and Walsingham used it as the basis of his account of the deposition proceedings. However, he also inserted into it two brief but revealing passages which throw light upon the nature of Richard's 'abdication' and Henry's claim. The passages in question are given below in square brackets.

The Record and Process of the renunciation of King Richard the Second since the Conquest and of the acceptance of the same renunciation, together with the deposition of the same King Richard, here follow:

Be it remembered that at about nine o'clock on Monday the feast of St Michael the Archangel, in the twenty-third year of the reign of King Richard II (*29 September 1399*), the lords spiritual and temporal and other great persons, namely Richard le Scrope archbishop of York, John bishop of Hereford, Henry earl of Northumberland, Ralph earl of Westmorland, Hugh Lord Burnell, Thomas Lord Berkeley, the prior of Canterbury, the abbot of Westminster, Sir William Thirning and John Markham, justices, Thomas Stowe and John Burbach, doctors of law, Thomas Erpingham and Thomas Gray, knights, and William Ferriby and Denis Lopham, notaries public,[1] who had initially been deputed, with the consent and counsel of the lords spiritual and temporal, the justices, and others learned in civil and canon law and in the laws of the kingdom gathered together in the usual meeting-place of the Council at Westminster, to undertake the following act, came into the presence of the said King Richard in the Tower of London. And there, in the same king's presence, it was recited by the earl of Northumberland, acting on behalf of and with the permission of all the aforesaid, how the same king at an earlier time, at Conway in North Wales, being then at liberty, had promised lord Thomas archbishop of Canterbury and the aforesaid earl of Northumberland that he was

---

1 The composition of the deputations to Richard in the Tower is a topic on which there has been some debate: Sayles, 'Three Lancastrian narratives', 260-3, doubted whether the two justices, Thirning and Markham, were really present, suggesting that their names were added later in order 'to assert that the English judiciary did more than acquiesce in the revolution and that they approved.' However, it is difficult to believe that the prominent part ascribed to Thirning in the 'Record and Process' is purely (as Sayles put it) 'imaginary'. It is worth noting that Sir John Markham had been one of Bolingbroke's retainers since 1393 (S. J. Payling, *Political Society in Lancastrian England* (1991), 39).

willing to yield up and renounce his crowns of England and France and his royal majesty, on account of his own inability and insufficiency, which he himself admitted there; which was to be done in the best manner and form that could be devised according to the counsel of learned men. In reply to this, and in the presence of the aforesaid lords and others, the king replied easily that he was willing to carry out what he had formerly promised in this regard; he wished, however, to speak with his kinsmen Henry duke of Lancaster and the aforesaid archbishop before thus fulfilling his promise. He also asked to be given a copy of the Cession made by him, that he might study it for a while; a copy was therefore given to him, and the said lords and others returned to their lodgings.

Later on that same day, after dinner, after the king had grown impatient for the arrival of the duke of Lancaster, who delayed a long time, at length the duke of Lancaster, the lords and other persons named above, and the archbishop of Canterbury, came into the king's presence in the Tower, where Lords Roos, Willoughby, and Bergavenny were also present. And after the king had spoken apart for a while with the said duke and archbishop of Canterbury, with whom, it seemed to those present, he conversed with a cheerful expression, he at length called forward all who were there and announced to them that he was ready to perform the Cession and Renunciation which he had promised. And although he was informed that, in order to save him the trouble of reading such a lengthy document, he could allow his Cession and Renunciation, which was written down on a parchment schedule, to be read out for him by others, nevertheless he himself, willingly and, so it seemed, with a cheerful expression, took the schedule in his hands and announced that he wished to read it himself; and, quite distinctly, he read it out. Thus did he absolve his liegemen, and renounce, and yield up, and this he swore, and indeed he added further remarks and enlargements during the reading, and he signed it at the foot with his own hand, as can be clearly seen on the aforesaid schedule, the tenor of which follows in these words:

> In the name of God, amen. I, Richard, by the grace of God king of England and France and lord of Ireland, absolve all my archbishops, bishops, and other prelates of the church in the said kingdoms and dominions whatsoever, both secular and regular, of whatever dignity, degree, estate or condition they be, and all my dukes, marquises, earls, barons, knights, vassals, vavasours, and all my other liegemen whatsoever, whether ecclesiastical or secular, by whatever name they might be described, from their Oath of Fealty and Homage and any other oaths to me which they

have taken, together with all bonds of allegiance, regality, and lordship, or of any other kind, by which they are or have been bound to me ... And by these words I fully, willingly, directly, and totally renounce my right to the rule, governance and administration of these kingdoms and dominions, and all and every type of power and jurisdiction in them, together with the name, honour, regality and majesty of kingship ... Saving the rights of my successors as kings of England in these kingdoms and dominions in all the foregoing for all time ..., I confess, acknowledge, recognise, and from my own certain knowledge truly admit that I have been and am entirely inadequate and unequal to the task of ruling and governing the aforesaid kingdoms and dominions and all that pertains to them, and that, on account of my notorious insufficiencies, I deserve to be deposed from them. And I swear upon these Holy Gospels, physically held here by me in person, that I shall never contravene the aforesaid Renunciation, Resignation, Demission and Cession, nor in any way, by word or deed, on my own behalf or, so far as I am able, through any other person, either openly or secretly challenge them, or allow them to be challenged; but I shall regard the same Renunciation, Resignation, Demission and Cession as established and accepted by me in perpetuity, and shall firmly hold and observe them in each and every part, as God and these Holy Gospels shall judge me. Written by me, the aforesaid King Richard, with my own hand.

And immediately the same king added to this Renunciation and Cession in his own words that, were it in his power, he should like the duke of Lancaster to succeed him to the throne. Yet, since his power to decide such things, as he himself said, was now minimal, he asked the aforesaid archbishop of York and bishop of Hereford, whom he also appointed as his spokesmen to convey and announce his Cession and Renunciation to the estates of the realm, that they should declare his will and intention in this matter too to the people. And as a sign of his will and intention he publicly removed from his finger his golden signet ring, and placed it on the aforesaid duke's finger, declaring that he wished this deed of his to be made known to all the estates of the realm.[2] When this had been done, all who were there bade him farewell and left the Tower to return to their lodgings.

On the following day, Tuesday the feast of St Jerome, in the great hall at Westminster, which had been suitably prepared for the holding of a parliament, in the presence of the aforesaid archbishops of Canterbury and York, the duke of Lancaster, and the other dukes and lords both spiritual and temporal whose names are written above, as well as a great assembly of the people of the realm gathered there for the

2 The signet was the personal seal of the king, and a symbol of kingship.

G

holding of parliament, with the duke of Lancaster occupying his proper and accustomed place, and the royal throne, solemnly bedecked with cloth of gold, standing vacant and without any president, the aforesaid archbishop of York and bishop of Hereford, in accordance with the king's injunction, publicly announced that the Cession and Renunciation had indeed been made by the king, and that he had signed it with his own hand, and had handed over his own signet; and they caused the Cession and Renunciation to be read out there, first in Latin and then in English. Whereupon the estates and people there present were immediately asked by the archbishop of Canterbury, who, on account of the dignity and prerogative of his metropolitan church of Canterbury, has the privilege of speaking before all the other prelates and magnates of the realm in such matters, if they wished, for their own welfare and for the good of the realm, to accept that same Renunciation and Cession. To which the same estates and people replied that, considering the reasons given by the king himself in that Renunciation and Cession, it seemed most expedient to them, and, unanimously and without dissent, they accepted the Renunciation and Cession, each one singly, and then jointly together with the people. Following this acceptance it was publicly declared there that, as well as accepting this Cession and Renunciation, it would be of great benefit and advantage to the realm if, in order to remove any scruple or malevolent suspicion, the many wrongs and shortcomings so frequently committed by the said king in his government of the kingdom, which, as he himself confessed in his Cession, had rendered him worthy of deposition, were to be set down in writing in the form of articles, publicly read out, and announced to the people. The greater part of these articles was thus publicly read out; of which the full tenor is as follows: (*There follows a copy of Richard's coronation oath.*)

Here follow the charges against the King, for which he was deposed[3]

(1) Firstly, the king is charged for his evil government, namely, that he gave the goods and possessions of the crown to unworthy persons, and otherwise indiscreetly dissipated them, as a result of which he had

---

3 For more generalised discussion of the charges against the king see A. Tuck, *Richard II and the English Nobility* (1972), Chapter 7; Given-Wilson, *Royal Household*, 246-51; Barron, 'Tyranny of Richard II'.

to impose needlessly grievous and intolerable burdens upon the people, and committed innumerable other crimes. By his assent and command, certain prelates and other temporal lords were chosen and assigned by the whole parliament to labour faithfully at their own costs for the just government of the kingdom; the king, however, made an agreement with his supporters, proposing to impeach of high treason the said lords spiritual and temporal thus employed about the government of the kingdom, and coerced the justices of the realm with threats of life and limb to confirm his wicked plans, intending to destroy the said lords.[4]

(2) Item: the king when he was formerly at Shrewsbury caused to come before him and others that supported him, in a chamber, various persons including the majority of the justices, where, through fear and threats, he induced, compelled, and forced them each to answer certain questions on his behalf concerning the laws of the kingdom, against their will, and otherwise than they would have answered had they not been under compulsion but at liberty; by authority of which questions the king planned to proceed to the destruction of the duke of Gloucester and the earls of Arundel and Warwick and other lords against whom he had conceived a great hatred because they wished him to be under good rule. By divine providence, and through the resistance and power of the said lords, the king was prevented from carrying out his plans.

(3) Item: when the lords temporal, in order to defend themselves, resisted the king's evil designs, the king set a day for parliament to see justice done to them, whereupon they, putting their hope and faith in the meeting of parliament, retired peaceably to their houses; but the king then secretly sent the duke of Ireland with his letters and his standard into Cheshire in order to raise to arms there a great number of men, and he incited them to rise up against the said lords and the magnates of the kingdom and the servants of the republic, thus challenging the peace which he had publicly sworn to keep, as a result of which deaths, imprisonments, quarrels and numerous other evils occurred throughout the kingdom; by which acts he committed perjury.

(4) Item: although the king pardoned the duke of Gloucester and the earls of Arundel and Warwick and all their supporters, in full

---

4 This and the next two charges refer to the Commission of Government (November 1386); the Questions to the Judges (August 1387); and the Radcot Bridge campaign (December 1387).

parliament and with its assent, and for many years behaved towards them in peaceful and benevolent fashion, yet he continued to bear hatred in his heart towards them, so that when an opportunity came he ordered the seizure of the duke of Gloucester – his own uncle, the son of the celebrated Edward former king of England, and constable of England – who had come humbly forward to meet his lord king in solemn procession, and the said earls of Arundel and Warwick; the said duke he sent abroad to the town of Calais, to be imprisoned by the earl of Nottingham, one of those who had appealed him, and there he caused him, without response or any legal process, to be secretly suffocated, strangled, and barbarously and cruelly murdered. The earl of Arundel, although he pleaded both a charter of general pardon and a charter of pardon which had been granted to him, and requested that justice be done to him, he wickedly ordered to be decapitated, having surrounded the parliament with a great number of armed men and archers whom he had gathered there for the purpose of overawing the people; the earl of Warwick and Lord Cobham he committed to perpetual imprisonment, and confiscated, from them and their heirs, their lands and tenements, both those held in fee simple and those held in tail,[5] expressly contrary to justice and to the laws of his realm, and to his oath, granting them to their appellants.

(5) Item: at the time when the king in his parliament caused the duke of Gloucester and the earls of Arundel and Warwick to be adjudged, in order that he would be free to pursue his cruel designs and wicked will against them and others, he gathered together a great number of malefactors from the county of Chester, some of whom travelled through the realm with him, both within the royal household and separately from it, cruelly killing some of the king's subjects, beating and wounding others, plundering the goods of the people, refusing to pay for their provisions, and raping and ravishing both married and unmarried women. And although serious complaints were made to the king about the excesses committed by them, yet he made no attempt to stop them, but rather supported these men in their crimes, trusting in them and their protection against all others of his kingdom; so that his faithful subjects had great reason to grieve and to be indignant.

(6) Item: although the king caused a proclamation to be made throughout the kingdom that he had had his uncle the duke of Gloucester and the earls of Arundel and Warwick seized and arrested

---

5 For this accusation see C. D. Ross, 'Forfeiture for treason in the reign of Richard II', *EHR* (1956), 560-75.

not for any conspiracies or insurrections committed by them within
the kingdom of England, but for numerous extortions, oppressions
and other deeds done by them at a later time contrary to his regality
and to his royal majesty, for, as he said, it was not his intention that
any member of the duke's or the earls' following, or any person that
had ridden with them at the time of those conspiracies and insurrections should be harassed or molested on account of that;[6] nevertheless
he later impeached the said lords in parliament, not for any such
extortions or oppressions, but for the aforesaid conspiracies and
insurrections, for which they were adjudged to death, and he compelled with threats of death many of their followers, and many of those
who had ridden with them at that time, to make fine and redemption
as if they were traitors, which was to the great destruction of many of
his people. Thus did he craftily, maliciously and fraudulently deceive
the said lords, their followers, and the people of the realm.

(7) Item: although many of these people, while making fine and
redemption in this manner, had obtained from the king letters patent
pardoning them fully, yet they received no benefit from these letters of
pardon until they paid new fines and redemptions in order to save their
lives, by which they were gravely impoverished; which derogated
greatly from the name and honour of kingship.

(8) Item: in the last parliament held at Shrewsbury, the king, desiring
to oppress his people, subtly procured and caused to be granted that
the power of parliament should, with the assent of all the estates of the
realm, be delegated to certain persons who, once the parliament had
been dissolved, were to terminate certain petitions which were
pending but had not been decided in parliament; by authority of this
concession, however, they proceeded, by the king's will, to deal with
other general business relating to that parliament, which was deroga-
tory to the state of parliament, to the prejudice of the whole realm, and
a pernicious example. And in order that these actions might seem to
have proper authority, the king of his own volition ordered the Rolls
of Parliament to be erased and altered, contrary to the intention of the
aforesaid grant.[7]

(9) Item: notwithstanding that the said king swore at his coronation
that, 'he would cause to be done in all his judgements equitable and
rightful justice and discretion, in mercy and in truth, according to his

6 *London Letter-Book H*, 437-8.
7 For this charge see Edwards, 'The parliamentary committee of 1398', 321-33.

power,' nevertheless the said king, among other things, harshly and
mercilessly decreed and ordained that no person should intercede or
plead with him to try to secure a pardon for the exiled Henry duke of
Lancaster, under great penalties. In so doing, he acted against the
bond of charity, and rashly violated his oath.

(10) Item: although the crown of England, and the rights of that
crown, and the kingdom itself, have always been free, so that neither
the lord pope nor any other foreign person, had any right to meddle
with them, nevertheless the king, in order to win support for his
wrongful statutes, sought the pope's confirmation for the statutes
made in the last parliament; he requested, therefore, apostolical letters
in which grave censures were threatened against any person attempting in any way to contravene these statutes;[8] all of which is contrary
to the crown and the royal dignity, and is known to be injurious to the
statutes and liberties of the realm.

(11) Item: although Henry, now duke of Lancaster, at the king's
command presented his bill of accusation against the duke of Norfolk,
which concerned the estate and honour of the king, and duly
prosecuted it, to the extent that he was quite ready, as commanded by
the king, to proceed to a duel; and indeed the king publicly, in the
presence of all those who had gathered to witness the duel, pronounced and declared that he had done his duty honourably and to the
full extent that was required of him; nevertheless the king, without
any legitimate cause, ordered the said duke of Lancaster to be banished
for ten years, contrary to all justice, to the laws and customs of his
kingdom, and to the law of arms pertaining thereto, thus damnably
committing perjury.

(12) Item: the king graciously granted by his letters patent to Henry,
now duke of Lancaster, that he would be allowed to sue through his
general attorneys for livery to be granted to him of any inheritances
or successions which might fall in to him during his absence in exile,
and that his homage would be respited, for which he would be asked
to pay a reasonable fine; later, however, the king wrongfully revoked
these letters patent, contrary to the laws of the land, thus committing
perjury.

(13) Item: notwithstanding that it had been ordained that each year the

---

8 It was the papal legate Pierre Dubois, bishop of Dax, who was in England in 1398-
  99, who confirmed the acts of the 1397-98 parliament and pronounced censures
  against those who contravened them (Adam Usk, 163).

king's officers, justices and others of his council should choose and nominate to the king sheriffs in each of the counties of the realm according to their discretion and knowledge, for the benefit and welfare of the kingdom, yet the king insisted, of his own unbridled volition, that men should be made sheriffs who had not been in any way elected or nominated, some of whom were his familiars, and others of whom he knew would be entirely amenable to his will, which was solely to his and their advantage; which was a major grievance to his people, and contrary to the laws of his realm, and by which he notoriously committed perjury.

(14) Item: when the king borrowed large sums of money from various lords and others in the kingdom, he promised repayment at a certain term; by individual letters patent, moreover, he promised on his good faith to each person from whom he had borrowed money that the money would be repaid within that specified time. Yet he did not keep his promise, and many of these sums are still outstanding, whereby his creditors feel much aggrieved, and not just they but many others in the kingdom regard the king as faithless.

(15) Item: whereas the king of England used to live honestly upon the revenues of the kingdom and the patrimony belonging to the crown, without oppressing his people except at times when the realm was burdened with the expense of war; this king, despite the fact that throughout almost the whole of his time there were truces in operation between the kingdom of England and its enemies, not only gave away the greater part of his said patrimony to unworthy persons, but, because of this, was obliged to impose grants upon his realm almost every year, which greatly oppressed his people and impoverished his nation; nor did he use these grants for the benefit or welfare of the English kingdom, but he dissipated it prodigiously upon the ostenation, pomp and vainglory of his own person. He also owed great sums of money in the realm for victuals for his household, and for other purchases, despite the fact that his wealth and riches were greater than can be remembered for any of his progenitors.

(16) Item: the king, not wishing to uphold or dispense the rightful laws and customs of the realm, but preferring to act according to his own arbitrary will and to do whatever he wished, at times when his justices or others of his council expounded to him upon the laws of the realm and asked him to do justice according to those laws, frequently replied and declared expressly, with an austere and determined expression, that his laws were in his mouth, or, at other times, that they were in

his breast; and that he alone could change or make the laws of his kingdom. And thus led astray by his own opinions, he frequently failed to do justice to his liegemen, but forced many, through fear and threats, to desist from the pursuit of common justice.

(17) Item: whereas various statutes were made in parliament, which ought to remain in effect until specifically revoked by a later parliament, the king, wishing to enjoy such liberty that he would not be bound by any statutes, but could do and act as arbitrarily as he pleased, craftily arranged for a petition to be put forward by the commons in parliament that he should, in general terms, be granted the right to enjoy the same liberties as any of his predecessors;[9] by the authority of which petition and grant he frequently acted and gave orders contrary to statutes which were still in effect, thus expressly and knowingly acting contrary to his coronation oath, as appears more fully below.

(18) Item: despite the fact that it had been ordained by statute that no sheriff should remain in office continually for more than one year, nor be readmitted to that office again for three years, the king, acting sometimes for his personal advantage, and sometimes for the advantage of others, caused and allowed some sheriffs to retain their offices for two years, and others for three years, which was contrary to the letter and the spirit of the aforesaid statute, whereby he committed perjury. And this is notorious, public and famous.

(19) Item: although according to both statute and the custom of the realm the people of each county ought to be free to elect and appoint knights of the shire to attend parliament, there to put forward their grievances and request remedies as seems expedient to them, yet the king, wishing to be free to impose his own arbitrary will upon his parliaments, frequently sent orders to his sheriffs telling them to send to parliament as knights of the shire men nominated by the king himself, whom he then often induced, sometimes by fear or threats, sometimes with bribes, to agree to things prejudicial to the realm and burdensome to the people – in particular, the grant to the king of the wool subsidy for the term of his life, and another subsidy for a number of years, which greatly oppressed his people.

(20) Item: the king, wishing to be free to act according to his arbitrary

---

9 Possibly a reference to the rather puzzling remark recorded in 1392 by the *Westminster Chronicle* (p. 484): 'at the same time, the king was given full power to rule his kingdom as he wished for all time to come.'

will in all things, unlawfully commanded all his sheriffs to swear an oath which went further than their ancient and accustomed one, namely that they would obey all and whatsoever mandates he sent to them under the great seal, the privy seal, or by signet letter. And if the sheriffs happened to hear of any person in their bailiwicks, of whatever status, who either publicly or privately was speaking ill of the king or saying things which redounded to his discredit or scandal, they were to have him arrested and kept securely in prison until they received further orders from the king. This can be found on record, and might lead to the destruction of many liegemen of the realm.

(21) Item: the king, wishing to subject his people and acquire their goods by craft, so that he would gain great wealth, forced the people of seventeen counties of the realm to submit themselves to the king as traitors, by letters under their seals; by colour of which letters he obtained great sums of money from both the clergy and the people of those shires, which they granted to him in order to secure his favour. And although, in order to please the people, he ordered those letters obligatory to be restored to them, yet he still forced their proctors, to whom they had granted full power to bind them and their heirs to the king, to submit themselves to him under their seals, in the name of the people. Thus did he deceive his people, and cunningly extort their goods from them.

(22) Item: although the king swore at his coronation to uphold the liberties granted to the English church, nevertheless, on account of his expedition to Ireland, he strictly enjoined many churchmen, such as the abbots and priors of his realm, that some of them should provide him with horses, others wagons or carts, and others great sums of money, for that expedition, as expressly set down in his letters, which were written in such a threatening manner as to ensure that these churchmen complied with his demands; whereby they were greatly impoverished and oppressed, to the manifest prejudice of the liberties of the church; by which pretext he committed perjury.

(23) Item: in many great councils of the kingdom, when the lords of the realm, justices and others were charged faithfully to counsel the king on matters concerning his welfare and that of his kingdom, the aforesaid lords, justices, and others, when offering their advice according to their discretion, were often so sharply and violently rebuked and reproved by the king that they dared not speak the truth in giving their advice on such matters.[10]

10 Item 23 is omitted from Walsingham's text, presumably in error.

(24) Item: the treasure, crowns, relics and jewels, that is, the goods belonging to the kingdom, which by ancient custom ought to be kept in the Royal Archive, for the king's honour, the preservation of the realm, and in case of any unforeseen event, were removed and carried out of his realm by the king on his expedition to Ireland without the consent of the estates of the realm, as a result of which the kingdom might have been greatly impoverished, had not these goods been fortuitously recovered from him against his will. Moreover, he ordered the rolls containing the records of his estate and government of the kingdom to be deleted and erased, to the great prejudice of the people, and the disinheritance of his crown; and this was done, so it is credibly thought, in order to sustain and preserve his evil rule.

(25) Item: the king was so variable and dissimulating in both word and letter, and so inconstant in his behaviour, especially in his dealings with the pope, and with kings, and with lords and others both within and beyond his own kingdom, that virtually no living person who came to know him could or wished to trust him. Indeed, so faithless and deceitful was he reputed to be, that he was a scandal not just to his own person and to the whole realm, but above all to foreigners throughout the world who heard about him.

(26) Item: although the lands, tenements, goods and chattels of each free man should not, according to the laws in force since ancient times, be seized except as a consequence of forfeiture, nevertheless the king, seeking to undermine those laws, frequently declared in the presence of many lords and others of the community of the realm that the lives of each of his subjects, together with their lands, tenements, goods and chattels were his, and subject to his will, regardless of any forfeiture, which is entirely contrary to the laws and customs of the kingdom.

(27) Item: although a statute was ordained, which has hitherto been maintained, 'that no free man should be arrested, etc., or in any way destroyed, nor should the king proceed or order any process against him, unless it be by lawful judgement of his peers, or by the law of the land',[11] yet by the will, command and ordinance of the king many of his liegemen, being maliciously accused of having allegedly said things either openly or privately to the disgrace, scandal or dishonour of the king's person, were seized, imprisoned, and brought before the constable and marshal of England in the Court of Chivalry; in which court the said liegemen were not permitted to enter any response

11 Clause 39 of Magna Carta.

except that they were not guilty, nor to defend themselves otherwise than by their bodies, despite the fact that those who accused and appealed them were young, strong and healthy, whereas the accused were aged, impotent, lame or infirm. From this the destruction not only of various lords and magnates of the realm, but of each and every person belonging to the community of the realm, could have resulted. Thus when the king wilfully contravened this statute of the realm, he undoubtedly thereby committed perjury.

(28) Item: although the people of the kingdom of England were, by their bond of allegiance, sufficiently bound and obliged to their king that if they committed any sort of offence he had the power to correct and punish them according to the laws and customs of the realm, yet he wished so harshly to oppress and subject his people, in order that he should be more free to pursue and exercise his foolish and illegal desires, that he sent out letters to all the shires in the realm ordering that all his subjects, both spiritual and temporal, should swear general oaths which were hateful to them, and which might in truth have resulted in the final destruction of his people; and that they should confirm these oaths by putting them in writing under their seals. In order to avoid the king's wrath, and out of fear of death, the people of the kingdom complied with this royal order.

(29) Item: when parties who were having cases of a purely ecclesiastical or spiritual nature heard in a church court tried to procure royal prohibitions from the chancellor of England to impede such legitimate processes in these courts, yet the chancellor rightfully refused to grant them, the king himself often, through letters of his signet, strictly forbade those ecclesiastical justices from proceeding in such cases, thus wickedly infringing the liberties of the church as approved in the Great Charter, which he had sworn to uphold; whereby he committed perjury and damnably incurred sentence of excommunication, as pronounced by the Holy Fathers against violaters of this sort.

(30) Item: the king in parliament, with armed men standing around in a threatening manner, adjudged Thomas Arundel archbishop of Canterbury, primate of all England and his spiritual father, who was through the king's cunning absent at the time, to perpetual exile, without any reasonable or legitimate cause, without lawful process, and contrary to the laws of the kingdom which he himself had sworn to uphold.

(31) Item: perusal of the king's testament, written under his great and

privy seals as well as his signet, revealed among other things the
following clause: 'Item, we wish that once the debts of our household,
chamber and wardrobe have been paid, for which we leave twenty
thousand pounds, and when fuller provision has been made by our
executors for the lepers and chaplains whom we appointed to be
maintained at Westminster and Bermondsey, for which purpose we
leave five or six thousand marks to be spent by the said executors; the
remainder of our gold should pass to our successor, on condition that
he approves, ratifies, confirms, upholds and strictly observes each and
every one of the statutes, ordinances, establishments and judgements
made and given in our parliament held on the seventeenth day of
September in the twenty-first year of our reign at Westminster, or in
the same parliament when it was continued at Shrewsbury, and all the
ordinances, judgements and establishments made or given on the
sixteenth of September in our twenty-second year at Coventry or
afterwards on the eighteenth day of March at Westminster by
authority of the same parliament, together with any ordinances or
judgements which might in future be promulgated under the authority
of the same parliament. If on the other hand, our successor will not
perform the above, or refuses to do so, which we cannot believe will
happen, then we wish that Thomas duke of Surrey, Edward duke of
Aumale, John duke of Exeter, and William le Scrope earl of Wiltshire,
once they have paid the debts of our household, chamber and
wardrobe, and set aside five or six thousand marks, as mentioned
above, should have and keep the remainder, for the defence and
maintenance of the aforesaid statutes, ordinances, establishments and
judgements to the utmost of their ability, even unto death if need be;
for each and every one of which injunctions we burden their consciences, as they would wish to answer at the day of judgement.'
Which article clearly demonstrates that the king tried unswervingly
to uphold and maintain those wrongful and iniquitous statutes and
ordinances, which are repugnant to all law and reason, not only in his
life but even in death, regardless of the danger to his soul and to his
kingdom, and to the ultimate destruction of his liegemen.[12]

(32) Item: in the eleventh year of King Richard's reign, in the chapel
of his manor at Langley, in the presence of the dukes of Lancaster and
York and many other lords, the king, openly expressing the wish that
his uncle the duke of Gloucester, also present there, should have faith

12 For the terms of the king's will see J. Nichols, *Collection of the Wills of the Kings and
Queens of England* (1780), 191-202; and *Foedera*, viii, 162.

in his good intentions, swore of his own volition upon the holy sacrament of the Lord's Body which had been placed upon the altar there, that he willingly and entirely pardoned the duke of Gloucester for any offences which he might have been said to have committed against the king's person, and that he would never try on that account to condemn or harm him. Later, however, notwithstanding this oath, the king ordered the aforesaid duke to be cruelly and horribly murdered for these alleged offences, thus damnably committing perjury.[13]

(33) Item: after one of the knights of the shire[14] had made a speech in parliament impeaching Thomas archbishop of Canterbury before the king and all the estates of the realm of various offences which he was unjustly said to have committed against the king's majesty, and although the said archbishop immediately declared himself ready to answer the charges, and requested the king that he be allowed to do so, believing himself capable of establishing his innocence, the king, scheming by all possible means to ruin and bring down the archbishop, as is clear from what followed, genially and cheerfully called the archbishop forward to the royal throne and earnestly advised and requested him not to say anything for the time being, but to wait for a more appropriate and opportune moment. And for the next five days and more the king continued wickedly and fraudulently to deceive the archbishop, constantly advising and persuading him not to come to the parliament but to remain undaunted at his house, promising him faithfully that nothing to his injury or disadvantage would be done during his absence. Yet the king in that same parliament, with the archbishop absent and unable to make any sort of response, sentenced him without reasonable cause to be banished during the king's pleasure, contrary to the laws of the land and to all justice; whereby he committed perjury.[15] Later the king, wishing to excuse his duplicity in this affair, held a number of placatory conversations with the archbishop in which he denied his own responsibility for the injuries done to him, and tried to place the blame on others. On one of these occasions, when the archbishop was conversing with the king and the duke of Norfolk and other lords and magnates of the realm, he observed sadly that he was not the first to suffer exile, nor would he

13 See Gloucester's confession, above, Doc. 4(a).

14 John Bussy, the speaker, according to the *Vita* (above, Doc. 1).

15 The original charge probably ended here; what follows seems to have been added later, presumably on Archbishop Arundel's information.

be the last, for he thought it likely that the duke of Norfolk and other lords would soon be following in his footsteps; he continually asserted to the king, moreover, that the consequences of these actions would ultimately fall upon his own head. At this the king's face dropped in astonishment, and he replied somewhat rashly that he regarded it as far from impossible that he should be driven out of his kingdom by his liegemen; but, he added presently, were such a thing to happen he would wish to betake himself to wherever the archbishop was at the time. Moreover, in order that the archbishop should trust in his words, the king showed him a great golden necklace which was in some intricate way attached to the neckline of his tunic, beneath his outer garments, telling the archbishop that as a token of his good faith he would send this necklace to him as a sign that he was about to come to where he was. And in order that the archbishop should trust him fully, he sent him a message advising him secretly to send the king all the jewels and other goods of his chapel, which the king would keep in safe custody in case anybody should try by authority of the sentence of exile passed against him to seize them. This the archbishop did, with the greatest secrecy, and the king, having inspected them, had them placed in chests which were locked and sealed by one of the archbishop's clerks, the king keeping the chests but sending the keys with the clerk to the archbishop. Later, however, and without the archbishop's knowledge, the king ordered the chests to be broken open, and disposed of the goods as he wished. The king also promised the archbishop that if he were to present himself for exile at Southampton, he would at the very least have his exile revoked at once, through the intercession of the queen. Nevertheless, if it should happen that he was made to go into exile, the king would without fail recall him to England before Easter next, nor would he under any circumstances confer his archbishopric upon any other person. All this the king faithfully promised, swearing it upon, and physically touch-ing, the cross of St Thomas the Martyr, former archbishop of Canterbury. But notwithstanding his promises, the king compelled the archbishop to go into exile, and immediately wrote to the pope specifially requesting his translation. In this way, and by other frauds and wrongful deeds, was the archbishop, a man of good faith, wickedly deceived.

Following this all the estates assembled there were asked both individually and jointly to give their opinion on the aforesaid, and it seemed to them, bearing in mind also the king's own confession of inadequacy and the other things mentioned in his Renunciation and Cession, that the wrongs and defects specified were fully sufficient and notorious to justify the king's deposition; all the aforesaid estates unanimously agreed, therefore, that there was abundant cause, for the security and peace of the people, and the welfare of the realm, to depose the king. Whereupon the said estates and communities there and then unanimously and without dispute publicly deputed and appointed certain commissioners, namely the bishop of St Asaph, the abbot of Glastonbury, the earl of Gloucester, Lord Berkeley, Thomas Erpingham and Thomas Gray, knights, and William Thirning, justice, to carry out this sentence of deposition, and to depose King Richard from all royal dignity, majesty, and honour, on behalf of, in the name of, and by authority of, all the aforesaid estates, in the same way as had been done in similar cases by the ancient custom of the kingdom. The commissioners presently assumed their task and, sitting as a tribunal in front of the royal throne, after some discussion of the matter wrote down the sentence of deposition, which, at the wish and command of the assembly and of his fellow commissioners, was read out by the bishop of St Asaph[16] in the following words ... (*The formal sentence of deposition recited the king's 'many perjuries, his cruelty, and his numerous other crimes,' as well as his confession of inadequacy and his 'voluntary' admission that he merited deposition.*)

In order that nothing which ought to be done should be left undone, the aforesaid estates, having again been individually questioned, then expressed the wish that the persons nominated above as commissioners should be appointed as their proctors, jointly and together to go and resign and yield up the homage and fealty which they had formerly performed to King Richard, and to intimate to him as much as was thought necessary of all the aforesaid matters concerning his deposition and renunciation. Immediately after this, since it was clear from the foregoing and what followed from them that the realm of England with its appurtenances was vacant, the said Henry duke of Lancaster rose from his place and, standing erect so that he could be seen by the people, humbly made the sign of the cross on his forehead and on his breast and, after first invoking the name of Christ, claimed this realm of England, now vacant as aforesaid, together with the crown and all its members and appurtenances, in his mother tongue, in the following words:

---

16 John Trevor, bishop of St Asaph 1395-1410; but he joined Glendower's Welsh rebellion against Henry and was formally deprived of his see in 1404.

(*English*) In the name of the Father, Son, and Holy Ghost; I, Henry of Lancaster challenge this Realm of England, and the Crown with all its members and appurtenances, inasmuch as I am descended by right line of the blood coming from the good lord King Henry the third, and through that right that God of his grace has sent me, with the help of my kin and my friends, to recover it; which realm was on the point of being undone by default of governance and the undoing of the good laws.

Following this challenge and claim, the lords spiritual and temporal and all the estates there present were individually and jointly asked what they thought of this challenge and claim; to which the same estates, together with all the people, unanimously and without any difficulty or delay agreed that the aforesaid duke should reign over them. Whereupon the king promptly showed to the estates of the realm the signet of King Richard, which, as mentioned earlier, had been willingly handed over to him as a token, and the archbishop, taking the aforesaid King Henry by the right hand, led him to the royal throne. After the king had knelt for a short while to pray before the throne, the aforesaid archbishop of Canterbury, assisted by the archbishop of York, seated the king upon the throne, to tremendous and joyful applause from the people. Presently the said archbishop of Canterbury, having with difficulty, on account of the joy of all present, imposed silence upon them, preached a short sermon, as follows: 'Vir dominabitur populo ...' (*The theme of Arundel's sermon was the folly of youth and the wisdom of age. For example: 'When a boy reigns, therefore, wilfulness reigns, and reason is exiled. And where wilfulness reigns and reason is exiled, constancy is put to flight, and then great danger threatens. From this danger we are now liberated, for a man is ruling.'*)

When this sermon was over, the lord King Henry, in order to set at peace the minds of his subjects, then and there publicly spoke these words: (*English*) 'Sires, I thank God and you, the lords spiritual and temporal, and all the estates of the land; and I wish you to know that it is not my will that any man should think that by way of conquest I would disinherit any man of his inheritance, his franchise, or any other rights that he ought to have, nor would I put him out of that which he has and has had by the good laws and customs of the realm; excepting those persons that have acted contrary to the good purpose and the common profit of the realm.'

[He had proposed to claim the kingdom by conquest, but Lord William Thirning, justice, said that this was quite impossible, for by doing so he would arouse the anger of the entire population against him. This was because if he claimed the kingdom in this way, it would appear to the people that he had the power to disinherit anybody at will, and to change the laws, establishing new ones and revoking old ones, as a result of which no one would be secure in his possessions].[17]

(*King Henry announced that parliament would meet on the following Monday (6 October), and that his coronation would be held on the next Monday (13 October); king, lords and commons then retired to the White Hall to celebrate.*) Afterwards, on the following Wednesday (*1 October*), the proctors who had been appointed as aforesaid came into the presence of Richard, former king, in the Tower, to do as they had been ordered, and Lord William Thirning, justice, speaking on his own behalf and on behalf of his fellows and co-proctors, in the name of all the estates and the people read out in full to Richard his admission of renunciation, together with the schedule of, and reasons for, the sentence of deposition. He also resigned and yielded up homage and fealty to him, in the following words.

Here follow the words spoken by William Thirning to Sir Richard, former king of England, in his chamber in the Tower of London, on the Wednesday next after the feast of St Michael the archangel:

(*English*) My lord, it is well known to you that a parliament of all the estates of the realm was summoned to Westminster, to begin on the morning of Tuesday the feast of St Michael the archangel – that is, yesterday – as a result of which summons all the estates of the land gathered there; which estates unanimously agreed to appoint these same persons that come before you here and now as their proctors, and gave them full authority and power, and charged them to say the words that we shall say to you, in their name and on their behalf: namely, the bishop of St Asaph for archbishops and bishops; the abbot of Glastonbury for abbots and priors and all other men of holy church, secular and regular; the earl of Gloucester for dukes and earls; the Lord Berkeley for barons and bannerets; Sir Thomas Erpingham, chamberlain, for all the southern bachelors and commons of this land; Sir Thomas Grey for all northern bachelors and commons; and my fellow John Markham and me to come with them on behalf of all these estates. And so, my lord, these words that we shall say to you, and the act that we shall perform, are not ours alone, but the words and the act of all the estates of this land, and it is our charge, and done in their name.

And he answered that he knew well that we would say only that with which we were charged.

17 These paragraphs are found only in Walsingham's version of the text.

My lord, you remember well that on Monday, the feast of St Michael the archangel, right here in this chamber, and in whose presence, you renounced and yielded up the estate of king, and the lordship and all the dignity and worship that belonged to it, and absolved all your lieges of their allegiance and the obedience which they owed to you, in the words that are contained in the same Renunciation and Cession, which you read yourself, by your own mouth, and affirmed by your oath and by your own writing. Whereupon you appointed as your proctors the archbishop of York and the bishop of Hereford, to announce and present in your name this Renunciation and Cession to all the estates and people that were gathered at Westminster on account of the aforesaid summons. This was duly done yesterday by these lords your proctors, and, once it had been heard and properly understood, this Renunciation and Cession was clearly and freely accepted and fully agreed upon by all the aforesaid estates and people. Moreover, my lord, at the request of all these estates and people, certain articles relating to the defaults in your governance were read there: and when they had been read to, and clearly understood by, all the aforesaid estates, they considered them to be so demonstrably true and notorious that, for these reasons, as well as many others, so they declared, and bearing in mind also your own admission, in your Renunciation and Cession, that you were not worthy, nor sufficient, nor capable to govern, on account of your own demerits – as is clearly stated there – they thought that this constituted reasonable cause to depose you. Whereupon the commissioners that they appointed there – as was duly recorded – declared and decreed and adjudged you to be deposed and deprived, and did indeed depose and deprive you of the estate of king, and of your lordship as specified in the aforesaid Renunciation and Cession, and of all the dignity, worship, and administration that belongs to it. We, therefore, as proctors to all the aforesaid estates and people, duly charged by them and by the authority given by them to us, and in their name, yield up to you, on behalf of all the estates and people aforesaid, liege homage and fealty, together with all allegiance and all other bonds, charges, and services that pertain to it; so that none of these estates and people, from this time forward, shall either bear you faith or do obedience to you as their king.

And he answered by saying that he looked not thereafter; but that he hoped, after all this, that his cousin would be a good lord to him.

[However, when Lord William Thirning said to him that he had renounced all the honours and dignity pertaining to a king, he replied that he did not wish to renounce those special dignities of a spiritual nature which had been bestowed upon him, nor indeed his anointment; he was in fact unable to renounce them, nor could he cease to retain them. And when William Thirning replied to this that he had himself admitted, in his own Renunciation and Cession, that he was not worthy, or adequate, or able enough to govern, he said that this was not true, it was simply that his government had not been acceptable to the people. But William replied by telling him that this had clearly been stated in the aforesaid Cession and Renunciation, and reminding him of the form in which this confession of his had been written down there. Hearing this, the king simply smiled and asked to be treated accordingly, and not to be deprived of the means with which to sustain himself honourably].[17]

18. The protest of the Bishop of Carlisle

Source: Traison et Mort, 220–2

Language: French (trans. B. Williams)

Although perpetuated by Shakespeare, the following story has, like many of the 'facts' so graphically presented in this chronicle, frequently been questioned. Thomas Merks, bishop of Carlisle, had already, by 16 September, been deprived of the revenues from his bishopric,[1] and before early December he was to be demoted from his see. That he offended Bolingbroke in some way is thus unquestionable. Moreover, he was apparently present in the assembly of 30 September (above, Doc. 16). Whether he made so public a protest as that recorded here is, however, more questionable. It is more likely, as Walsingham states (below, Doc. 20(a)), that he was deprived and arrested because of suspicions that he had been involved in the death of the duke of Gloucester, and it may be that the author of the Traison *misconstrued rumours that he had heard about what Walsingham describes as the 'most excellent speech' which Merks made defending himself from that charge. The author was clearly confused between the deposition proceedings of 29–30 September and the parliament which met on 6 October; although he seems to have placed the bishop's speech before the formal deposition of the king, he made no distinction between this assembly and the parliament.*

Item, on the morrow when the duke was seated on the throne, where King Richard had been accustomed to sit, he sent one of the dukes to tell a knight, called Sir Baldwin Pigot,[2] to summon the lords of the council and the commons. It is true that the bishop of Carlisle, who was of the order of St Benedict, rose from his seat and demanded leave to speak, which when he had obtained, he said as follows: 'My lords, consider well before you give judgement upon what my lord the duke has set forth, for I maintain that there is not one present who is

---

1 *CCR, 1396-9*, 508.

2 Sir Baldwin Pigot of Bedfordshire, knight of the shire in the parliaments of 1397-98 and 1401, though not apparently in 1399 (*CCR, 1396-99*, 303; *CCR, 1399-1402*, 107, 330).

competent and fit to judge such a sovereign as my lord the king whom we have acknowledged our liege lord for the space of twenty years and more, and I will give you my reasons; there never was, nor is in this world, any false traitor nor wicked murderer, who, if he be taken prisoner by the hands of justice, is not, at the least, brought before the judge to hear his sentence. My lords, you have well and truly heard the accusations that my lord the duke has made against King Richard; and it appears to me that you are about to give judgement, and to condemn King Richard, without hearing what he has to answer, or even his being present. Moreover, I say that my lord the duke has more erred and offended against King Richard than has the king against him; for we know full well that my lord the duke was banished ten years by the council of the realm, and by the consent of his own father, for the great crime which he and the duke of Norfolk committed; and he has returned to the country without the king's permission: and moreover I say he has done still worse, for he has seated himself on the throne, where no lord ought to sit other than the lawfully crowned king of England; wherefore I declare that you ought to bring King Richard in presence of the full parliament to hear what he has to say, and to see whether he be willing to relinquish his crown to the duke or not.' Then the duke of Lancaster commanded that they should lay hands on the bishop, and convey him to prison at St Albans. And, after the bishop was led away to prison, the duke demanded sentence upon King Richard ...

19. The protest of the Percies

Source: Hardyng's Chronicle, 349-54

Language: English and Latin

John Hardyng, soldier, diplomat, and lifelong servant of the Percy family, began writing his verse chronicle in the 1440s, and in 1457 presented it to King Henry VI. Following the change of dynasty in 1461 he wrote a second version, adding a number of explanatory passages in prose, which he presented to King Edward IV in 1464. The prose addition appended to the following passage is found only in the second, 'Yorkist' version of the chronicle. Although doubts are naturally raised by the fact that Hardyng was writing over half a century after the events he describes, and by his attachment to the Percy cause, there are nevertheless a number of intimations in the sources that Bolingbroke swore an oath of some sort concerning his intentions during his campaign of 1399. The Dieulacres chronicler, for example, in his account of the battle of Shrewsbury in 1403, states that Henry Percy the younger ('Hotspur') claimed that Bolingbroke had sworn to the Percies 'upon the relics of Bridlington, that he would never try to seize the throne, and had said that if anyone could be found who was more worthy of the crown than he was, he would willingly stand down for him; the duchy of Lancaster, he had declared, was all that he wished for'.[1]

Hardyng's chronicle is divided into chapters, each consisting of a number of stanzas. Each paragraph below represents one stanza. The extracts are from chapters 195-6: Bolingbroke has moved on from Ravenspur to Doncaster, where he was met by the earl of Northumberland, Sir Henry Percy, the earl of Westmorland, and a number of other lords.

The duke swore in good faith upon the sacrament there to claim no more than his mother's inheritance, his father's lands, and those of his

---

1 Dieulacres Chronicle, 179. See also Sherborne, 'Perjury and the Lancastrian revolution'. The Dieulacres chronicler also states that Hotspur 'had absented himself from the festivities on the day of the coronation, which had undoubtedly been carried out against his wishes.' But the fact that he was made a Knight of the Bath on the eve of the coronation, and that he and his wife received gowns for the coronation, casts doubt upon this statement (*GEC*, ix, 714).

wife; and to desist from taxes and tallages during his lifetime, except in cases where the baronage and all the estates of parliament considered it necessary and fully consented thereto.

He also swore that good and proper restraint would be placed upon the king's government; and that, because of their infamy and misrule, the Cheshiremen would be dismissed from his household, and officers of proven integrity would be appointed to govern both his household and his royal estate; these were the very points that he swore in his oath there.

Then they rode on to Bristol, where Scrope and Bussy and Sir Henry Green were at that time, and they beheaded them; but Bagot escaped. Then the king, at Flint, summoned great numbers of people to muster for him, but they took his wages and went to join Duke Henry, with whom they willingly rode forth.

Meanwhile the earl of Northumberland negotiated with the king at Conway, to persuade him to meet with Duke Henry in England; and he brought the king, humbly attired, to the duke. Saying little, they rode on to Chester, where the king was placed under guard, and from there they marched south to London.

Chapter 196: How Duke Henry of Lancaster was made king by resignation, renunciation and deposition, and by election of parliament, and was crowned at Westminster on St Edward's day, in October

They put him in the Tower, where he resigned his right, his realm, and his royal crown to Duke Henry, which no one then impugned; he made there a clear renunciation of all his right, as a result of which, and on account of his misrule, the parliament then by solemn ordinance deposed him.

Then they decided on a free election; but on account of the youth of Mortimer – who was at that time by rightful descent earl of March, and nearest heir of England to King Richard, as was clear at the time[2]

---

2 Edmund Mortimer, born 6 November 1391, great-grandson of Lionel duke of Clarence (second surviving son of Edward III), and heir to the earldom of March.

– and on account of Duke Henry's might, they chose him king, as nobody can deny.

At that time the earl of Northumberland had, on the advice of Duke Henry, sent his troops home, as had his son Henry, who wished to act truly;[3] for they did not think that the duke would in any way go against the oath which he had taken. He and his followers, however, as was clear at the time, kept their troops with them until he was crowned king.

The earls of Northumberland and Worcester, Sir Henry Percy, and the earl of Westmorland all advised him not to do anything contrary to his oath; and although he listened to their request in the evening, on the following day he took private counsel and decided that he would undoubtedly be crowned king.

(*In the second version of his chronicle Hardyng inserted at this point a prose addition explaining the above points and relating them to the Percy rising of 1403. After a short preamble, the prose addition begins with a recitation of the manifesto with which the Percies apparently challenged the king on the field of Shrewsbury in July 1403.*)

(*Latin*) We, Henry Percy earl of Northumberland, constable of England and warden of the West March of England towards Scotland, Henry Percy our first-born son, warden of the East March of England towards Scotland, and Thomas Percy earl of Worcester, spokesmen and defenders of the public weal, declare, state, and will prove with our own hands before our lord Jesus Christ our supreme judge on this present day, against you, Henry duke of Lancaster, who wrongfully and without any legal title except that which is born of your own iniquity and the violence of your followers presume to call yourself king of England, and your accomplices and supporters, that when, following your exile, you returned to England, you swore an oath to us at Doncaster upon the holy gospels, which you personally held and kissed, concerning the kingdom and the status of king, excepting only your own inheritance and that of your wife in England; and that our lord King Richard would remain king for the term of his life, under the direction, and by the good advice, of the lords spiritual and temporal. But then you imprisoned your lord, and our king, in the Tower of London until, under threat of death, he resigned the kingdoms of England and France and renounced all his right to the said kingdoms and to all his other lands and lordships beyond the sea. By authority of this

3 According to the records of the exchequer, both Northumberland and Hotspur were given wages for troops who had not only ridden with them in the summer of 1399 but had also remained with them during the October parliament (P.R.O. E403/564, 17 December, 1 March).

resignation and renunciation you then, on the advice of your followers, and supported by the clamour of a crowd of common people whom you and your accomplices had gathered together at Westminster, had yourself crowned king of the aforesaid kingdoms, and ordered all the royal castles and lordships to be seized. All of which was contrary to your oath, whereby you are perjured and false.

Item: we declare, state, and shall prove that whereas you swore to us upon the same gospels, at the same time and place, that while you lived you would not permit any tenths to be levied from the clergy, or fifteenths from the people, or any other tallages from the kingdom of England for the use of the kingdom unless it were with the agreement of the three estates of the realm in parliament, and only then in cases of great necessity, in order to resist enemies of some sort, and for no other reason; nevertheless, contrary to that oath of yours, you ordered the levy of numerous tenths and fifteenths, as well as other impositions and tallages, from the clergy, from the community of England, and from the merchants, under threat from your royal majesty; whereby you are perjured and false.

Item: we declare, state, and shall prove that whereas you swore upon the same gospels, at the same time and place, that our lord and yours, King Richard, would, while he lived and ruled, enjoy his royal prerogatives, you traitorously, without either his consent or the authority of the lords of the realm, subjected him for fifteen days and nights to starvation, filth and cold in your castle of Pontefract, and thus murdered him; which is a terrible thing to hear of among Christians, and whereby you are perjured and false.

Item: we declare, state, and shall prove that at the time when our lord and yours, King Richard, was so foully put to death as described above, you, contrary to your oath, unjustly seized and usurped by force the kingdom of England and the name and honour of king of France from Edmund Mortimer earl of March, who was then the closest, most immediate, and direct heir by succession to England and France, following the death of the said Richard; whereby you are perjured and false ...

(*English*) Many men have been misled, and are still greatly confused, upon the following point: they claim that Edmund, earl of Lancaster, Leicester and Derby, was the elder son of King Henry III, but, being hunchbacked, was unable to become king, as a result of which his younger brother Edward became king with his consent;[4] this is alleged by some to be supported by an untrue chronicle which was fabricated during the time of King Richard II by John of Gaunt duke of Lancaster, whereby he hoped to make his son Henry king, when he saw that he might not be chosen as King Richard's heir apparent.

Yet I, John Hardyng, the author of this book, heard the earl of Northumberland, who was killed at Bramham Moor in the time of King

---

4 See Adam Usk's account of Bolingbroke's attempt to exploit the 'Crouchback legend' (above, Doc. 15).

Henry IV,[5] say that this same King Henry, on the feast of St Matthew
before he became king (*21 September 1399*), advanced the claims of this
same chronicle, thereby asserting his title to the crown by descent from the
said Edmund. Whereupon all the chronicles of Westminster and of all the
other well-known monasteries were brought in to the council at Westminster and examined by the lords, and it was proven by reference to all these
chronicles that the said King Edward was the elder brother, and Edmund
the younger brother; nor was he hunchbacked or in any other way crippled,
but the comeliest person in England apart from his brother Edward.
Whereupon that chronicle which King Henry had produced was rejected
and discounted.

I also heard the earl say that the said King Henry had made King
Richard resign his right to him in the Tower of London under threat of
imprisonment and in fear of his life, and had made him draw up a
renunciation of his right. These instruments were shown to the council,
and to the parliament which met at Westminster on the day after the
following feast of Michaelmas, where, on account of his power and
ambition, and with the support of certain of the lords and commons, he was
crowned, contrary to the oath which he had made to the earl of
Northumberland and other lords in the Whitefriars at Doncaster, and
against the will and the advice of the said earl, his son, and Sir Thomas
Percy earl of Worcester; for which they were later to die ...

I also heard the said earl of Northumberland say on a number of
occasions that he heard Duke John of Lancaster petition, in the presence of
both the lords in councils and parliaments, and of the knights elected to be
members of the common house, that he should be acknowledged as heir
apparent to King Richard, since the king was unlikely to have any issue of
his body. To which the lords spiritual and temporal and the commons in
the common house replied, after taking spiritual advice, that the earl of
March, Roger Mortimer, was his next heir to the crown by full descent of
blood, and that they would have no other; whereupon they asked the
question, 'Who is it who dares to suggest that the king will have no issue?',
for he is young and able to have children. Being thus disappointed, the
duke of Lancaster with his council therefore fabricated and forged the
aforesaid chronicle saying that Edmund was the elder brother, in order to
supply his son Henry with a title to the crown;[6] and he tried to persuade
the aforesaid earl of Northumberland and his brother Sir Thomas Percy to
go along with it, since they were descended, through a sister, from the
same Edmund;[7] but they refused to do so.

I heard the earl say on a number of occasions to various people that this

5 The battle of Bramham Moor, near Tadcaster, at which Northumberland was slain,
  was fought on 19 February 1408.

6 The *Continuatio Eulogii*, 369-70, recounts a similar debate as having occurred
  during one of the parliaments of the 1390s.

7 Northumberland was the son of Henry Lord Percy (d. 1368) and Mary, sister of
  Henry duke of Lancaster (d. 1361).

fabricated chronicle was circulated by the duke to several abbeys and friaries, to be kept by them to support his son's claim to inherit the crown, which claim he first put forward after he had brought King Richard to the Tower; but Earl Percy rejected that claim.

Part three: October 1399 to February 1400

20. The first parliament of Henry IV, October–November 1399

The parliament of October–November 1399 was chiefly concerned with two matters: the trials of those most closely associated with the deposed king, and the death of the duke of Gloucester. Not surprisingly, these two matters were closely linked, for it was upon those who had enjoyed Richard's confidence that suspicion of involvement in Gloucester's murder fell. The Rolls of Parliament record the excuses of the appellants, the sentence passed upon them, and the infamous confession of John Hall detailing the manner of Gloucester's death. The more circumstantial accounts given by Walsingham and the author of the Great Chronicle of London *(this part of which, although finally composed around 1500, was based on materials compiled in the early fifteenth century) go much further than the Rolls of Parliament in depicting the atmosphere of near-hysteria generated by the accusations and counter-accusations which the bitterly divided nobles hurled at each other. Both authors seem to some extent to have used official records, although Walsingham also probably based parts of his account on information provided to him by the bishop of Carlisle (who was resident at St Albans both before and after the parliament). It was clearly a parliament thirsting for blood – even more so once the grim details of Gloucester's suffocation had been made public – and it seems to have taken all the new king's political skill to stop it degenerating into violence. In the end, however, the only blood to be spilt was that of the unfortunate John Hall, whose only real crime, if what he said about his part in Gloucester's murder is to be believed, was having been in the wrong place at the wrong time.*

It is with the coronation itself, however, that Walsingham begins his account of the new reign: more specifically, with the bizarre story of the miraculous holy oil used to anoint the new king. The story is yet another example of the lengths to which the new regime went in order to justify Henry's rule; it was, perhaps, Richard's refusal to accept that he could renounce 'those special dignities of a spiritual nature which had been bestowed upon him, nor indeed his anointment' (above, Doc. 17) which prompted Henry and his supporters to make a Lancastrian of the Blessed Virgin.

(a) According to Thomas Walsingham

Source: *Annales Ricardi Secundi*, 297-331

Language: Latin

(*Parliament met on 6 October, but was promptly adjourned until after Bolingbroke's coronation, which took place on 13 October*) ... And, as an omen of even better fortune to befall him in the future, so it is believed, he was anointed with that heavenly oil which the Blessed Mary, the Mother of God, had once given to the Blessed Thomas (*Becket*) the Martyr while he was in exile, and which he had entrusted to the keeping of a certain saintly monk ...

(*The oil, kept in a golden eagle and a phial of stone, was deposited by St Thomas at a monastery in Poitiers, along with a schedule upon which he had written down a prophecy made to him by the Blessed Virgin, to the effect that a future English king who was anointed with this oil would recover Normandy and Aquitaine, and would drive the infidels from the Holy Land. It was rediscovered during the reign of Edward III and stored away to be used at the coronation of his eldest son, the Black Prince – who, however, predeceased his father. At the time of Richard II's coronation attempts were made to find the oil, but they proved fruitless.*) After many years of the aforesaid Richard's reign had passed, the king, curiously searching through the relics and other possessions of his forebears in the Tower, began opening and inspecting a number of chests, and at length came across one which was locked with a number of different locks to which nobody could find the keys. He ordered this chest to be broken open, therefore, to find out what was in it, and discovered there this eagle, containing the phial and the schedule written by the Blessed Thomas. When he realised the power which the oil possessed, he immediately, like the immature and glory-seeking youth that he was, asked Thomas of Arundel, the archbishop of Canterbury, to re-anoint him with this oil, thinking that he would thereby triumph gloriously against his enemies, and wishing to anticipate this divine prophecy and fulfil it himself, for whom it was in no way intended.

The archbishop, however, a man of wise counsel, absolutely refused to do as the king asked, as was indeed almighty God's intention. It was enough, he explained to the king, that he had already received his holy anointing once at the hands of the Metropolitan at his first coronation, and he should not do so again, for it might happen that by an act of such presumption he would in fact lay himself open to God's wrath ...

When he returned for the last time from Ireland, and handed himself over under certain conditions to the duke of Lancaster, and then went on to Chester castle, the archbishop insisted that he hand the eagle and phial over to him; and, although unwillingly, he did so, saying that it was now clear to him that it was not God's will that he should be anointed with the aforesaid oil, but that such a worthy blessing should instead be accorded to another. The archbishop, therefore, kept these treasures in his reverend custody until the coronation of the present king, who thus became the first king to be anointed with this precious liquid sent from heaven. And as a result of this many people believe that he was indeed that king, chosen by God, for whom this oil was so miraculously provided, and that greater things were promised to him than to any who had come before him ...

(*Parliament reconvened on 14 October. On 15 October the acts of the 1397-98 parliament and of the parliamentary committee were revoked, those of the 1388 parliament were reaffirmed, and those who had been convicted in 1397-98, or their heirs, were restored to their inheritances.*) On Thursday (*16 October*), the knights of parliament made a request that all the evil counsellors of the former King Richard should be arrested. On the same day Sir William Bagot was brought in for questioning. On being asked whether he still stood by the bills which he had written and sent to the king, he began by saying that he did, and then went on to accuse the duke of Aumale of being one of King Richard's evil counsellors, and one of the principal accomplices to many of the king's evil designs: 'It was you,' he declared, 'who said at (*blank*) that if the duke of Gloucester, the earl of Arundel, the earl of Warwick, and others, were not killed, the king would never be able to exercise his regal power to the full.' And he added that King Richard had said that he wished to place the kingdom in good hands by resigning from it himself and committing its government, along with the crown, to the duke of Aumale, since he was the noblest and wisest man in the whole kingdom; to which the duke of Norfolk had replied that it would be both better and more correct if the duke of Hereford were to take the king's place, not only because he was more closely related to the king, but for many other reasons too. But King Richard retorted that he would never do this, 'For,' he asserted, 'Hereford is a worthless man at heart, and will always remain so. Besides, if he were to rule the kingdom, he would want to destroy the whole of God's holy church.' King Henry, hearing himself being thus defamed by such testimony, immediately replied that, with the grace of God, he would show any such prediction to be quite false, for he had taken a vow to uphold, protect and support God's church with as much zeal as any of his predecessors. He did say, nevertheless, that he hoped to see men chosen as rectors of churches who were worthy of their position, unlike many of those who had been appointed in his predecessors' times.

Unable to tolerate the accusations which William Bagot was making against him, the duke of Aumale rose from his seat and threw his hood into the middle of the hall, challenging him to a duel to prove his innocence, but on this occasion the king told him to go and retrieve his hood.

William Bagot was then asked why he had either offered or given his consent to so much of the bad advice given to the king, which he knew in all honesty and good faith that he ought to have resisted. To which he replied hotly – indeed rather too boldly and candidly – 'Is there anyone among you all who, if King Richard had demanded such-and-such a thing from you, would have dared to disagree with him, or not to comply with his order?' But John Norbury, treasurer of the realm, was not prepared to allow William to get away with excuses of that sort for his crimes, and answered, 'Yes, indeed, I for one, even if it would have meant that I lost all my goods and my life as well.' Then Bagot, trying to justify his own behaviour by reference to the misdeeds of others, said that it was not just he who should be made to answer like this to the charges laid against him, for there were several others present in parliament who ought by right to be asked about these matters as well. Hearing this, the dukes of Surrey and Exeter, suspecting – as well they might – that this remark was intended to implicate them, instantly rose to their feet, threw down their hoods, and offered battle against William Bagot or anyone else who wished to accuse them of the death of the duke of Gloucester or of offering evil counsel to the king. But the king once again ordered them to retrieve their gages. Bagot, however, continued to insist that not only the lords temporal but the lords spiritual too were just as guilty in these matters as he was, trying in particular to exonerate himself from any part in the death of the duke of Gloucester by maintaining that the blame for this ought to be shared by those who had given their consent to the deed in parliament. It was clear, however, that in this regard he was pointing the finger principally at the duke of Aumale. The duke vehemently denied it, seeking to excuse himself by whatever means he could, but Bagot said that if they really wanted to know who was

H

responsible they ought to question a valet named Hall, who at present was being held in Newgate prison, and get him to tell them everything he knew about the duke of Gloucester's death. When he had said this, order was given that William Bagot should be kept in custody until Saturday, and that meanwhile, on Friday, a discussion of these matters should be held among the lords, spiritual as well as temporal, without whom it would be impossible to decide the case.

On the Friday, therefore, the lords spiritual and temporal, with the exception of the three above-mentioned dukes, appeared before the king in the white chamber, where each of the lords temporal was asked individually whether, as requested in the commons' petition, these three dukes and the other appellants who had appealed the duke of Gloucester, etc., ought to be arrested. The first to reply was Lord Cobham who, after speaking at some length about the evils of recent years, said, among other things, that with such a king, such leaders, and such rulers, the condition of the English people had sunk lower even than that of heathen peoples, who, although infidels to the Christian faith and thus erroneous in their beliefs, nevertheless speak the truth, acknowledge the truth, and act according to the truth. The English, however, although they are Christians and should therefore profess the truth and act accordingly, nevertheless, for fear of the loss of their worldly goods, or of being ruined through exile, or even of death – which may befall even the constant – never dare to speak or act according to the truth under such rulers. And he went on to say that it was clear to him that since the king himself, who was the chief and foremost among so many worthless and evil counsellors, had quite rightly been deposed and punished for this sort of crime, so also should those who had encouraged or incited or persuaded him to commit such deeds be arrested and made to suffer whatever punishment it was thought that their wicked counsel deserved, which should be decided by sober deliberation in a council of the realm. For these people, glorying in the evils of their time, used to describe themselves as the king's foster-children, and, with insufferable disdain, even took to announcing this in public, as they did for example when they presented their appeal with the words, 'We, the foster-children of King Richard, etc.'.[1] 'But alas!' declared Cobham, 'as the foster-parent is, so shall the

---

1 An interesting illustration of this occurs in a petition from the duke of Aumale to the king concerning the office of constable, which was granted by the king on 6 January 1399, and in which Aumale describes himself three times as the 'humble liegeman and foster-child' ('humble liege et nurri') of the king: R. L. Atkinson, 'Richard II and the death of the Duke of Gloucester', EHR (1923), 564.

foster-children be! As God is my witness,' he concluded, 'I do not say this because I seek revenge for the injuries which they have inflicted upon me, but because I stand for common justice, and I declare to you upon my conscience that if my own father who begat me was guilty of crimes of this sort, I would without hesitation say to you that he should be punished for them.' And when Lord Cobham had finished speaking, and he and the others had been asked for a decision on these matters, each one of them replied individually that he was of the same opinion, namely that all the aforesaid appellants should be arrested.

On one occasion when the record of the judgement given against the duke of Gloucester, the earl of Arundel and the earl of Warwick in that fateful parliament held in the twenty-first year of King Richard's reign was read out, and mention was made, among other things, of the way in which the earl of Warwick had publicly confessed to being a traitor to the king, the said earl, blushing with shame at his behaviour on that occasion, rose to his feet and, standing so that all could see him, asked the king if the record could be corrected, swearing that no such words had ever passed his lips; it had been someone else, he said, who had advised him to make this confession, but he had rejected the advice offered by such a person. To which Ralph Nevill, earl of Westmorland, who was standing nearby, immediately said, 'I trust that you are not suggesting to me that it was I who was at that time trying to persuade you to say such things' – for the earl was, by the king's command, in Nevill's custody at the time. 'Absolutely not,' replied the earl, 'the person who tried to persuade me is now dead.'

On another occasion when this record was read out again, and the same things were repeated about the earl of Warwick's ignominious confession, he again got up and declared that he had never made such an admission. The king, however, thinking it wrong to go on with such pretences when the evidence of the record was so obviously true, ordered him to say no more on the subject, for at the time when he made his confession, he had also admitted that the holy abbot of St Albans and a monk at Westminster had advised him that he ought to attend to that business, for which he was, by the king's judgement (*condemned*).[2] After hearing this, the earl decided to stop pressing for the deletion or annulment of the record. Also, because the same record made mention of the duke of Gloucester, etc., as being traitors as well, Lord FitzWalter rose to his feet and said that he was prepared to do battle with anyone who accused the duke of Gloucester of treachery;

2 This or some similar word is missing from the manuscript.

and Lord Morley did the same.[3] The king, however, wishing to calm everyone down, had a chest brought in containing the blank charters which King Richard had so craftily extorted from the lords and commons of the realm, and ordered the chancellor to cancel them so that they could never be used to oppress the people.

On the feast of St Luke the Evangelist (*Saturday 18 October*), William Bagot was again brought in for questioning, whereupon Thomas Percy, acting for the steward of the realm, asked him how he proposed to explain away – for he certainly could not deny – his conspiracy and plot against the life of the duke of Lancaster, father of the present king.[4] William replied that he had charters of pardon which covered this, granted to him not only by King Richard but also by the duke himself, the latter having granted it to him at the instance and request of the king. Percy then asked him whether his charter from the king covered this matter only, or all the rest of his crimes as well, both specific and general. He replied that it was a general pardon covering all matters, and that it could be found on record. When ordered to produce the charters, however, he said that he had left them at Chester. It was decided that he should be kept in custody until the following Tuesday.

On the same day the commons once again petitioned that all those, ecclesiastics as well as laymen, who had been known to be King Richard's evil counsellors, should be arrested, and especially those who through their false and deceitful computations and prophecies had led that king astray.[5] To this King Henry replied that some of them were already in custody, and the rest could be arrested at will if the commons would care to be more specific about whom they were referring to. In the meantime, he told them, they should spend the next few days, from this Saturday until the following Tuesday, making careful search and inquiry into these matters, for Monday was the octaves of his royal coronation, when, with his bishops in attendance, the king would be washed, the amice which had been placed upon his head at the time of the royal anointing would be removed, and the other traditional rites and ceremonies would be performed on his

---

3 Walter Lord FitzWalter (1386-1406), and Thomas Lord Morley (1379-1416). Both served under Gloucester, and had been dubbed knights by him on his French expedition of 1380 (Goodman, *Loyal Conspiracy*, 75, 124).

4 For this episode see above, pp. 19–20.

5 '... dementaverunt dictum regem.' An alternative translation might be '... caused the king to lose his mind.'

person, as a consequence of which they could not attend parliament that day.

(*John*) Hall, valet, was then led in, manacled and shackled, and interrogated about the death of the duke of Gloucester. He admitted that he had been one of those present at the duke's death, along with many others, but it had been against his will, and he had had no prior knowledge of the deed. He had been called from his bed and brought before the duke of Norfolk, who ordered him to accompany the others to the murder; when he refused to do so, the duke struck him a great blow on the head and swore that he would be hanged the next day if he didn't obey. 'For it is the king,' said the duke of Norfolk, 'and the duke of Aumale, who have ordered his death, and so it must be done.' Thus he went along to join the others, and then on with them to the place where the murder took place.

Hearing this, the duke of Aumale rose to his feet and asked permission from the king to defend himself, for Hall's words had implied that he had to some extent consented to the duke's death. After he had tried for some time, and in very long-winded fashion, to exonerate himself, finally Lord FitzWalter, having been given permission to speak, said to him, 'It was you who appealed him of treason, you who brought accusations against him, and you who made the king hate him; and for all those reasons it was you who brought about his death – which, with the king's permission, I shall prove in battle.' The duke of Surrey, trying both to win the approval of his accomplice, the duke of Aumale, and to establish his own innocence, said to Lord FitzWalter, 'You talk too much, and are constantly interfering. Why are you so eager to accuse us on the grounds of this appeal, when in fact there was no way that we could have avoided doing what we did at the time? When we were so much in the king's power, and in so many ways under his authority, how could we dare to disobey any command that he gave us? And were not you and all the other lords present as well, and did you not consent to his death too?' To which Lord FitzWalter said, 'No, you are wrong about me, I was not present at that parliament, nor did I ever consent to that judgement, as I believe the lords here present will bear witness.' Whereupon all those who were present agreed that it was true that he had not been present at the parliament.[6] The duke of Surrey somewhat shamefacedly resumed his seat therefore, and

6 This is a puzzling assertion, for FitzWalter's name is among those who swore at Westminster abbey on 30 September 1397 to uphold the acts of the parliament (*RP*, iii, 356).

Lord FitzWalter addressed the duke of Aumale again: 'You, Aumale, were the cause of the duke of Gloucester's death. You were midwife to his murder. And this I shall prove by battle. There is my hood!', and so saying he threw down his hood, to which the duke of Aumale responded with equal vehemence by throwing down his own hood. Seeing this, Lord Morley, Lord William de Beauchamp, the earl of Warwick himself, and nearly all the rest of the earls and barons also threw down their hoods to challenge Aumale on this point, whereupon there was such a mighty tumult and clamour from the commons offering battle on the same point that the king was afraid that the duke was about to be put to death before his very eyes. Rising therefore to restrain the lords, he first begged, then warned, and finally ordered them not to try to do anything which was against the law, but to act legally and only after proper discussion. Anything that might be done by any other means was as reprehensible as the crimes of those whom they were currently accusing. Impressed by this speech, the lords ceased their tumult and quietened down. Judgement was then given against the aforesaid Hall, who was condemned to drawing, disembowelling, having his bowels burned, hanging, beheading, and quartering.

On the Tuesday following the octaves of the king's coronation (*21 October*), the commons petitioned that the former king Richard should be brought into their presence to answer for the crimes of which he was accused, but the king said that he did not wish to reply to this until all the prelates were present ...

On the morrow of the feast of the Apostles SS Simon and Jude (*29 October*), shortly after midnight, the former king Richard was, with great secrecy, moved from the Tower of London to a different location.

On the same day all the lords temporal gathered in parliament, and with them was the bishop of Carlisle.[7] When they had taken their seats, the record of the appellants' proceedings against the duke of Gloucester, etc., in the parliament held in King Richard's twenty-first year was read out. After listening to this the duke of Aumale rose to his feet there and declared that, although it was true that he had been one of the appellants, he had never consented to the death of the duke of Gloucester. Lord FitzWalter, on the other hand, said that he had indeed been the cause of the duke's death, and repeated his offer to prove this in battle. The dukes of Surrey and Exeter, the marquis of

---

7 This is the start of the formal trial of the appellants, the records of which are in Doc. 20(b). The six accused lords had been arrested on 20 October (*CCR, 1399-1402*, 28).

Dorset, and the earls of Gloucester and Salisbury said the same, namely that while they admitted their role as appellants, none of them had agreed to the duke's death. Thomas Lord Morley, however, rose to speak against the earl of Salisbury, claimimg that it was he who had caused the duke's death, and that he would prove this in battle: 'For you,' he asserted, 'liar and turncoat that you are, betrayed the duke's counsel to the king. He confided greatly in you, yet you shamefully engineered his indictment!' and so saying he threw down his gage of battle against Salisbury. To this the earl replied with equal vehemence by throwing down his own gage against Lord Morley and declaring himself quite ready to do battle to prove his innocence on this matter. However, since no further information was forthcoming on this question for the moment, it was decided that further discussion of it should be postponed until the Monday after the feast of All Saints (*3 November*), in the presence of the constable and marshal.

Following this the bishop of Carlisle rose to defend himself against the various misdeeds of which rumour-mongers were accusing him, and which he proposed to show to be untrue. The king told him that he was under no obligation to stand trial on that count, and that it was more appropriate that he should appear before an ecclesiastical court, but he, after protesting that his action should not in any way prejudice the laws or liberties of the church, nevertheless repeatedly asked that his defence should be heard, and went on to deliver a most excellent speech exonerating himself from the numerous crimes which rumour had imputed to him, including complicity in the death of the duke of Gloucester. He also complained of the fact that he had been under arrest for a long time. He was quickly told that he had not in fact been placed under arrest, but had simply been sent to a secure refuge for his own safety, in order to allay the hatred towards his person which had grown up amongst the populace; as from now, however, he was free to go wherever he wished. Nevertheless he was still advised, for his own safety, to go back to the abbot of St Albans, in whose community he had already, by the king's order, spent some time, and remain there until the popular clamour had subsided and the world was more favourably disposed towards him. And so he did this for a while ...

(*On 3 November the judgement against the appellants was read out by William Thirning.*) After sentence had thus been passed against the lords there was considerable muttering and criticism of the king, the archbishop, the earl of Northumberland, and others of the council, to the effect that they had been bribed and had therefore spared the lives of men whom the people considered to be utterly wicked and thoroughly deserving of death.

At the same time a letter was unexpectedly found in the king's chamber which contained, among other things, a threat to raise a rebellion against the king if he did not put the above-mentioned lords to death. The parliament, which was about to be dissolved, was therefore prolonged so that the king could call together the lords, the peers of the realm, and ask them if any of them knew anything about the letter. They all swore that they knew nothing whatsoever about it. The king then asked the knights of parliament if they had offered any advice on, or given their consent to, the opinions expressed in the letter, but they all declared on oath that they too had known nothing about it. Reassured by these replies, the king then dissolved parliament

(b) According to a London chronicler

Source: *The Great Chronicle of London*, ed. A. H Thomas and I. D. Thornley (1983 reprint), 75-81.

Language: English

On the Thursday (*16 October*) the commons came in and rehearsed all the errors made in the last accursed parliament, and five in particular: the first error, they said to the king, is that you yourself were ready to wager by battle an appeal between you and the duke of Norfolk, but that notwithstanding this you were exiled for a term of years without reasonable cause; the second error is that our Metropolitan, the archbishop of Canterbury, was forejudged without right of reply; the third error is that the duke of Gloucester was murdered and then forejudged after his death; the fourth error is that the earl of Arundel claimed his charter of pardon and it was not allowed; the fifth error is that all the power of this evil parliament was placed in one person. Which errors, it seems to us, would never have been committed without the assent of those that were privy to the former king's counsel; wherefore they prayed that those persons might be arrested and kept in custody until it is decided what should be done.

BAGOT'S BILL IN ENGLISH

On the same day, William Bagot was brought to the bar, and a bill in

English written by him was read out, as follows:

These are the points which Sir William Bagot has acknowledged: the said William acknowledges that he had heard the king declare in various parliaments and to various knights that he was determined to have his way and his will in various matters in one parliament or another, otherwise he would dissolve parliament and, once it was dissolved, strike off the heads of those who had defied him in parliament. And with such strong and threatening words both the lords and the commons were forced to obey him and to accede to his wishes. The said William also acknowledges that the king said to him at Lichfield that his desire was to live long enough to see the crown held in such high respect, and obeyed with such lowly humility by all his lieges, as had been the case under previous kings, for he considered that he had been humiliated and disobeyed by both his lords and his commons, so that it might be chronicled forever that with skill and wisdom and strength he had recovered his royal dignity and his honourable estate; and should he achieve this, he would renounce his crown on the following day. And he went on to say that the most able, wise and powerful man that he could think of to whom to renounce it was the duke of Aumale, asking me if I agreed: but I said by my troth that I knew well that the people would not obey him. Whereupon the king told me that he thought that I would support the duke of Hereford, but that if Hereford became king he would be as great a tyrant to the holy church as there ever was. So I held my peace, daring to say no more; 'and yet,' said the king, 'there have been many good Confessors among both his ancestors and mine, who never persecuted the holy church.'

The same William also declared that in the month of October in the twentieth year (*1397*) he was riding along Savoy Street towards Westminster behind the duke of Norfolk when the said duke asked him whether I knew anything about what had happened to the duke of Gloucester; and I said, 'no, by my troth, but the people say that you murdered him.' To which he swore great oaths that it was not true, that he had in fact saved his life, contrary to the wishes of the king and certain other lords, for more than three weeks, and that he had never stood in greater fear of his life than at the time when he returned from Calais to the king's presence, because the duke was not then dead. Then the king ordered one of his own men and a number of other lords' men to go with him to Calais to make sure that the murder was carried out. And all the time (*Norfolk*) swore, as he would answer before God, that it was never his wish that Gloucester should be killed, but that it was done solely out of dread of the king and fear for his own life. He also went on to say that there was no man in the kingdom of England that the king valued so highly as the duke of Aumale, for he had acted as his principal accomplice in the arrest of the lords, and in the subsequent parliament, the forfeitures, and all other such matters.

The same William also said that he had heard the king declare, and even take a vow, at King's Langley last March (*1399*), to the effect that as long as he lived the present duke of Lancaster would never return to England;

he would rather restore to their estates the sons of the duke of Gloucester, the earl of Arundel, the earl of Warwick, and all the others who had been forejudged at the last parliament for standing up to his power and his malice. And so he decided absolutely there to revoke his letters patent concerning the taking of his homage by attorney and the payment of his fine through general attorneys. And concerning these matters, together with the details of many other matters, the said William sent a messenger, Roger Smart, to the duke of Lancaster in France, telling him to inform him that the king was his sworn enemy, and that he would have to help himself by force; and the said Roger has acknowledged these matters before Peter Bukton and another person who informed him about it. William also said that he had heard the duke of Aumale say to Sir John Bussy and Sir Henry Green that he would gladly give twenty thousand pounds to see this man dead; and they asked him, 'Which man?', and he replied, 'The duke of Hereford: not because I am afraid of him, but because of the misery and trouble that he is likely to cause within this kingdom.'

When this bill had been read out, the duke of Aumale rose from his seat and said that, concerning the points raised in it ... (*at this point a folio has been torn out of the manuscript*). And concerning the other point, the duke of Aumale declared that, 'If the duke of Norfolk maintains that I sent two yeomen to Calais to see to the duke of Gloucester's death, then I say that he lies falsely, and I shall prove it with my body.' Whereupon he offered his pledge, and threw down a hood which he had borrowed, which was handed over to the constable and marshal of England. And the king gave the duke of Norfolk permission to return, in order to determine this wager of battle ...

THE APPEAL OF THE LORD MORLEY

Then Lord Morley rose from his seat and said to the earl of Salisbury that he had been the chief counsellor of the duke of Gloucester, and he had also been the chief counsellor of King Richard, and thus was he false and traitorous to his master; 'And that I shall prove with my body,' and he offered his pledge, and threw down his hood upon the ground. The earl of Salisbury repeated to Lord Morley that he was never a traitor, nor had he been false to his master, nor had he revealed his counsel; and that he lied falsely, and he would prove it so; and he threw his gloves down upon the ground. Whereupon their pledges were handed over to the constable and marshal of England, and the parties were arrested and a day assigned to them ...

And afterwards the Lord FitzWalter came and requested a day and a place to decide his appeal against the earl of Rutland. To which the king replied that he would send for the duke of Norfolk: 'And when he has come, we will proceed with your matter.'

(c) According to the Rolls of Parliament

Source: RP, iii, 415-53

Language: French

On Thursday 23 October, the archbishop of Canterbury on behalf of the king charged all the lords spiritual and temporal, and all others then present, upon their allegiance, that the matter which they were about to discuss was confidential and should not be revealed by them to any living person. They were then asked by the earl of Northumberland what they thought ought to be done with Richard, the former king, to ensure the security of the king and all the estates of the realm, and how he might be securely guarded, saving his life, for the king does not in any way wish to deprive him of his life. And when each of the lords spiritual and temporal whose names are below had been individually examined on this matter, they replied that they thought that he should be kept in secure and secret custody in a place where there were no other people about, that he should be guarded by trustworthy and responsible persons, that under no circumstances should anyone who had been familiar with him when he was king be about his person, and that all this should be done with the greatest possible secrecy. (*There follow the names of twenty-two prelates and thirty-six lay lords who assented to this.*)

Be it remembered that in the parliament held at Westminster on Monday the feast of St Faith the virgin (*6 October*), in the first year of King Henry IV, the commons declared to the king that it was hardly possible that Richard, former king of England, who had been deposed because of the many great defaults and offences in the government of his royal estate, could have committed the said offences without the support of others who were about his person, and that the commons had been led to believe that various records had been drawn up at the parliament held at Westminster in the twenty-first year of his reign, which made mention, at least in part, of his misdeeds, and contained the names of those others who were to blame; and they asked the king if these records could be brought into parliament and read out, in order to throw light on this question. This the king granted them, saying too that those persons who were mentioned in these records should also be made to come into parliament, and that the records should be read in their presence, and their answers to them heard; and if anyone wished to make any specific allegations concerning these persons, he would be duly heard, as would any answers given to him, and the king would then do justice to them. These records were then read out in parliament in the presence of the aforementioned persons, namely Edward duke of Aumale, Thomas duke of Surrey, John duke of Exeter, John marquis of Dorset, John earl of Salisbury, and Thomas earl of Gloucester.

When these records had been read out, the duke of Aumale informed the king that he had duly heard an appeal and certain records which concerned his person, among others; and he requested the king, since the appeal which had been brought by himself and the other appellants, and the record of the answers given by those who had been appealed, and the judgements of the lords who had been present in parliament and had given judgement, had all been read out in that same parliament, that the names of the lords responsible for these judgements should be read out in this parliament, and that they should be questioned as to whether they, or any of them, had been persuaded, requested, required, or constrained by the said duke of Aumale, or by anyone acting in his name, on any matter concerning these judgements, or if they were in any other way prevented from speaking freely; and if any of them wished to argue that he was, the duke of Aumale was ready to defend himself in whatever way the king should decide. He added, moreover, with regard to the death of Thomas former duke of Gloucester, that he had never been a party to his death, nor did he advise it, assent to it, or agree to it; and if anyone wished to gainsay him, he was ready to defend himself in whatever way the king should decide. The duke of Aumale also said, in relation to the aforesaid appeal, that he was never involved in the making, drawing up, approval, or promotion of it, indeed he knew nothing about it until shortly before the time when it was presented to the former king in the hall of Nottingham castle,[8] but was constrained by the king to present it in the form that it then was. Moreover, he had said at the time, both to the deceased duke of Lancaster and to his father the duke of York, that he had been ordered that day to do something that made him sadder than he had ever been before, but that for fear of death he dared

8 On 5 August 1397.

not contravene the king's order, just as the lords who gave judgement on the appeal dared not contravene the former king's wishes when they gave their judgement.

As for the judgements given against the earls of Arundel and Warwick, both what had been done by himself and the other appellants, and the answers made by these earls, were on record, but, bearing all these things in mind, he prayed that the king would do justice to him. Moreover, he never advised or assented to the banishment of the present king, which seemed to him entirely against right and justice, nor to the repeal of his patent, which was done contrary to his wishes.[9] At the time when the former king first mentioned this plan to the duke of Aumale, he remembered being greatly saddened by the idea, and even came to London to ask Lord William le Scrope, who was treasurer at the time, to approach the former king in an attempt to dissuade him from such an unfortunate course of action. He also spoke to Lord Lovell at the time, telling him that if the king went ahead with his plan it would cause universal amazement, which clearly shows that he did not agree with it. And he begged the king to ask Lord Lovell about this. As for the lordships belonging to the present king which the former king had committed to the duke of Aumale, he said that he made no attempt to use the letters which the former king issued to him in the hanaper[10] until after he had gone to Ireland, when Robert Waterton advised the duke of Aumale's ministers that they ought to take possession of these letters from the hanaper, not only for the duke of Aumale's benefit but also for the benefit of the present king. Nor did the duke of Aumale remove any (*Lancastrian*) minister from his office apart from Robert Nevill of Hornby, whom he replaced with Robert Waterton.[11] Nor did the duke of Aumale, or anyone acting on his behalf, ever receive a single penny from the profits of these lordships. As for the judgements given against the others, those who were not appealed, he had no part in them, nor did he consent to them. And if anyone wished to gainsay him

9 It is specifically stated on the official roll that all of the six accused apart from the duke of Surrey (who was in Ireland) consented to the repeal of Bolingbroke's letters patent on 18 March 1399 (*RP*, iii, 372).

10 The hanaper was the office of the chancery in which fees were paid and letters issued (from the 'hamper' in which letters were kept).

11 Nevill, a Yorkshire knight and long-standing Lancastrian servant, was constable of Pontefract under John of Gaunt; Waterton was one of Bolingbroke's closest associates (Walker, *The Lancastrian Affinity*, 289; Given-Wilson, *Royal Household*, 191).

on any of these points, the duke of Aumale was ready to defend himself in whatever way the king should decide. And as to the question of whether or not he bore a grudge against the present king, and whether he was for him or against him, he placed himself entirely at the king's mercy and at his command.

(*The dukes of Surrey and Exeter, and the marquis of Dorset, also disclaimed responsibility for initiating the appeal, denied any involvement in Gloucester's death, and claimed to have been opposed to the exile of Bolingbroke and the repeal of his letters patent.*)

Item: John earl of Salisbury said to the king that he had heard the process of an appeal brought by certain persons of whom he was one, which he regretted. However, he said that he had in no way been involved in the planning or promotion of this appeal, and had known nothing about it until ordered by the former king to present it in the form that it then was; which order he dared not out of cowardice disobey, but went ahead with it, in the same way that the lords, also out of fear, gave judgement on the appeal. And although he was well aware that he had not acted loyally, it was fear of his life that prevented him from speaking the truth. He also said that although the present king, in the bill of appeal which he had brought against the duke of Norfolk in that same parliament, had mentioned that the earl of Salisbury had plotted the death of the most noble lord the duke of Lancaster – on whom may God have mercy – yet were the duke of Norfolk present, or anybody else who wished to make the same accusation on his behalf, he was ready to defend himself like a gentleman in whatever manner the king should decide. Yet inasmuch as he had failed, for fear of his life, to conduct himself loyally, he cried mercy of God, of the king, of the crown, and of all parties.

Item: Thomas earl of Gloucester said to the king that he had heard the appeal of which he was one of the appellants; and concerning this appeal, he said that on St Oswald's day (*5 August 1397*), when the former king was sitting dining in the great hall of Nottingham castle, and the earl of Gloucester was also sitting dining at a side table in the same hall, the king sent a message to him to get up and come to him. When he did so, the king ordered him to go outside the castle gate and do as the other lords there were doing. Whereupon the earl of Gloucester went to his chamber in the keep of the castle, donned his hauberk, girded himself with his sword-belt, and took about six valets with him, because he thought that he was going to have to make an arrest. When he came outside to the gate he found the other appellants there, among whom was William le Scrope reading the bill of appeal, most of which had already been read before his arrival. Presently the king sent for them to come forward, and asked them why they had tarried so long. Thus was the name of the earl of Gloucester added to the appeal, but by whom he had no idea. Afterwards, in fear of his life, he had not dared to disobey the former king's order to present the appeal. As to the death of the duke of Gloucester, he said that he never advised or assented to it, nor did he know anything about it until it was announced to the whole realm. And as to the judgements given against the earls of Arundel and Warwick, and the exile of the present king and the repeal of his patent, and all the other judgements given in parliament, none of these were done on his advice, but were entirely contrary to his wishes and intentions. This he was ready to prove, should anyone wish to gainsay him; for any wrong that he had done, however, he placed himself at the king's mercy.

Following this, Lord William Thirning, chief justice of the common bench, at the king's command, and with the advice and assent of the lords of parliament, gave judgement in parliament against the aforesaid Edward duke of Aumale, Thomas duke of Surrey, John duke of Exeter, John marquis of Dorset, and Thomas earl of Gloucester,[12] in the following words:

(*English*) My lords, you are well aware that, at the instance and the request of the commons, the king granted and commanded that certain records of the parliament held in the twenty-first year of King Richard the second should be read out, and that certain persons mentioned in those records should be told to come and hear them, and to make answer to them; and that, once both they and the answers given to them had been heard, if any man, of any state or condition whatsoever, wished to comment upon them, he should be allowed to have his say, as would any who wished to make further reply, and then the king would do them justice. These records were duly read out in this present parliament, and the answers of certain lords, that is to say, of the aforesaid dukes of Aumale, Surrey and Exeter, of the marquis, and of the earls of Salisbury and Gloucester, were heard, each of them answering personally for himself, before the king and all the estates in this present parliament; at which time no person of any estate or condition made any comment upon them, apart from Lord Morley to the earl of Salisbury, and Lord FitzWalter to the duke of Aumale. Whereupon

12 It will be noted that the earl of Salisbury was not included in the judgement. This was because it had been decided in the Court of Chivalry that he was to submit himself to trial by battle with his accuser, Lord Morley. The combat was to have taken place at Newcastle in February 1400, but was pre-empted by Salisbury's death in January (Adam Usk, 206).

the king said that he would take advice concerning the aforesaid records
and what was contained in them, and concerning the answers of the
aforesaid lords, from all his other temporal lords and his other counsellors,
and then proceed as he thought best by their advice, for the circumstances
of the parliament required that he act with speed.

In the morning, therefore, the king gathered all his temporal lords and
the others of his council together to discuss this matter. And since the
answers of those lords named in the records were sound in their intent and
in their denials of responsibility – that is to say, because each of them
individually said that he was not the promoter or instigator of the bill
containing the appeal, nor did he know anything about it until it was
shown and read to him, which occurred in various places and at various
times, as was explained here before the king and all of you; and because
they were commanded by the then king to do it, and thus did it in fear of
their lives, and to avoid what perils might have befallen them had they not
done so; and because some of them begged the king and the lords to take
account of their youth at that time; and because each one of them
disclaimed all responsibility for, and consent to, the death of the duke of
Gloucester – the king, in order to be entirely clear as to the truth of this
matter, and to arrive at the best and most equitable judgement, decided, on
the advice of his lords temporal and his other counsellors, to summon those
same lords appellant, all except the earl of Salisbury, and to charge them
individually and in private, with none of the others present, by the faith and
the allegiance that they owed to him, to tell him truly who were the
promoters and instigators of the appeal and the other things included in
the record, and of a number of other matters not mentioned in the record.
And their answers were duly noted by the king and the lords; whereupon the
king once more reminded them, upon their faith and allegiance, that they
should try to think further about these matters and to remember all that they
could about them, and that if anything else, in addition to what they had told
him, came to their minds, then they should tell him about it ...

(*The lords temporal advised the king that a sentence should be passed on the
appellants which ensured his own and the realm's security; the lords spiritual,
also consulted, advised an exemplary sentence but not capital punishment. The
judgement of the lords was that Aumale, Surrey and Exeter should lose their
dukedoms, Dorset his marquisate, and Gloucester his earldom. They were also
sentenced to the loss of all lands and goods which they had acquired from
either the lords convicted in 1397 or from the king since that time, and were
placed under severe constraint as far as the giving of liveries was concerned.*)

Moreover, the temporal lords, with the assent of the king, adjudge and
award that if any of these same lords appellant should ever be an adherent
to the deposed former king, Richard, whether it be by counsel, or any other
sort of help, against either his deposition or any of the other acts or

ordinances of this parliament concerning the person of the same Richard, that they do so under pain of treason, and shall be treated as traitors. Since, moreover, there have been numerous complaints among the people that various of their followers have committed great crimes, extortions and acts of oppression against the people, inasmuch as it has been said that some of the men who were with them, by authority of their lordship and of the great position of their lords, have taken much more by extortion and oppression of the king's people and by the maintenance of quarrels than all the rest of their own livelihood amounted to; the lords, with the assent of the king, adjudge and award that a proclamation be made throughout the realm, that if any man wishes to make a complaint against these lords, or against any of those who are or who have been their followers, concerning any extortions, wrongs, or oppressions done to them, let them come, and justice shall be done to them.

(*French*) Item: John Hall, who was in the custody of the marshal of England, was brought by the marshal into parliament, and Walter Clopton, chief justice of the king,[13] said to this John Hall, by command of the king, that he had acknowledged certain things before James Billingford, clerk of the crown, which things had been set down in writing and read to him. At the king's command, these things were then read out in parliament, as follows:

Be it remembered that on Friday 17 October, in the first year of King Henry IV, John Hall, former valet of Thomas duke of Norfolk, having sworn upon the holy gospels to tell the truth, in a chamber in the constable's house in the inner palace of Westminster, acknowledged before James Billingford, in the presence of Henry earl of Northumberland, constable of England, and Thomas earl of Worcester, that in the month of September (*1397*), the said duke of Norfolk and a certain John Colfox, one of the duke's esquires,[14] paid a visit to John Hall's chamber in the town of Calais. John Colfox told him to get out of his bed and come with him to see his lord the duke, which he did. The duke asked him why he had taken so long, and whether he had heard anything about the duke of Gloucester, to which John Hall replied that he presumed that he was dead. No, said the duke of Norfolk, he was not dead, but the king had charged him with murdering Gloucester; and he added that the king and the duke of Aumale, who was then earl of Rutland, had sent across certain of their esquires and valets to be there, and that he wanted John Hall to be there in the name of the duke of Norfolk. John Hall begged not to be made to do this, saying

---

13 Clopton was Chief Justice of the King's Bench.

14 This was in fact Nicholas Colfox: on 7 November he was deprived of a grant which Mowbray had given him, but he was later pardoned for his alleged role in Gloucester's murder (*CPR, 1399-1401*, 57; Legge, *Anglo-Norman Letters*, 446, and references cited there).

that he would rather lose all his goods and be dismissed than to have to do such a thing; to which the duke of Norfolk said that either he would be there, or he would lose his life, and gave him a great cuff across his head. So the duke of Norfolk, John Colfox, and John Hall went to the church of Our Lady of Calais, where they found William Hamsterley and (*blank*) Bradeston, esquires of the duke of Norfolk, William Serle, valet of the former king's chamber, (*blank*) Frauncis, valet of the duke of Aumale's chamber, William Roger and William Denis, valets of the duke of Norfolk, and another valet staying with the duke of Aumale who John Hall thinks was called 'Cook of the Chamber'.[15] John Hall was told there that all the others had already sworn to reveal to no one what they were about to do, and they made him swear too, upon the body of Christ, in the presence of one William, who was chaplain of St George at the church of Our Lady of Calais and cousin to John Lancaster,[16] one of the duke of Norfolk's esquires, that he would keep counsel in this affair.

Having thus taken the oath, they all went together with the duke of Norfolk to the hostel called Princes Inn, where the duke of Norfolk showed the said John Colfox, William Hamsterley, Bradeston, William Serle, Frauncis, William Roger, William Denis, Cook of the Chamber, and John Hall into a lodging within the hostel, and went on his way together with various others who were not known to John Hall. Soon after they had arrived there, John Lovetoft[16] appeared with several more esquires whom John Hall did not know, bringing with him the duke of Gloucester, whom he handed over to William Serle and Frauncis at the inner door of the hall, saying, 'Here are Serle and Frauncis.' To which the duke of Gloucester replied, 'Now I know that I shall be all right,' and he asked William Serle how he was. 'Well enough,' replied Serle, 'and many greetings.' William Serle and Frauncis took the duke of Gloucester from John Lovetoft, who then left, and led the duke to a side chamber, saying that they wished to speak with him. And they told him that it was the king's will that he should die; to which the duke of Gloucester replied, 'If that is the will of my lord, so be it.' William Serle and Frauncis then told him to take a chaplain, and he duly confessed himself to a chaplain. After this, they made the duke of Gloucester lie on a bed, and the said William Serle and Frauncis placed a featherbed over him; William Roger, William Denis and Cook of the Chamber held down the sides of the featherbed, while William Serle and Frauncis pressed down upon his mouth until he was dead. Meanwile John

---

15 William Hamsterley fled on 20 October, and all his lands and goods were declared forfeit to the king (*CCR, 1399-1402*, 532); Serle, an executor of Richard II's will, escaped to Scotland but was handed over to King Henry in 1404 and suffered a cruel death (*Annales Ricardi Secundi*, 390-1; Given-Wilson, *Royal Household*, 181-2, 229); a William Denys, possibly the one referred to, was dead by January 1401 (*CPR, 1399-1401*, 404), but I have not been able to trace the others mentioned here.

16 For Lancaster and Lovetoft see Rickhill's account below. No action seems to have been taken against either of them. Lancaster had a grant from Mowbray to him confirmed in May 1400, and Lovetoft's annuity of £20 at the exchequer was confirmed in February 1401 (*CPR, 1399-1401*, 294, 453).

Colfox, William Hamsterley and Bradeston went down on their knees close to where the duke lay, weeping and praying for his soul, and John Hall kept guard at the door of the lodging. Soon after he died the duke of Norfolk arrived, and saw that he was dead; whereupon John Hall heard him say that it would be a far better thing to have the aforesaid duke of Gloucester still alive now. And John Hall is ready to prove, either by his body or otherwise at the king's pleasure, that all these things are true.

When the king and all the lords temporal present in parliament had heard this admission made by John Hall, it seemed to them that he merited the harshest death to which he could possibly be sentenced, since the duke of Gloucester was so great a personage. With the assent of the king, therefore, the lords temporal adjudged the said John Hall to be drawn from Tower Hill to Tyburn Forks, and there disembowelled and his bowels burned in front of him, and then hanged, beheaded and quartered; and his head should be sent to Calais where the murder was committed, and his quarters sent to wherever else the king should determine. Whereupon the marshal of England was commanded to carry out the execution; and so it was done, that same day.

Item: on Tuesday 18 November, the commons prayed the king that William Rickhill should give his answer to the petition which they had previously submitted to the king in the following words: (*The petition recited that Rickhill, a former justice of the common bench, had been arrested for his part in securing the duke of Gloucester's confession in 1397; Walter Clopton, the present chief justice of the king's bench, was ordered to cross-examine him about his part in the affair. He claimed to have been ordered by King Richard on 17 August 1397 to go to Calais with the earl marshal, Thomas Mowbray, there to do whatever Mowbray commanded. He and Mowbray crossed to Calais, in separate ships, on Friday 7 September, where Mowbray showed him a commission from the king, also dated 17 August, ordering him to visit Gloucester and to make a written record of all that Gloucester might say to him; this was the first he knew of the fact that his visit to Calais was connected with the duke of Gloucester.*) ... William was astonished to see this commission because, as he said to the earl marshal, the duke of Gloucester was dead: his death had been announced to all the people, in Calais as well as in England. The earl replied to William that in fact the duke was still alive, and he told him to come to Calais castle on Saturday, the feast of the Nativity of Our Lady (*8 September*). But William said to the earl that he had no desire to visit the duke or to speak with him unless it were in the presence of sufficient persons who would bear witness to the truth of whatever William might say to the duke, and whatever the duke might say or give to him. The earl marshal therefore assigned John Lovetot and John Lancaster, esquires, to be witnesses for William in this matter, and to see and hear everything that passed between him and the duke. So William arrived at Calais castle between five and six o'clock in the morning on Saturday the feast of Our Lady, and the keeper of the castle allowed him to enter. There he found John Lovetot and John Lancaster, the witnesses assigned to him. Later, between eight and nine o'clock, the said William, John Lovetot and John Lancaster entered the hall of the castle; John Lovetot and John Lancaster went to the chamber behind the screen in the hall, and informed the duke of Gloucester that William had come with a message from the king, and wished to speak with him. Meanwhile William remained in the hall along with various menials who were waiting on the duke, namely Thomas Whitehead and Nicholas Miles, chaplains, Reynold Rumbold and Robert Wade, clerks, John Cok esquire, and various others, until he was called forward by the witnesses to come to the duke in his chamber ...

(*Rickhill then recounted his interview with Gloucester, his departure from the castle, and his return the same evening to hear and collect Gloucester's confession. Gloucester asked him to return next morning, which Rickhill promised to do.*) ... on the following morning William again arrived at the castle gate, planning to go in as agreed between him and the duke the previous evening, but a valet standing on the walls called out to him that he could not enter until he had spoken with Thomas, the earl marshal. Soon afterwards, therefore, on the same day, William approached the earl marshal and asked him for permission to visit and speak with the duke. The earl replied that first he wished to speak with the keepers of the castle. A little later, still on the same day, the earl sent the aforesaid John Lovetot and John Lancaster to William with a message to the effect that he would not be allowed any further visits or conversations with the duke. William then begged Lovetot and Lancaster, as they wished to answer before God, that should it be necessary they would bear witness truly to all these matters, and that William had done as was asked of him properly and loyally; and they answered that they would ...

(*Rickhill left Calais the following Tuesday, 11 September, and delivered Gloucester's confession to the king on Sunday 16 September, the day before parliament opened, receiving from the king an acknowledgement under the great seal.*) ... the reason why William requested this acknowledgement was because he was afraid that the document which he had delivered to the king might be altered or amended, or its contents damaged or erased; he now showed this acknowledgement under the king's great seal to this present parliament. In the parliament held at Westminster in the twenty-first year, those of the articles in the document which suited the king's purposes were read out, but those which were contrary to the king's interests were not, and no mention was made of them ... (*Rickhill went on to protest about his name being publicly associated with Gloucester's confession, for he had done nothing except what he was ordered to do. He had passed on Gloucester's confession exactly as it had been given to him, as could be proved by comparing it with the original which Rickhill had kept for himself, which was now in the possession of Sir Peter Courtenay. The lords concluded that he had behaved entirely honourably throughout the affair, and fully acquitted him.*)

21. The 'Epiphany Rising' and the death of the king

The two most substantial chronicle accounts of the events of January-February 1400 are those of Thomas Walsingham and the author of the Traison et Mort. *Both are characteristically detailed, though neither is without its problems. For example, Walsingham's lengthy description of the earl of Huntingdon's wanderings through Essex is very difficult to reconcile with the fact that he died not on 15 January as the chronicler asserts, but on 9 or 10 January, and it is hard to know how Walsingham could have acquired such detailed information about his movements. Equally, the story in the* Traison et Mort *of the accidental discovery by the duke of York of his son's sealed indenture of conspiracy seems little more than a device by the author to defame further the earl of Rutland — although it is worth noting that the Dieulacres chronicler also blamed Rutland for betraying the plot.[1]*

As to the manner of Richard's death, the heroic fate ascribed to him in the Traison et Mort *— and later adopted by Shakespeare — can be quickly dismissed. Apart from the fact that the author could not possibly have had access to the information which he presents, it is worth pointing out that when Richard's body was exhumed in the nineteenth century no marks of violence were found upon it. However, it is difficult not to be equally sceptical about the story which the Lancastrians put about, and which Walsingham passed on, namely that the king starved himself to death. There can, in fact, be little doubt that Richard was murdered, probably on Henry's orders.*

(a) According to Thomas Walsingham

Source: *Annales Ricardi Secundi*, 322-31

Language: Latin

In the year of grace 1400, and the first year of the reign of King Henry the fourth since the Conquest ..., the earls of Kent, Salisbury and Huntingdon, displaying singular ingratitude to a king who, contrary

1 Dieulacres Chronicle, 173-4

to the wishes both of many of the lords of the realm and of the commons, had spared their lives, now went from bad to worse and began holding meetings and conspiracies in various places at which they plotted a surprise attack on the king, under the guise of Christmas festivities or jousts, while he was at Windsor castle. Their plan was to put him and all his sons to a cruel death and, once they had got hold of King Richard, to put him back on the throne; they also hoped, through such abominable deeds, to be restored to the ducal titles and lands of which they had quite properly been deprived. By divine intervention, however, their plan was miraculously foiled, for the king was forewarned of their traitorous conspiracy and, quickly removing himself from Windsor, made with all haste for London. The earls of Kent and Salisbury, however, thinking that the king knew nothing of their plans, set out at dusk on the Sunday evening (*4 January*) after the feast of the Circumcision intent on carrying out their wicked plot against the king, and arrived before the castle with an armed force of about four hundred men-at-arms and archers, ready to commit their hideous crime as soon as possible. But when they found out that the king, having been forewarned of their evil and deceitful plans, had already left, they were greatly downhearted and dismayed, and sought, as rapidly as they could, some escape from their plight. Spurring on their horses, therefore, they rode as rapidly as they could to the manor of Sunning, near Reading, where the queen, the daughter of the king of France, was staying at the time. They arrived at the gates there at about nine o'clock on the feast of the Epiphany (*6 January*) and, leaving their men-at-arms and archers outside to wait for them, the two earls took a handful of followers with them and went into the hall, to the great surprise of all the queen's servants, who had no idea what all this meant ...

(*Kent exhorted the queen and her followers to join the rising against the king, claiming that Henry had fled to the Tower of London and that Richard had escaped from prison and was waiting at Pontefract with 100,000 men.*) At length, after receiving permission to leave, (*Kent*) mounted his horse and rode firstly to Wallingford and then on to Abingdon, where he told the same lies as he had told before in a desperate attempt to persuade the people to take up arms and follow him in King Richard's service. But as soon as the earl and his men had left each place, and before those whom he had exhorted could take up arms, a new rumour would come to the effect that King Henry was getting ready to pursue the earl with an enormous force of soldiers. And as this rumour kept on growing stronger, experience told them that it was likely to be closer to the truth.

The earl of Kent, therefore, along with the earl of Salisbury, Lord (*Ralph Lumley*)[2] and some other followers, took their weaponry and fled with all haste until they came under cover of night to the town of Cirencester. But the inhabitants of that town, becoming suspicious of their display of arms, and believing, quite rightly, that they were not telling the truth, during the night secretly blocked all the entrances and exits from the lodging where they were staying. Meanwhile the earls, fearing that if they stayed there until morning they would be in great danger, tried to get out and slip away unnoticed in the middle of the night, but when they saw that every way out had been blocked with beams and other great pieces of wood, they began an attack with lances and arrows, trying to drive off the townspeople who were preventing them from leaving. The townspeople continued to surround them, however, and now they too began to shoot arrows at the lodging – some through the windows, some at the doors and gates – with the result that no place was safe for them, and not only were they unable to get out, they were not even able to look out. This fight lasted from the middle of the night until three o'clock on the following day, when the earls eventually gave up, handed themselves over to the townspeople, and surrendered, begging not to be put to death before they had had an opportunity to speak to the king. They were accordingly led to the abbey, where they heard mass and were given breakfast for the day. During the afternoon, however, at about the hour of vespers, a certain priest who was one of their followers started a fire in some houses in one of the streets of the town, in the hope that while the townspeople were busy trying to put it out the earls could seize the chance to escape. It was in vain, however, for the townspeople, anticipating such a ruse, abandoned the houses to the flames and rushed instead to the abbey to make sure that those whom they had spent so much effort in capturing should not be allowed to get away. By this time Thomas Lord Berkeley had arrived and was preparing to take them to the king, which he would undoubtedly have done had the fire not been started in the town, but this wanton act so infuriated the townspeople, and indeed others who had begun to arrive from various parts of Gloucestershire and elsewhere, that no words could dissuade them from their determination to see the earls put to death. They even

2 The text reads 'Domino (blank) Bunney', but Ralph Lord Lumley (1384–1400) is meant.

threatened Lord Berkeley with death if he did not hand those traitors to the king over to them. Eventually, therefore, when the sun was almost setting, they were duly handed over, and the earls of Kent and Salisbury were beheaded at the hands of the people; by which act the Lord took his revenge upon them with such punishment as their bad faith and lack of belief merited. For they were both unfaithful to their king, who had spared them, and, what was worse, they were ungrateful to him who had shown them so much mercy. And if what is commonly said is true, then the earl of Salisbury, who all his life had been a follower of the errors of the Lollards, a despiser of holy images, and a spurner of the sacraments, ended his miserable life without the sacrament of confession.[3]

Lord John Holand, earl of Huntingdon, the former duke of Exeter, had not ridden with the other earls to Windsor castle on the day when they had planned to kill the king, but lurked instead in London awaiting the outcome of events, ready, so it was said, if things turned out as they had planned, to go to their aid with a large force of men-at-arms. Once he heard that the plan had gone wrong, however, he tried to escape in a little boat, but He who commands the wind and the tide stirred up such a violent and contrary wind against him that there was no way that he could prevail against it and make his escape along the Thames. Seizing a horse, therefore, he rode as fast as he could to Hadleigh castle in Essex, where Aubrey de Vere, the earl of Oxford, was staying with his wife, the countess of Oxford;[4] but he could not tarry long there, because his pursuers were searching everywhere for him. Slipping out of the castle secretly, therefore, accompanied by a knight called John Schevele[5] whom good fortune had raised in a few years from the rank of groom to such heights, he came across a mill where he hid for two days, desperately searching for a way to allay God's wrath so that he could escape by sea. Every time he tried to sail out to sea, however, he was driven back to shore again by the strength of the wind, until eventually, despairing of escaping by sea, he abandoned this idea and travelled back inland until he came by night to the house of an esquire whom he knew called John Pritwell.[6] While he was dining there,

---

3 John Montague earl of Salisbury was well known for his Lollard sympathies; see the comments of K. B. McFarlane, *Lancastrian Kings and Lollard Knights* (1972).

4 Aubrey de Vere, earl of Oxford 1393-1400; his wife was Alice, daughter of John Lord FitzWalter.

5 This was in fact Sir Thomas Shelley (*CCR, 1399-1402*, 42).

6 John Prittlewell's annuity of 40 marks at the exchequer from Richard II had been confirmed by Henry IV on 20 November 1399 (*CPR, 1399-1401*, 337)

however, a crowd of locals suddenly rushed in, seized him, and, leading him off to Chelmsford, sentenced him, by judgement of the common people, to the most shameful of deaths ... (*Although initially saved by the intervention of the countess of Hereford and Sir Gerard Braybrook, and given refuge in Pleshey castle, Holand was eventually beheaded at the insistence of the locals at nightfall on 9 or 10 January,[7] on the spot where the duke of Gloucester had been arrested in 1397.*)

Also at this time, Thomas Lord Despenser, the former earl of Gloucester, was suddenly captured while trying to escape, and, having been taken to Bristol, was beheaded at the behest of the common people, despite the fact that he had sent messengers from there in the hope of saving his life until he had had a chance to speak with the king.

Meanwhile the king, who never lacked courage or boldness of purpose, having left his children in the Tower of London in the care of the mayor and citizens[8] set off in strength in pursuit of the aforesaid lords, and soon arrived at the head of a splendid army at Oxford. On his way he had heard news of the capture and well-deserved punishment of those who had committed treason against him, that is, that without any effort on the part of him or his army, they had been swiftly overcome, not through his ingenuity but through God's. When this news was confirmed, therefore, he raised his hands high and gave thanks to God for so favouring him, not only for setting him up in the kingdom without bloodshed, but also now for delivering him from the clutches of his enemies without putting either himself or his followers in any serious danger; for he knew that all these things had happened not through human agency but miraculously, through divine intervention. Several others who had joined the rebels were also brought to Oxford, where, after being interrogated, they were led off to their deaths.

Soon after this the clerks (*Richard*) Maudeleyn and William Ferriby were sentenced in London and put to death by being drawn, hanged and beheaded, and the knights Bernard Brocas[9] and John Schevele

---

7 Walsingham gives 15 January, but Huntingdon was dead by 10 January at the latest (*GEC*, v, 198).

8 The mayor of London was Thomas Knolles. The *Vita Ricardi Secundi*, 163, credits him with the discovery of the plot; he later received £10 from the king for defending the Tower of London with 30 soldiers for ten days at the time of the rising (P.R.O. E403/564, 4 February).

9 Sir Bernard Brocas, a knight from Hampshire and former life-retainer of King Richard's (Given-Wilson, *Royal Household*, 284).

suffered a similar fate, as did a number of others whose names are unknown to us. The bishop of Carlisle, when accused of giving advice and support to the traitors, was unable to answer for his behaviour and was also condemned to death, although later, in the Tower, the king relented and granted him his life. The abbot of Westminster and Roger Walden – who had previously been archbishop of Canterbury, though God alone knows how – were interrogated and made to answer for themselves, but later set at liberty.

When Richard, former king of England, who had been imprisoned in Pontefract castle, heard of the disasters which had befallen his brother John Holand and the others, he apparently became so depressed that he determined to starve himself to death. He is said, therefore, to have abstained from food to such a degree that the orifice leading to his stomach contracted, so that when later, on the advice of friends, he tried to satisfy his natural longings by eating, he found himself unable to eat anything because his appetite had been completely suppressed, with the result that he wasted away through natural debility, and finally died at the aforesaid castle on St Valentine's Day (*14 February*). His body was taken from there to London, and was exhibited at all the important places on the way – that is, at those places where they spent the night; or at least that part of his body by which he could be recognised was exhibited, namely from the base of his forehead down to his throat. When they came to St Albans, where they spent the night, the community held a solemn requiem service for his soul, and in the morning the abbot celebrated mass; then he was taken on to St Paul's church in London where the king attended his obsequies both on the first day, and then again, along with various nobles of the realm and citizens of London, on the following day. Then, as soon as mass was over, the body was taken back to Langley[10] to be buried among the friars, arriving there at dead of night. Soon after this messengers arrived from the king to the abbot of St Albans ordering him, on the king's behalf, to make his way there by the following morning so that he could, along with the bishop of Chester and the abbot of Waltham, be present at the king's last funeral rites. This he duly did: and thus, without ceremony and almost unattended, was this royal corpse committed to the grave.

10 King's Langley in Hertfordshire; the Dominican house there was under the patronage of the English kings.

CHRONICLES OF THE REVOLUTION

(b) According to the *'Traison et Mort'*

Source: Traison et Mort, 229-51

Language: French (trans. B. Williams)

Item, it is true that the eighth day before Christmas, thirteen hundred
fourscore and nineteen, the following parties were dining in the rooms
of the abbot of Westminster;[11] that is to say, the first duke was the
duke of Exeter, earl of Huntingdon; the second the duke of Surrey, earl
of Kent; the third the duke of Aumale, earl of Rutland. The first earl
was the Lord Despenser, earl of Gloucester; and the second the earl of
Salisbury. The late archbishop of Canterbury, named Walden, was also
there, and so was the good bishop of Carlisle, the abbot of Westminster, and Maudeleyn who resembled King Richard, with Master Pol,
King Richard's physician, and a wise baron, Sir Thomas Blount.[12]
When the lords had finished dinner, they went into a side council-
chamber, and a secretary was present who had prepared six small
deeds, which were all cut and indented one to fit the other; to which
each of the said lords affixed his seal, and swore by their souls to be
faithful to one another even unto death, and to restore King Richard
to his kingdom and lordship, or to die in the attempt. They resolved
to surprise King Henry and his sons at a tournament to be held on the
day of the Three Kings, for which purpose they were to assemble on
New Year's Day at a town called Kingston, ten leagues from London;
and that Maudeleyn should ride with them, to represent King Richard.
Item, King Henry sent letters to all the lords of his kingdom, inviting
and commanding that they would come to the feast of the new king at
his castle of Windsor ...

On the first Sunday of the year (*4 January*), the duke of Exeter, the
duke of Surrey, and the earl of Salisbury met at Kingston, with eight
thousand archers and three hundred lances of men-at-arms, the flower
of all England; and, on setting off from Kingston, the lords sent letters
to the duke of Aumale earl of Rutland, in London, urging him not to
fail to be at Colnbrook on the night of the Kings. The duke of Aumale
was dining, the first Sunday of the year, with his father the duke of
York; and, after he had seated himself at the table, he placed the
indenture of their confederacy on the table. When the duke saw it, he

11 William Colchester.

12 Sir Thomas Blount of Oxfordshire had been a knight of Richard II's chamber since
at least 1384 (Given-Wilson, *Royal Household*, 282).

demanded, 'What letter is that?' The earl, taking off his bonnet, replied, 'My lord, do not be angry, it does not touch you.' 'Show it to me,' said the duke to his son, 'for I will know what it is.' Aumale then handed the letter to his father. And when the duke of York saw the six seals, he read the letter throughout; which done, he said, 'Saddle the horses directly. Hey, thou traitor thief, thou hast been traitor to King Richard, and wilt thou now be false to thy cousin King Henry? Thou knowest well enough that I am thy pledge-borrow, body for body, and land for goods, in open parliament; and I see plainly that thou goest about to seek my destruction. By St George, I had rather thou shouldst be hung than I.' And so the duke of York mounted on horseback to ride to Windsor to reveal the matter to King Henry, and to show him the letters which he had taken from his son. The duke of Aumale, seeing that his father was gone to King Henry at Windsor, set off himself, and arrived there a good time before his father, who was advanced in years; he then caused the castle-gates to be shut, and carried the keys with him to King Henry, before whom he bent the knee, beseeching his forgiveness. The king replied, 'Fair cousin, you have done nothing amiss.' Then he declared unto him the power of the confederated lords, their names, and the whole of the conspiracy; how he and his sons were to have been seized, and King Richard and his queen restored, and that he had been a party to the enterprise; for which he begged for mercy and forgiveness.

'If this be true,' said Henry, 'we pardon you; but if I find it false, upon our word you shall repent it.' Whilst they were talking together, the duke of York arrived, and presented to the king the indenture he had taken from his son; and when the king saw the indenture with its six seals, he ordered eight horses to be saddled, for he would go to London presently. The king mounted on horseback, and reached London at nine o'clock at night: on his road he met the mayor with four attendants, hastening to inform him that the lords had taken the field with six thousand followers. A proclamation was immediately issued that all those who were willing to serve their king and the city of London should repair to the council-house, enrol their names, and swear to serve loyally; promising, for fifteen days, eighteen pence for every lance and nine pence for each archer. By the morrow morning at eight o'clock, more than sixteen thousand men were enrolled and paid, and ready to follow the king ...

(*On 6 January Henry marched out of the city and mustered his forces.*) The king drew up his army of twenty thousand men in order of battle, and ordered the earl of Rutland to go forward to reconnoitre his enemies, who were sixteen miles distant, and to bring him a positive report of them. He then appointed a vanguard of four thousand archers and two hundred lances, in two divisions: giving the command of one to his brother the marquis,[13] and of the other to Sir Thomas Erpingham, and sending them by different routes. To the rest he gave orders that no person should be so bold as to pass his horse, on pain of losing his head, for he wished to be the first to come to blows. When Rutland left the king, he went straight to Colnbrook, where he found the brother of King Richard (*Huntingdon*) and the other lords, to whom he gave to understand that King Henry was out of London ready to take the field with two thousand archers; and the lords thought that the king had not even so many men as the earl had told them, and agreed in council that they should go to Wales or Chester, where they would be strong enough to fight all England. The earl of Rutland pretended that he was willing to live and die with them. When the lords and their army had passed the two bridges of Maidenhead, four leagues beyond Colnbrook, the two vanguards of King Henry came in sight; and the earl of Rutland, perceiving that they were so near, returned towards them, crying out, 'They all flee,' making pretence that he had had a skirmish with those who passed the bridge: and the lords of King Richard's party perceiving that the earl of Rutland was against them, held the bridge with the duke of Surrey, who is called earl of Kent, and begged the earl of Huntingdon that he would lead on the army until they had fairly passed Henley and Oxford, and he would hold the bridge with those of the rearguard who were best mounted in spite of them. The vanguard of King Henry could not succeed in passing the bridge of Maidenhead; and the duke of Surrey skirmished so well that he captured from them two pack-horses, two baggage-wagons, and a chariot of the king's; he would not let a single person pass the bridge for three days[14] before King Henry came up: and when he knew that the king had arrived, he and his companions held the bridge bravely till night, and then stole away quietly, taking with him all of the town, both horse and foot, to serve King Richard. The earl of Huntingdon had already gone on with all the army, clearing the town of its provisions and victuals, that King Henry and his people might not find any. The duke of Surrey rode with such speed that he reached Oxford

13 John Beaufort, earl of Somerset; he had been deprived of his marquisate in November 1399.

14 This cannot fit with the known chronology of the revolt: Williams suggested that the chronicler meant to write 'trois heures' instead of 'trois jours'.

the same night; and, after leaving that city, he overtook on the morrow King Richard's brother and the other lords with the people of Woodstock; and they marched to a town called Cirencester. There the army encamped in the fields, but all the lords went to lodge in an inn …

(*The townspeople of Cirencester, discovering the treachery of the earls, barricaded them in the inn, and a skirmish ensued; Huntingdon, Despenser and Maudeleyn escaped through a window and set fire to some houses before fleeing.*) The earl of Huntingdon found his steward with about a dozen horses, and immediately mounted, and went away towards Essex to flee from the kingdom; and the Lord Despenser fled towards Wales, his own country; and Maudeleyn thought to go to Scotland. The lords who remained in the town of Cirencester held the house bravely, and defended themselves valiantly until the morrow morning at eight o'clock, when they were forced to surrender. There were captured Sir Thomas Blount, Sir Benedict (*Cely*),[15] and thirty other knights and esquires, whom they bound securely together, and led them away on foot by the sides of their horses, which the villeins rode. When the lords were captured, the townspeople cut off the heads of the duke of Surrey and the earl of Salisbury and stuck them on long poles; and in this manner carried them from Cirencester to Oxford, where they found King Henry lodging in the abbey of the Carmelites, outside the town, to whom they brought the heads and the prisoners …

Item, it is true that on the day of the Kings (*6 January*), when King Henry had taken the field, outside London, with all his people who were about to combat the lords who had risen to support King Richard, he commanded a knight called Sir Peter Exton[16] to go and deliver straightaway from this world John of London,[17] called Richard, for it behoved that the sentence of parliament should be accomplished. The knight, having taken leave of King Henry, rode to the castle where he found King Richard confined, who was seated at table awaiting his dinner; and Sir Peter called King Richard's esquire trenchant, and forbade him on the part of King Henry to dare to taste any more of the king's meat, saying he might let him eat alone if he

15 Sir Benedict Cely, or Sely, came from Sussex and had been one of Richard II's chamber knights since at least 1395 (Given-Wilson, *Royal Household*, 283).

16 No person of this name is known to have existed; possibly it was a corruption for Peter Bukton, who apparently acted as Richard's gaoler for a time (Short Kirkstall Chronicle, 126).

17 Apparently an illusion to the reports of Richard's illegitimacy which some chroniclers alleged were circulating at the time (Adam Usk, 180-1).

chose, for he should never eat again. The esquire returned to the room where King Richard was seated, who was unwilling to eat because he was left alone, and his esquire would not perform his office as usual. 'What is the news?' said the king. The esquire replied, 'I know of none except that Sir Peter Exton is come; what tidings he has brought I know not.' King Richard then begged the esquire to carve him some meat and to taste it, as was his duty. The esquire went down upon his knees before the table, and, begging King Richard's pardon, hoped he would excuse him, for they had forbidden him by King Henry's order; upon which King Richard went into a passion, and, seizing one of the table-knives, struck the esquire on the head with it, exclaiming, 'Cursed be Henry of Lancaster and thou!' As he uttered these words, in rushed Sir Peter Exton to the room where King Richard was, with seven men, each man having a lance in his hand. It is true that King Richard, perceiving Sir Peter Exton and his seven armed men, put the table back from him, and, springing in the midst of them, wrung an axe from the hands of one of them who came there to murder him; with which King Richard right valiantly and vigorously defended himself, and in so doing slew four out of the eight men; when Sir Peter leaped upon the chair where King Richard usually sat at meals whilst he was in prison, where he waited, his axe in his hand, till the king came near to him. The king defended himself so well that it was great marvel how he could so long make head against them, for they were all armed; but King Richard defended himself right vigorously like a good and loyal knight, till at last in defending himself he retreated towards the chair where Sir Peter Exton was, who gave him his death-blow, for he smote him such a blow on his head that King Richard fell backwards on the ground. The king exclaimed, 'Lord, have mercy on me!' after which he gave him yet another blow on his head. And thus died noble King Richard without confession, which was a great pity, and he that says otherwise does not speak discreetly. When the king was dead, the knight who had given him his death-blow went to sit down beside the corpse and began to weep, saying, 'Alas! what is it that we have done? We have murdered him who has been our sovereign lord for the space of twenty-two years. Now I have lost mine honour, and I shall never go into any country but I shall be reminded of it.' On the morrow the corpse of King Richard was carried to Pontefract,[18] and there was he interred like a poor gentleman. God have mercy on him!

18 The author thought that Richard was murdered at Gravesend castle in Kent.

22. The 'Epiphany Rising': contrasting fortunes

Although Thomas Walsingham and the author of the Traison et Mort *provide the most detailed accounts of the rising, they leave a number of questions unanswered. How, for example, was the plot uncovered? The intriguing story involving a London prostitute which is told in the* Continuatio Eulogii, *when taken together with the letter which Archbishop Arundel (from whom the author of the* Continuatio Eulogii *may well have acquired his information) wrote to his monks at Canterbury, is not perhaps as implausible as it seems at first sight. How, too, were the townsmen of Cirencester alerted to the plans of the rebel earls? Was it, as John Norbury's letter states, through quick thinking on the part of Walter Hungerford, or was it through that 'certain esquire of Cirencester' one of whose servants had attended the festivities at Windsor? Also, was the author of the* Traison *correct in saying that Huntingdon and Despenser had been present at the Cirencester debacle before fleeing to Essex and South Wales respectively? Almost certainly not: the monk of Evesham, who probably heard about Despenser's death from neighbouring Tewkesbury abbey (where Despenser was buried), and was well-placed to know what happened at Cirencester, suggests that he had remained at Cardiff awaiting the outcome of events.*

(a) The discovery of the conspiracy

Source: Continuatio Eulogii, 385-6

Language: Latin

The king held Christmas at Windsor; a certain esquire from Cirencester who was greatly skilled in arms sent a member of his household, as was his custom, to the king's court so that he could report back to him on the warlike deeds done at the jousts there.[1]

---

1 The man referred to may be John Cosyn of Cirencester, a former servant of the duke of Gloucester who was retained for life by the king in November 1399. On 24 January 1400 he was granted an annuity of 100 marks at the exchequer for 'manfully resisting' the earl of Kent and the other rebels at Cirencester (*CPR, 1399-1401*, 86, 127, 182-3).

After the feast of the Lord's Circumcision (*1 January*), the archbishop of Canterbury left Canterbury to join the king for the feast of the Epiphany at Windsor. At this time a member of the king's household spent the night with a London prostitute; in the morning she said to him, 'Goodbye, my friend, for I shall not be seeing you again.' He asked her why that was, and she replied, 'The earls of Huntingdon, Kent and Salisbury are waiting near Kingston with many other knights to ambush and kill the king, the archbishop of Canterbury, and all the rest of you when you return from Windsor, and to put King Richard back on the throne.' 'How do you know this?' he asked her. She replied, 'A member of one of their households slept with me the other night, and he told me.' Hurrying to the king, therefore, he told him about this conversation, and they called an immediate halt to the jousts. Hearing this, the man from Cirencester reported it back to his master. The king sent a messenger to warn the archbishop, who turned back to Reigate; then, changing his plans, the king hurried to London at night by a different route, sending out orders to all the men of the shires to join him as soon as possible. A member of the archbishop's household was passing through Kingston when the earl of Kent spotted him from the window of his lodgings and, ordering him to be brought into his presence, asked him, 'Where is your master?' 'At Reigate castle,' he replied. 'And where is the king?' 'In London,' he replied. 'You speak the truth,' said the earl, 'they have fled out of fear of us. If I had encountered your lord, I would have stripped him of his crown.' And he ordered his servants to take the man's horse and money. Then he and the earl of Salisbury and their followers rode to Cirencester, proclaiming along the way that King Richard was coming....

(b) A narrow escape for the Archbishop of Canterbury

Source: Letter from Archbishop Arundel to the Convent of Canterbury Cathedral, in *Literae Cantuariensis*, iii, 73–5

Language: Latin

My dearest sons and brothers ... In order that the workings of God the father be clearly revealed before your eyes as wonderful and praiseworthy, we shall familiarise you with the details of what recently happened to us. On Sunday 4 January we were making our way from our manor of Croydon to join our lord king, and, having arranged to spend the night in the town of Kingston upon Thames, we had sent on ahead our baggage-train, including our jewels, and some of our officials, so that they could get on with preparing whatever needed to be got ready, when, as we were approaching the town, quite unaware of any sort of deceit, we were by divine mercy forewarned of a secret and abominable ambush which had been laid by certain people who thirsted after our blood. Abominable indeed is the word for an ambush of this sort, in which a nephew, with the calculated villainy of a traitor, attempts an armed attack against his uncle, like a son against his father[2] ... However, the divine power could not leave this sort of dreadful crime unpunished for long without taking revenge, so, without wasting time, he struck with sudden fury at this would-be parricide, this foul ingrate; as a result of which, the authors of this crime – whom we can identify as the earls of Kent and Salisbury, and Lords Ralph Lumley, Thomas Blount and Benedict Sely – were seized, along with some others, at Cirencester, by the virtuous common people of the neighbourhood, who have made all these facts publicly known; nor indeed did they simply capture them, but, lest others might arrive and succeed in snatching their prisoners from their grasp, they also beheaded the aforesaid earls and Ralph Lumley, leaving the rest to our lord king's judgement ... (*We have also heard*)[3] that the earl of Huntingdon, Lord Thomas Shelley, and various others are being held prisoner by royal officials in Essex and Kent; may each one of them receive the reward that his behaviour deserves, and may the severity of the punishment torment their wicked souls ... Written at our residence in London on the 10th day of January.

(c) The capture of Sir Walter Hungerford

Source: Anglo-Norman Letters, ed. Legge, 64.

Language: French

From John Norbury to the archbishop of Canterbury.

Very reverend father in God and my most honoured lord, I commend myself to your lordship. Since you wish to hear news of these matters, may it please you to know that the earl of Kent came across Walter Hungerford,

2 The earl of Kent was the son of Alice, the archbishop's sister.

3 The original is damaged at this point.

knight,[4] and made him swear against his wishes to take his side, and took him in his company to Cirencester; the said Walter, however, having been thus coerced, secretly alerted the bailiffs of that town and begged them to get together to arrest these rebels and malefactors against our lord the king. The bailiffs and people of the town assembled therefore, and, on the night of the feast of the Epiphany, seized the said earl of Kent, the earl of Salisbury, and all those who had banded together to follow them; they are all safely in custody, and my lord Botiller[5] and I will be there next Thursday to take custody of them and lead them to our lord the king at Oxford. Very reverend father, etc. Written, etc. (*no date*).

(d) The fate of Lord Despenser

Source: Vita Ricardi Secundi, 164–5

Language: Latin

During the following week Lord Thomas Despenser too was beheaded, in the following manner. He was staying around this time at his castle of Cardiff in Wales when the king sent some men-at-arms with orders to bring him to London, voluntarily or otherwise. But he, realising that he was under suspicion, made what arrangements he could for his belongings and, taking all his jewels with him, secretly fled before these men-at-arms could get to him, hoping to escape overseas; and, having found a ship, he put out to sea. The captain of the ship, however, who had been bribed, and who was a traitor even to his lord, and still more so to the faithless, had stowed away about twenty well-armed men in secret places on the ship.

Once they had set sail and travelled a fair distance from the shore, the captain said to him, 'Where are you planning to go to, my lord?' 'Abroad,' he replied. To which the captain said, 'I shall have to take you to Bristol.' 'Under no circumstances will you dare to do any such thing,' he replied, 'for before you do so you will die by the sword.' But the other said, 'There is no point in your continuing to argue about it, for whether you like it or not that is where you are going.' There

---

4 Sir Walter Hungerford was a king's knight and the son of Sir Thomas Hungerford, former steward of the duchy of Lancaster. Although a Gloucestershire jury later found him guilty of joining the rebel earls, his claim that he had been coerced into riding to Cirencester with them was accepted by the king (*Calendar of Inquisitions Miscellaneous, 1399-1422*, 30; *CPR, 1399-1401*, 385).

5 Possibly Sir Thomas Botiller, or Butler, of Gloucestershire.

ensued a violent quarrel between them, hearing which, those concealed below suddenly rushed up from their hiding-places and began to attack him and his men, and although he tried desperately to defend himself, and even managed to wound some of them, they were too numerous and too strong for him, and he was overcome. Thus at length they brought him back by force in the ship to Bristol, where they handed him over to the custody of the town's mayor.

On the second day after this all the people gathered together and shouted out to the mayor, 'Bring out this traitor to the king and the kingdom, and let him be put to death.' Although the mayor tried hard to save him from their clutches, there was nothing he could do about it, and in the end they dragged him out to the cross which stands in the market-place and beheaded him.[6] Then they took his head away and placed it on top of London bridge. Later, however, at the request of his mother, a reputable lady, it was taken down and buried with the rest of his body at Tewkesbury, next to his father ...

---

6 The mayor of Bristol was Thomas Knappe; Despenser was said to have been wearing 'a furred gown of motley velvet or damask' when he was seized outside Knappe's house (*CPR, 1399-1401*, 197). He died on 13 January.

23. Rumours and omens of Richard's fate

The secrecy surrounding Richard's death reaped its inevitable harvest: the monk of Evesham, although no supporter of the fallen king, still found it hard to believe that he had starved himself to death. The confusion expressed by Adam Usk, who declared almost in the same breath that Richard both 'mourned even to death' and was 'tormented ... with starving fare', was to be taken up and exploited by supporters of the deposed king such as Jean Creton. This uncertainty was to fuel numerous conspiracies and rebellions against the Lancastrian regime during the next few years, the most common story being that Richard had been spirited away from Pontefract and given refuge in Scotland, whence a steady stream of calls to arms to his supporters began to emanate. The probable author of these was in fact William Serle, an esquire of the former king's chamber who escaped to Scotland and apparently forged the royal signet there. It was only after Serle's capture and execution in 1404, according to Walsingham, that the rumours that Richard was still alive abated.[1] Nevertheless, as late as 1416 a London hosteller called Benedict Wolman was sentenced to be hanged because he conspired 'to bring Thomas Warde, otherwise called Trumpyngtone, whom they declared to be the late King Richard II, from Scotland into England, with the view of placing him on the throne'.[2]

Richard's downfall also brought forth the customary crop of epitaphs, obituaries and claims of prophecies fulfilled. The monk of Evesham took the opportunity to pen the only substantial description that survives of the king's physical appearance and characteristics. Adam Usk, as so often, sought refuge in prophecies of doom. But it is fitting that the last word should be left to Jean Creton. At the time he completed his chronicle, Creton seems sincerely to have believed that Richard might still be alive. Shortly after this, however, he was sent by the French King Charles VI on a mission to Scotland to discover whether there was any truth in these rumours; and, as he apparently later told Jean Froissart, he discovered that there was none.[3] Creton's own admission

1 *Annales Ricardi Secundi*, 390-1. See the extended discussion of this matter and the documents printed by Williams in the introduction and appendix to the *Traison et Mort*, lii-lxxiii, 267-77; see also D. W. Dillon, 'Remarks on the manner of the death of Richard II', *Archaeologia* (1840), 75-95.

2 *London Letter-Book* I, 165-6.

3 Palmer, 'Authorship, date and historical value', 151-4.

of his former gullibility merely serves to confirm the truth of what all but a few diehards must really have believed all along, namely that Richard had perished in some dismal fashion, probably during the first two weeks of February 1400, in Henry Bolingbroke's castle of Pontefract.

(a) A king who deserved his fate

Source: *Vita Ricardi Secundi*, 166–7

Language: Latin

After a while this miserable story of the destruction of the aforesaid lords (*the rebel earls*) reached the ears of the deposed King Richard, who was at that time in Pontefract castle. He had placed all his trust in them, hoping that through them and with their help he might be restored to his former eminence, but when he realised that his hopes had been thus dashed and there was now no chance of escaping, he declined into such grief, languor and weakness that he took to his bed and refused any food, drink or other sustenance. Thus on St Valentine's day, 14 February, in the year (*1400*), the twenty-third year of his reign, he died there in prison. Others say, however, and with greater truth, that he was miserably put to death by starvation there. Thus was the fateful judgement spoken by the Lord in the gospels fulfilled with respect to this king: 'He who lives by the sword shall die by the sword.' For since he had in the past so thoughtlessly condemned many people to die by the earthly sword, so it came about that in the end he himself died, childless and friendless, by the sword of hunger; and he was buried at Langley.

This King Richard was of average height, fair-haired, with a pale complexion and a rounded, feminine face which was sometimes flushed; he was abrupt and stammering in his speech, and, because he spurned the advice of his elders and betters and preferred to take counsel from the young, he was capricious in his behaviour. He was prodigious with gifts, extravagantly ostentatious in his dress and pastimes, and unlucky as well as faint-hearted in foreign warfare. Towards his servants he often displayed great anger; he was also puffed up with pride, consumed by avarice, much given to luxury, and fond of burning the candle at both ends, sometimes staying up half the night, and at other times right through until morning, drinking and indulging himself in other unmentionable ways.

He imposed crushing tenths, taxes and similar subsidies upon his people almost continuously through his reign, so that scarcely a year passed in which he did not hold a parliament to secure whole or half tenths and fifteenths; yet when, under the pretext of defeating the enemy, he had acquired enormous wealth for the crown, it was all spent on his own foolish wantonness. Nevertheless there are two things to be said in his favour: firstly, that he favoured and promoted God's church and churchmen, especially the black monks, and secondly, that for the salvation of his soul he acquired rents to the value of 500 marks to be made over to Westminster church for the maintenance of his anniversary, even though he is not buried there.[4] May God have mercy on his soul. Amen.

(b) Auguries of Richard's fate

Source: Adam Usk, 191–202

Language: Latin (trans. E. M. Thompson)

The lord Richard, late king, after his deposition, was carried away on the Thames in the silence of dark midnight, weeping and loudly lamenting that he had ever been born. And a certain knight there present said to him: 'Remember that thou, in like manner, didst entreat the earl of Arundel in all things most spitefully' ...

Then, too, I saw with King Henry a greyhound of wonderful nature, which, on the death of his master the earl of Kent,[5] found its way by its own instinct to King Richard, whom it had never before seen and who was then in distant parts; and whithersoever the king went, and wheresoever he stood or lay down, it was ever by his side, with grim and lion-like face, until the same king, as is before told, fled at midnight by stealth and in craven fear from his army; and then, deserting him, and again led by instinct and by itself and with no guide, it came straight from Carmarthen to Shrewsbury to the duke of Lancaster, now king, who lay at that time in the monastery with his army, and, as I looked on, it crouched before him, whom it had never

---

4 Richard's body was later removed by Henry V from King's Langley to the tomb which he had prepared for himself and his first wife Anne in Westminster abbey.

5 Thomas earl of Kent (d. 1397), Richard's half-brother. Froissart (*Chroniques*, xvi, 187) tells a different version of this story of the greyhound, saying that it was called 'Blemach' and that it forsook Richard for Henry during their meeting at Flint.

seen before, with a submissive but bright and pleased aspect. And when the duke had heard of its qualities, believing that thereby his good fortune was foretold, he welcomed the hound right willingly and with joy, and he let it sleep upon his bed. And after the setting aside of King Richard, when it was brought to him, it cared not to regard him at all other than as a private man whom it knew not; which the deposed king took sorely to heart ...

(*Usk describes the failure of the 'Epiphany Rising'.*) And now those in whom Richard, late king, did put his trust for help were fallen. And when he heard thereof, he grieved more sorely and mourned even to death, which came to him most miserably on the last day of February, as he lay in chains in the castle of Pontefract, tormented by Sir (*Thomas*) Swynford with starving fare.[6]

At the coronation of this lord three ensigns of royalty foreshadowed for him three misfortunes. First, in the procession he lost one of the coronation shoes; whence, in the first place, the commons who rose up against him hated him ever after all his long life: secondly, one of the golden spurs fell off; whence, in the second place, the soldiery opposed him in rebellion: thirdly, at the banquet a sudden gust of wind carried away the crown from his head; whence, in the third and last place, he was set aside from his kingdom and supplanted by King Henry.

(c) Jean Creton's scepticism at the news of Richard's death

Source: Metrical History, 217–241

Language: French

Soon after this (*the 'Epiphany Rising'*), they made good King Richard acquainted with the whole truth of this sorry business, which greatly saddened him – and no wonder. Then he wept and said, 'Make ready,

---

6 Sir Thomas Swynford, a knight of Henry's chamber, may indeed have been Richard's gaoler at Pontefract: shortly after this, an exchequer entry records that 'a certain valet of Sir Thomas Swynford' was paid his expenses 'for coming from Pontefract castle to London to inform the king's council of certain matters relating to the welfare of the lord king.' The immediately following entry notes a payment to another valet sent from the king's council to Pontefract to oversee 'the safekeeping and custody of the body of Richard, former king of England' (P.R.O. E403/564, 20 March).

death, and take me; no one can help me now, for I have lost my friends. Gracious Lord who was crucified, deign to have mercy on me, for I can live like this no longer.

The king was so vexed at heart by this evil news that from that time onwards he neither ate nor drank: and thus, so they say, it came to pass that he died. But, in truth, I do not believe it; for some declare for certain that he is still alive and well, shut up in their prison. It is a terrible wrong that they commit. Nevertheless, they had the body of a dead man carried openly through the city of London, accompanied by the sort of pomp and ceremony that befits a dead king, saying that it was the body of the deceased King Richard. Duke Henry made a great show of mourning there, holding the pall behind him, followed by all his kinsmen splendidly arrayed, showing no shame for the crimes they had committed against him. This will be an awful burden to them before God at the day of judgement, when he sentences the wicked to the everlasting flames of hell.

Thus, as you can hear, did they carry the dead body to St Paul's in London, with all the honour due to a king. But I certainly do not believe that it was the old king; I think it was Maudeleyn, his chaplain, whose face, size, height and build were so exactly similar to the king's that every one firmly believed that it was good King Richard. If it was him, however, I fervently pray, morning and night, to the merciful and holy God, that he will take his soul to heaven, for, in my opinion, he hated all kinds of sin, and every sort of vice. I never saw him deviate in the least from catholic faith and justice. For seven months I served him in any way that I could, to make myself worthy of the benefits that he had promised me.[7] In truth, the only reason why he was deposed and betrayed, was because he loyally loved his father-in-law the king of France with a love as true and sincere as any man alive. That was the root of the problem, and the cause of the envy – although they charged him with having evilly caused the deaths of the dukes his uncles, and of being neither prudent nor wise enough to govern the realm. I could tell you many other things that were commonly said about him, but I think that, as far as I could discover it, I have told you the truth. And I shall abide by my opinions even unto death. For, evil and unreasonable people as they are, the English mortally hate the French, if they dared to show it ...

7 If, as seems likely, Creton returned to France in September 1399, then he cannot have spent seven months with Richard, for, as he tells us himself ('Metrical History', 13), he did not reach England until the end of April at the earliest.

Let us now pray God, who humbly suffered his naked body to be suspended upon the cross for the redemption and restoration of sinners from the false enemies of hell, that he will speedily avenge the great wrongs, ingratitudes and injustices which the wicked English have committed against their king and queen. For I declare to you in truth that I have a great wish to see this happen, because of the wickedness which I have seen among them. And if everyone knew about their behaviour, and the way they hate the French, I firmly believe that within three months or less we should see a host of vessels filled with men and provisions setting out to make war against them ... Also, the good earl of Salisbury, at the time when he was captured with King Richard, earnestly begged and entreated me to publish the whole truth about their evil and treacherous behaviour, and I willingly and loyally promised him that I would do so. I have taken the trouble, therefore, to fulfil that promise, which I made to him at a time when he was in such fear and anxiety. Besides, I am sure that the true story of the capture of the king – the way he was falsely enticed out of his strong and fair castles in Wales through agreement with the earl of Northumberland, as I explained earlier – is not widely known. And I sincerely pray all those who shall read through to the end of this story which I have written about the English and their affairs, that if I am guilty of any inadequacies as a writer, either in prose or in verse, they will excuse me for it, for I am not skilled in these matters. Amen. (*This concludes Creton's history.*)

Appendix A: the duke of York's army, July 1399

The composition of the army assembled by the regent, Edmund duke of York, in July 1399, can be at least partially reconstructed from the payments recorded on the exchequer issue roll and from a series of accounts later submitted by those who brought troops (P.R.O. E403/ 562, 12 July, and E101/42/12, respectively). · York's army can be divided into three groups: (i) major retinues brought by lords and royal councillors; (ii) sheriffs' posses; (iii) lesser retinues brought by individuals – often men of quite humble standing. In some cases the period for which payment was made is given, and in most other cases it is possible to work out, from the amount of money received, the number of days (though not the actual dates) for which money was paid. For most of the retinues, the number of men-at-arms and archers is stated, but not usually for the posses. However, it is possible to estimate with reasonable accuracy, by comparison with more detailed accounts, roughly how many soldiers most of the sheriffs were being paid for.

From this it is possible to calculate that York authorised payments totalling £2,035 to be made to a total of about 3,300 men. The major retinues available to York were those of himself, John Beaufort marquis of Dorset, Michael de la Pole earl of Suffolk, Henry Despenser bishop of Norwich, Robert Lord Ferrers of Chartley, the abbot of Walden in Essex, and Sir William Elmham (who probably accompanied the bishop of Norwich from Suffolk): together, these numbered about 1,090 men. The councillors Bussy, Green, Bagot and Russell were paid sums which suggest that they had a total of about 500 to 550 men with them. Sheriffs from ten counties (none further north than Rutland) responded to York's summons, and their posses amounted to about a further 1,150 men. The lesser retinues, again overwhelmingly from central and southern England, probably provided a further 550 to 600 men. Thus some 3,300 men received payment from York. But how many of these he had together at any one time is less clear.

Most instructive here are those accounts which specify the dates for which leaders of retinues claimed payment for their men. York's first summons was issued on 28 June, for a muster at Ware in Hertfordshire. Payment was made from the day that the leaders left home to join the muster, and the accounts indicate that in most cases it took at least a week for them to gather their forces and set out: of those whose dates of payment are specified, only the royal councillor John Russell and the sheriff of Oxford and Berkshire, John Golafre, were able to set out before 5 July. On 12 July York moved from St Albans to Ware to collect his troops, and on the following day he seems to have moved north to Bedford; here he was joined by more forces, including those of the Northamptonshire knights John Holand, John Trussell and Guy Malory. Already, however, some of his troops may have been leaving him: Golafre, for example, despite having gathered his troops as early as 2 July, only received payment for them until 12 July. According to the *Vita*, Golafre himself remained loyal to the king, but the same may not have been true of his men. The fact that they were only paid until 12 July might suggest that they were among those who, as Walsingham put it, 'set off, as soon as they had gathered in any numbers, to find the duke of Lancaster and to fight for him at the wages of King Richard.'

From Bedford, York turned back via Aylesbury and Thame to Oxford, where he spent about four days (?16–19 July), and where the decision was taken to split the army, Lescrope and the other councillors going ahead to Bristol. York moved more slowly via Stow-on-the-Wold and Gloucester to Berkeley, which he probably reached on about 24 July. He continued to pick up some troops on the way – for example, Sir Amaury de St Amand, the esquire Robert Chorley, and several of the other minor retinues from Hampshire only seem to have joined him at Gloucester – but by the time of his meeting with Bolingbroke at Berkeley on 27 July, royalist support was beginning to crumble. One of the most detailed surviving accounts is that of John Browning, the sheriff of Gloucestershire: Browning left Gloucester on 10 July with 20 men-at-arms and 100 archers, joined York at Ware on 12 July, and then marched back to Bristol. Presumably he went with Lescrope and the councillors to Bristol, for he only claimed wages for his men for the period 10–24 July, and 24 July was four days before York (with Henry Bolingbroke) reached Bristol. Sir John Trussell's retinue, which had joined York at Bedford and then marched via Oxford to Bristol, was only paid until 26 July. The fairly brief lengths of time for which many of the other retinues were paid suggests that they too may have melted away some time before York's encounter with Bolingbroke.

Nevertheless, if the evidence of the accounts is to be believed, York clearly still had a fair number of soldiers with him when he met Bolingbroke, for most of those who received wages for specified periods claimed to have remained with him until between 28 July and 1 August. What happened to York's troops after 27 July is unclear. A small number of them, led by the bishop of Norwich and William Elmham, put up token resistance to the Lancastrian force, but their swift (and apparently bloodless) defeat marked the end of the regent's army as any sort of threat to Bolingbroke. Presumably most of them then either joined the winning side or simply drifted home. York himself accompanied Bolingbroke to Bristol, where he was present at the execution of Bussy, Green and Lescrope on 29 July. According to the *Vita*, York then remained at Bristol while Bolingbroke returned to Berkeley, Gloucester, and so northwards to Chester. Within a few days York had probably returned to Wallingford, where Queen Isabelle was staying, and whence a number of royal writs were issued during the first week of August.

The evidence of the accounts is insufficient to reach firm conclusions as to the reasons for York's failure to offer serious resistance to Bolingbroke, but, taken together with the remarks of the chroniclers, it is at least suggestive. Initially, it seems that quite a substantial force – probably numbered in thousands – gathered in Hertfordshire by 12– 13 July. This force was drawn almost entirely from the southern half of the country. Although troops continued to join York up until about 22 July, he was also suffering desertions, probably at a greater rate than he was winning recruits. It may be, therefore, that by the time he met Bolingbroke on 27 July, lack of numbers and low morale among his troops had made his position militarily untenable, leaving him no option but to allow the Lancastrian army free passage through the realm. On the other hand it may of course have been York's own indecision or lack of commitment to Richard's cause which was chiefly responsible in the first place for the crumbling of military support for the king. Nevertheless he clearly still had a fighting force of some magnitude with him on 27 July, even if he chose not to use it.

The Duke of York's army, July 1399

(a) *Lords' and councillors' retinues*

Name	Men-at-arms	Archers	Days paid
Edmund duke of York	100	200	· 30 days
John Beaufort, marquis of Dorset	100	200	20 days
Michael de la Pole, earl of Suffolk	29	109	5-31 July
Henry Despenser, bishop of Norwich	62	130	6-30 July
Robert Lord Ferrers of Chartley	10	50	19 days
The abbot of Walden (Essex)	1	39	20 days
Sir William Elmham	1	30	20 days
Sir John Bussy	*c.* 200		?
Sir Henry Green	*c.* 150		?
Sir William Bagot	*c.* 150		?
Sir John Russell	5	22	29 June-24 July

(b) *Sheriffs' posses*

Sheriff	County	Men-at-arms	Archers	Days paid
John Mulso	Northants	*c.* 250		?
John Worship	Beds. and Bucks.	*c.* 250		?
John Browning	Gloucs	20	100	10-24 July
Robert Russell	Worcs.	*c.* 100		?
Thomas Oudeby	Rutland	*c.* 100		?
William Audley	Hants.	*c.* 100		?
John Golafre	Oxford and Berks.	10	60	2-12 July
Richard Mawardyn	Wilts.	*c.* 80		?
Andrew Neuport	Cambridge and Hunts.	*c.* 70		?
Robert Turk	Herts.	1	10	12 July-1 Aug.

(c) *Minor retinues, by county*

Name	Men-at-arms	Archers	Days paid
HAMPSHIRE			
Sir Bernard Brocas	1	6	15
Nicholas Popham and Nicholas Merkant, esquires		4	20
Nicholas Bray, esquire		3	20
William Tauk, esquire	*c.* 20		?
William Kingsham and William Tangeley, esquires		6	20
Nicholas Valence, esquire		4	10
Philip Popham, esquire		1	10
John Norton, esquire		2	10
John Champflour, esquire		2	10
Sir Ingelram de Bruyn	1	26	10
Sir Amuary de St Amand	6	34	8
Robert Chorley, esquire		13	10

(*Total for Hampshire*: 14 knights and esquires, 129 men-at-arms and archers)

Name	Men-at-arms	Archers	Days paid
MIDDLESEX			
John Hall, esquire		1	12-29 July
John Lambkin, esquire		1	20
William Blake of Ruislip, valet		19	5-28 July
John Gedeney and John Pertryng, valets		38	5-28 July
Thomas Willesden, esquire			20
(*Total for Middlesex*: 3 esquires, 3 valets, 59 archers)			
NORTHAMPTONSHIRE			
Sir Guy Malory	2	18	6-30 July
Sir John Trussell	1	8	6-26 July
Sir John Holand	1	8	6-31 July
John Mantell, esquire		2	20
Sir John Withermale		3	24
John Maryns, esquire		4	24
Thomas Langport and Gerard Waldeneye, esquires		2	24
John Preston and John Hertewell, esquires		5	20
John Drayton, esquire		1	24
Laurence Dyne, esquire		3	20
William Trussell, esquire		2	20
(*Total for Northamptonshire*: 13 knights and esquires, 60 men-at-arms and archers)			
LINCOLNSHIRE			
George Everingham, esquire		6	20
Thomas Foxton, esquire		1	30
William Driby, esquire	7	30	10
(*Total for Lincolnshire*: 3 esquires, 44 men-at-arms and archers)			
DERBYSHIRE			
Sir William Meynell	?	?	?
John Statham, esquire			15
(*Total for Derbyshire*: 1 knight, 1 esquire, ? men-at-arms and archers)			
HERTFORDSHIRE: William Barker of Ashwell, Hugh Heymes of Baldock, Robert Wyght of St Albans, valets		57	12 July-1 Aug.
WARWICKSHIRE: Sir Thomas Astley and Sir Thomas Clinton		5	30
NORTHUMBERLAND: John Heron, esquire	1	7	·30
ESSEX: Sir Bartholomew de Boucher and John Squerry, esquire	c. 80		?
SOMERSET: Sir Edmund Seymour		6	10
CHESHIRE: Robert Massy, sergeant-at-arms		1	20
SHROPSHIRE: Sir Walter Bytterley	?	?	?
LEICESTERSHIRE: Sir Nicholas Hauberk	?	?	?
DEVON: Walter Clifton, valet			10
?CORNWALL: Richard Crees, esquire		9	20
Unidentified			
David Benbury, esquire	c. 25		?
Alan Scalby, valet			20
Sir Roger Siglem	?	?	?
John Paraunt, sergeant-at-arms	?	?	?
John Michell, sergeant-at-arms	?	?	?
Thomas Wodingfield, sergeant-at-arms	?	?	?

Appendix B: Bolingbroke's army in 1399

The following list of those who received wages for accompanying Bolingbroke on his march through England in the summer of 1399 is compiled principally from a Duchy of Lancaster account in the Public Record Office (DL.42/15, ff. 70-71), with some additional information taken from another Duchy account (DL.28/4/1, f. 19), and from the exchequer issue roll (E403/564, various dates). Almost all of those listed below were paid not only for 'coming to the king (Henry) after his arrival in England,' but also for 'remaining with him during the parliament at Westminster.' The list bears out the comment of the Dieulacres chronicler that 'numerous noble and warlike men from the north and from Lancaster, Derby and Stafford gathered with him (Henry)' (Dieulacres Chronicle, 171). In those cases where the ministers responsible for making payments are specified, they are mostly from the great northern and north midland honours of the Duchy of Lancaster, such as Tutbury, Pontefract, Lancaster, Bolingbroke and High Peak. Indeed, comparison of York's and Bolingbroke's armies suggests a significant element of division along regional lines in 1399, though this could have been due to the circumstances of the moment as much as to deep-rooted political affiliations. More than half of those listed below had also been retainers of John of Gaunt. Unfortunately the number of soldiers accompanying the recipient is never specified, though the total sum paid out – approximately £4,900 – was certainly large.

Commander	Wages (£)	Paid by receiver of
Earl of Northumberland	1,333	
Sir Henry Percy	666	
William Lord Willoughby	623	
Robert Waterton, esquire	285	Pontefract
Sir Walter Blount	233	Tutbury
William Lord Roos	200	
Sir Thomas Wendesley	160	High Peak
Earl of Westmorland	146	
John Curson, esquire	100	Tutbury

Sir Thomas Gerard	93	Lancaster
Sir Thomas Beck	86	Tutbury
Sir John Cokayn	66	Tutbury
Sir Roger Swillington	66	Pontefract
Sir Nicholas Montgomery	66	Tutbury
Sir John Dabrichecourt	60	Lancaster
Sir Robert Rokely and		
William Drummond	51	
Thomas Gresley, esquire	50	Tutbury
Sir Gerard Usfleet	40	Pontefract
Sir Thomas Hercy	40	Bolingbroke
Sir Nicholas Langford	40	Lancaster
Sir John Berkeley	33	
Sir William Dasteley	33	
Sir Thomas Aston	33	Tutbury
Thurstan del Boure, esquire	30	High Peak
Thomas Foljambe, esquire	30	High Peak
Sir Richard Stanhope	30	Bolingbroke
Thomas Clavell, esquire	26	Pontefract
Sir Robert Nevill	20	Pontefract
John Langford	20	Leicester
Sir Hugh Shirley	20	
Thomas Mereward	18	
Roger Bradbourn, esquire	17	High Peak
Bartholomew Montgomery, esquire	16	Lancaster
Henry Vanes, esquire	14	Bolingbroke
Richard Gascoigne, esquire	13	Knaresburgh
Simkin Franceys, esquire	12	Tutbury
Sir Hugh Husee	12	Bolingbroke
Henry Bothe, esquire	12	Tutbury
Edmund Barry, esquire	10	Norfolk
John Leventhorpe, esquire	10	Hertford
William Kettering	10	Pontefract
John Reynes, esquire	10	Norfolk
John Ayresworth, esquire	8	Lancaster
Ralph Burburgh, esquire	8	
John de Normanton	7	Tutbury
Henry Bradfield, valet	6	Tutbury
Aultyn Houby	6	Leicester
Thomas Cokfeld, esquire	5	Tutbury

Bibliography

Manuscripts

(a) British Library: Cotton Claudius B. ix (*Vita Ricardi Secundi*)
Cotton Tiberius C. ix (*Vita Ricardi Secundi*)
Harleian MS. 1319 (Metrical History)
Harleian MS. 3600 (Whalley Abbey Chronicle)

(b) Corpus Christi College, Cambridge: MS. 59 (The 'Manner of King Richard's Renunciation')

(c) Public Record Office: CP25 (Feet of Fines)
DL.28 (Duchy of Lancaster Accounts)
E361 (Exchequer Enrolled Accounts)
E101 (Exchequer Accounts Various)
E403 (Exchequer Issue Rolls)

Printed sources

Anglo-Norman Letters and Petitions, ed. M. D. Legge (Anglo-Norman Text Society, vol. iii, 1941).

Bower, Walter, *Scotichronicon*, vol. viii, ed. D. E. R. Watt (1987).

Calendar of Close Rolls 1396–99, 1399–1402 (HMSO 1927).

Calendar of Fine Rolls 1391–99, 1399–1405 (HMSO 1929, 1931).

Calendar of Inquisitions Miscellaneous 1399–1422 (HMSO 1967).

Calendar of Letter-Books of the City of London, ed. R. R. Sharpe, vols. H and I (1907–8).

Calendar of Papal Letters 1362–1404, ed. W. H. Bliss *et al.*, 2 vols (HMSO 1902–4).

Calendar of Patent Rolls 1396–99, 1399–1401 (HMSO 1909, 1903).

Calendar of State Papers Milan 1385–1618 (HMSO 1912).

Calendar of State Papers Venice 1202–1509 (HMSO 1864).

Choix de Pièces Inédites Relatives au Regne de Charles VI, ed. L. Douet-D'Arcq (Société de l'Histoire de France, vol. 119, 1863).

Chronicle of John Hardyng, ed. H. Ellis (1812).

Chronicon Adae de Usk, ed. E. M. Thompson (1904).

Chronicon Henrici Knighton, ed. J. R. Lumby, 2 vols (Rolls Series 1895).

Chronicque de la Traison et Mort de Richart Deux Roy Dengleterre, ed. B. Williams (1846).

Chronique de'Enguerran de Monstrelet, vol. i, ed. L. Douet-D'Arcq (Société de l'Histoire de France, vol. 91, 1857).

Chronique du Religieux de Saint-Denys 1380–1422, vol. ii, ed. M. L. Bellaguet (Documents Inédits Sur l'Histoire de France, 1840).

Creton, Jean, 'Metrical history of the deposition of King Richard the Second', ed. J. Webb, *Archaeologia* (1823).

Diplomatic Correspondence of Richard II, ed. E. Perroy (Camden Society Publications, 3rd Series, vol. xlviii, 1933).

English Chronicle from 1377 to 1461, ed. J. S. Davies (Camden Society Publications, 1st Series, vol. lxiv, 1855).

Eulogium Historiarum Sive Temporis, ed. F. S. Haydon, vol. iii (Rolls Series 1863).

Foedera, Conventiones, Litterae et Cuiuscunque Generis Acta Publica, ed. T. Rymer, 20 vols (1704–35).

Froissart, Jean, *Oeuvres*, ed. Kervyn de Lettenhove, 25 vols (1867–77).

Histoire du Roy d'Angleterre Richard, ed. J. A. Buchon (Collection des Chroniques Nationales Françaises, vol. xxiii, 1826).

Historia Vitae et Regni Ricardi Secundi, ed. G. B. Stow (1977).

Johannis de Trokelowe et Anon Chronica et Annales, ed. H. T. Riley (Rolls Series 1866).

Kirkstall Abbey Chronicles, ed. J. Taylor (Publications of the Thoresby Society 1952).

Literae Cantuariensis, ed. J. B. Sheppard, vol. iii (Rolls Series 1889).

Official Correspondence of Thomas Bekynton, ed. G. Williams, vol. i (Rolls Series 1872).

Proceedings and Ordinances of the Privy Council of England, ed. N. H. Nicolas, i (1834).

Rotuli Parliamentorum, ed. J. Strachey *et al.*, vol. iii (1783).

Salmon, Pierre, *Mémoires*, ed. J. A. Buchon (Collection des Chroniques Nationales Françaises, vol. xxiv, 1826).

Westminster Chronicle 1381–1394, ed. L. C. Hector and B. F. Harvey (1982).

Secondary sources

M. Aston, *Thomas Arundel* (1967).

R. L. Atkinson, 'Richard II and the death of the Duke of Gloucester', *EHR* (1923), 563–4.

C. Barron, 'The tyranny of Richard II', *BIHR* (1968), 1–18.

C. Barron, 'The deposition of Richard II', in *Politics and Crisis in Fourteenth-Century England*, ed. J. Taylor and W. Childs (1990).

A. L. Brown, 'The reign of Henry IV', in *Fifteenth-Century England 1399–1509*, ed. S. B. Chrimes, C. D. Ross and R. A. Griffiths (1972).

D. M. Bueno de Mesquita, *Giangaleazzo Visconti, Duke of Milan 1351–1402* (1941).

D. M. Bueno de Mesquita, 'The foreign policy of Richard II in 1397: some Italian letters', *EHR* (1941), 628–37.

M. V. Clarke and V. H. Galbraith, 'The deposition of Richard II', *BJRL* (1930), 125–81.

G. E. Cokayne, *Complete Peerage*, ed. V. H. Gibbs *et al.*, 13 volumes (1910–59).

E. Collas, *Valentine de Milan, Duchesse d'Orleans* (1911).

D. Crook, 'Central England and the revolt of the earls, January 1400', *HR* (1991), 403–10.

R. G. Davies, 'Richard II and the church in the years of tyranny', *Journal of Medieval History* (1975).

R. R. Davies, 'Richard II and the principality of Chester', in *The Reign of Richard II*, ed. F. R. H. du Boulay and C. Barron (1971).

D. W. Dillon, 'Remarks on the manner of the death of Richard II', *Archaeologia* (1840), 75–95.

J. G. Edwards, 'The parliamentary committee of 1398', *EHR* (1925), 321–33.

R. C. Famiglietti, *Royal Intrigue: Crisis at the Court of Charles VI 1392–1420* (1986).

V. H. Galbraith, 'Thomas Walsingham and the St Albans Chronicle 1272–1422', *EHR* (1932), 12–30.

J. L. Gillespie, 'Richard II's Cheshire archers', *Transactions of the Historical Society of Lancashire and Cheshire* (1974), 1–39.

J. L. Gillespie, 'Thomas Mortimer and Thomas Molineux: Radcot Bridge and the appeal of 1397', *Albion* (1975), 161–173.

C. Given-Wilson, *The Royal Household and the King's Affinity: Service, Politics and Finance in England 1360–1413* (1986).

C. Given-Wilson, 'Adam Usk, the monk of Evesham, and the parliament of 1397–8', *HR* (1993).

C. Given-Wilson, 'The manner of King Richard's renunciation: a "Lancastrian narrative"?', *EHR* (1993).

A. Goodman, *The Loyal Conspiracy* (1971).

A. Gransden, *Historical Writing in England II* (1982).

M. Harvey, *Solutions to the Schism: A Study of Some English Attitudes 1378 to 1409* (1983).

G. Hill, *A History of Cyprus*, 2 vols (1948).

G. A. Holmes, *The Estates of the Higher Nobility in Fourteenth-Century England* (1957).

E. Jarry, *La Vie Politique de Louis de France, Duc d'Orleans* (1889).

D. Johnston, 'Richard II's departure from Ireland, July 1399' *EHR* (1983), 785–805.

M. C. E. Jones, *Ducal Brittany 1364–99* (1970).

N. R. Ker, *Medieval Manusripts in British Libraries*, vol. iii (1969).

J. L. Kirby, *Henry IV of England* (1970).

F. Lehoux, *Jean de France, Duc de Berri*, vol. ii (1966).

K. B. McFarlane, *Lancastrian Kings and Lollard Knights* (1972).

P. McNiven, 'The Cheshire rising of 1400' *BJRL* (1969–70), 375–96.

P. Morgan, *War and Society in Medieval Cheshire 1277–1403* (Publications of the Chetham Society, 3rd Series, vol. xxxiv, 1967).

R. Mott, 'Richard II and the crisis of 1397', in *Church and Chronicle in the Middle Ages: Essays Presented to John Taylor*, ed. I. Wood and G. A. Loud (1991).

J. Nichols, *Collection of the Wills of the Kings and Queens of England* (1780).

M. Nordberg, *Les Ducs et La Royauté: Etudes sur la Rivalité des Ducs d'Orléans et de Bourgogne 1392–1407* (1964).

J. J. N. Palmer, *England, France and Christendom 1377–99* (1972).

J. J. N. Palmer, 'The authorship, date and historical value of the French chronicles on the Lancastrian revolution', *BJRL* (1978–9), 145–81, 398–421.

S. J. Payling, *Political Society in Lancastrian England* (1991).

E. Perroy, *L'Angleterre et le Grand Schisme D'Occident* (1933).

P. Pietresson de Saint-Aubin, 'Documents inédits sur l'installation de Pierre d'Ailly à l'evêché de Cambrai en 1397', *Bibliothèque de l'Ecole de Chartes* (1955), 138–9.

J. B. Post, 'Courts, councils and arbitrators in the Ladbroke manor dispute, 1382–1400', in *Medieval Legal Records Edited in Memory of C. A. F. Meekings*, ed. R. F. Hunnisett and J. B. Post (1978).

J. B. Post, 'The obsequies of John of Gaunt', *Guildhall Studies in London History* (1981), 1–12.

The Reign of Richard II, ed. F. R. H. Du Boulay and C. Barron (1971), 277–83.

A. Rogers, 'Henry IV and the revolt of the earls', *History Today* (1968), 277–83.

C. D. Ross, 'Forfeiture for treason in the reign of Richard II', *EHR* (1956), 560–75.

G. O. Sayles, 'The deposition of Richard II: three Lancastrian narratives', *BIHR* (1981), 257–70.

J. W. Sherborne, 'Perjury and the Lancastrian revolution of 1399', *Welsh History Review* (1988), 217–41.

A. R. Stanley, 'On an examination of the tombs of Richard II and Henry VI in Westminster Abbey', *Archaeologia* (1880), 309–27.

A. B. Steel, *Richard II* (1941).

G. B. Stow, 'Richard II in Thomas Walsingham's Chronicles', *Speculum* (1984), 68–102.

J. Tait, 'Did Richard II murder the Duke of Gloucester?', in *Historical Essays by Members of the Owens College Manchester*, ed. T. F. Tout and J. Tait (1902), 193–216.

J. Taylor, *English Historical Literature in the Fourteenth Century* (1987).

A Tuck, *Richard II and the English Nobility* (1973).

R. Vaughan, *Philip the Bold* (1962).

S. K. Walker, *The Lancastrian Affinity 1361–1399* (1990).

S. K. Walker, 'Letters to the Duke of Lancaster in 1381 and 1399' *EHR* (1991), 68–79.

J. H. Wylie, *History of England under Henry IV*, 4 vols (1884–98).

Index

(Members of the nobility are indexed by title, e.g, Huntingdon, not Holand. For the titles of earls, marquises and dukes see p. xvi)